OXFORD BIBLE ATLAS

Oxford Bible Atlas

FOURTH EDITION

Edited by

ADRIAN CURTIS

OXFORD

UNIVERSITY PRESS

OXFORD
UNIVERSITY PRESS

Great Clarendon Street, Oxford OX2 6DP

Oxford University Press is a department of the University of Oxford.
It furthers the University's objective of excellence in research, scholarship,
and education by publishing worldwide in

Oxford New York

Auckland Cape Town Dar es Salaam Hong Kong Karachi
Kuala Lumpur Madrid Melbourne Mexico City Nairobi
New Delhi Shanghai Taipei Toronto

With offices in

Argentina Austria Brazil Chile Czech Republic France Greece
Guatemala Hungary Italy Japan South Korea Poland Portugal
Singapore Switzerland Thailand Turkey Ukraine Vietnam

Published in the United States
by Oxford University Press Inc., New York

British Library Cataloguing in Publication Data

Data available

Library of Congress Cataloging in Publication Data

Data available

ISBN 0-19-100158-9
978-0-19-100158-1

1 3 5 7 9 10 8 6 4 2

Printed on acid free paper through Phoenix Offset,China

PREFACE TO THE FOURTH EDITION

The *Oxford Bible Atlas* has been a much valued companion of readers of the Bible since its first publication in 1962. This fourth edition is substantially revised yet it is very much the child of its predecessors. There are definite family resemblances, but also some differences. In some sections, the text has been changed completely, while in others it follows closely that of the third edition. Some amendments have been made to the maps, and the format of some of them has been changed. The most striking difference in the presentation is in the use of colour photography throughout. It is hoped that this will enhance the readers' appreciation of the lands of the Bible.

One of the difficulties in preparing such an atlas lies in what name to give to the area of land in the southern Levant with which it is most closely concerned, not least because many terms have come to have very particular political and religious connotations. Terms such as 'Promised Land' and 'Holy Land' have been coined from the perspective of those religions which regard the land as 'promised' or 'holy'. They have been avoided in this *Atlas* although it is acknowledged that many people's interest in the land is precisely because of its religious significance. The problem with the term 'Israel' is that it has meant different things at different times. Within the Bible itself, the term is used with a variety of senses—a people who traced their descent from the eponymous ancestor Israel (a name given to Jacob; cf. Gen. 32: 28), the land occupied by all the twelve tribes who claimed descent from the sons of Jacob, and the northern kingdom of Israel as distinct from the southern kingdom of Judah. So 'Israel' and 'Israelites' are used from time to time in this *Atlas* with the appropriate biblical sense for the context. A term which has often been used as a convenient geographical designation for the southern part of the east Mediterranean coastal strip is 'Palestine', from a name given to the area by the Romans and deriving ultimately from the word 'Philistine'. 'Palestine' is used in this *Atlas* with that geographical sense.

The dating scheme used in this *Atlas* follows that in *The Oxford History of the Biblical World* (edited by Michael D. Coogan, New York and Oxford: Oxford University Press, 1998). The Chronological Chart is that used in *The Oxford History of the Biblical World*, slightly adapted.

v

CONTENTS

Contents

Archaeology in Bible Lands

LIST OF MAPS

ABBREVIATIONS

HEBREW BIBLE (OLD TESTAMENT)

Gen.	Genesis	Ezr.	Ezra	Hos.	Hosea
Ex.	Exodus	Neh.	Nehemiah	Joel	Joel
Lev.	Leviticus	Esth.	Esther	Amos	Amos
Num.	Numbers	Job	Job	Obad.	Obadiah
Deut.	Deuteronomy	Ps.	Psalms	Jon.	Jonah
Josh.	Joshua	Prov.	Proverbs	Mic.	Micah
Judg.	Judges	Eccles.	Ecclesiastes	Nah.	Nahum
Ruth	Ruth	S. of Sol.	Song of	Hab.	Habakkuk
1 Sam.	1 Samuel		Solomon	Zeph.	Zephaniah
2 Sam.	2 Samuel	Isa.	Isaiah	Hag.	Haggai
1 Kgs.	1 Kings	Jer.	Jeremiah	Zeph.	Zephaniah
2 Kgs.	2 Kings	Lam.	Lamentations	Hag.	Haggai
1 Chr.	1 Chronicles	Ezek.	Ezekiel	Zech.	Zechariah
2 Chr.	2 Chronicles	Dan.	Daniel	Mal.	Malachi

APOCRYPHA

1 Esd.	1 Esdras
Tobit	Tobit
Judith	Judith
Sirach (Ecclus.)	Ecclesiasticus or the Wisdom of Jesus Son of Sirach
1 Macc.	1 Maccabees
2 Macc.	2 Maccabees

NEW TESTAMENT

Matt.	Matthew	Eph.	Ephesians	Jas.	James
Mark	Mark	Phil.	Philippians	1 Pet.	1 Peter
Luke	Luke	Col.	Colossians	2 Pet.	2 Peter
John	John	1 Thess.	1 Thessalonians	1 John	1 John
Acts	Acts of the	2 Thess.	2 Thessalonians	2 John	2 John
	Apostles	1 Tim.	1 Timothy	3 John	3 John
Rom.	Romans	2 Tim.	2 Timothy	Jude	Jude
1 Cor.	1 Corinthians	Tit.	Titus	Rev.	Revelation
2 Cor.	2 Corinthians	Philem.	Philemon		
Gal.	Galatians	Heb.	Hebrews		

BIBLE VERSIONS

NAB	New American Bible
NJB	New Jerusalem Bible
NRSV	New Revised Standard Version
REB	Revised English Bible
RSV	Revised Standard Version

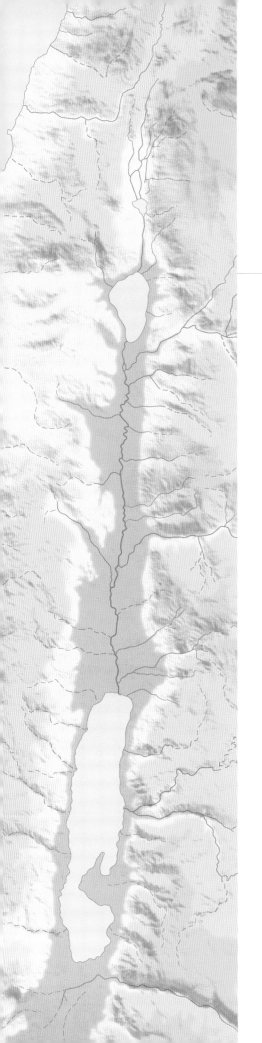

The Setting

The Text in Context

THE SETTINGS OF STORIES

Those who tell stories often set them in a particular time and place. In some works of fiction, where the setting too is entirely fictional, a map is provided to help the readers to follow the story; for example, with J. R. R. Tolkien's trilogy *The Lord of the Rings* comes a map of 'Middle Earth', the setting of the saga. Writers of historical novels are often at great pains to provide an accurate geographical setting, perhaps with a map, even if the contents are primarily fictional. And those who seek to recount the stories of real people and events do so with reference to the locations of the activities described. Therefore it is important for the readers of stories to have an awareness of their geographical setting. This is not simply to enable the reader to plot movement from place to place. The reader may be helped to know whether the setting is in a desert or in a forest, in a frozen waste or in the tropics, in a bustling city or an idyllic rural setting. So an appreciation of the setting may help the understanding of the story. If this is true of other types of literature, it is certainly true of the Bible.

FROM GARDEN OF EDEN TO NEW JERUSALEM

The Bible contains much material which purports to tell of past events, of people, of what things they had said or what deeds they had done, and very often where they had said or done these things. This is particularly true of narrative material, but other types of literature, such as prophetic oracles against foreign nations, or letters written to new churches, may allude to or presuppose geographical settings and geographical knowledge. The beginning of the Book of Amos (Amos 1–2) takes on greater significance when read with a geographical awareness. The announcement of God's judgement starts some distance from Israel, in Damascus, Gaza, and Tyre, but then comes closer, to Edom, Ammon, and Moab, then to the immediate neighbour Judah, and finally to Israel itself.

The Bible opens with a poetic and stylized account of creation, but then comes another creation story. This story is set in a place, a garden in Eden, a region which, from the perspective of the teller, is in the east (Gen. 2: 8). Very few would seek to place Eden on a map, seeing it as belonging to the realm of myth, but it is noteworthy that it does reflect a geographical interest, both in the indication of the direction ('east') and in the description of the river which flowed out of Eden, its four branches, and where they flowed (Gen. 2: 10–14). Similarly, the New Jerusalem, described almost at the end of the Bible (Rev. 21: 10–22: 5), would not be located on a map, but an awareness of what Jerusalem was actually like would help the appreciation of how different the New Jerusalem would be.

But in between, and once a few more pages have been turned after the account of the Garden of Eden, the stories are given a geographical setting which can more easily be related to what is known of the ancient world. This prompts the question of the extent to which the stories preserved in the Bible are descriptions of actual events and real people. The issue has been and continues to be much debated. Of course the answer will vary depending on the particular story. To some extent, it could be argued that this is not an issue relevant to the preparation of an atlas. What matters is not whether something happened but whether it is given a real rather than fictional geographical setting, and whether it is possible to use a knowledge of geography and of archaeology to illuminate the context in which the story is set. It has been argued that, if a story has preserved accurately the context in which it is set, why can it not have preserved accurately the details of the people about whom the stories are told? And if that is the case, then surely the Bible can be seen as a reliable historical source. But this is to overlook the fact that different types of material can be given geographical (and indeed 'historical') settings. There is perhaps inevitably a danger of circular argumentation, particularly when the Bible itself is one of the ancient sources used to reconstruct the context. Some have argued that that the Bible should not be used in the task of reconstructing a picture of events in the southern Levant in the time of which it purports to tell. But the Bible is a relatively ancient source, and to dismiss it for lack of objectivity would be to dismiss other ancient sources written for particular and sometimes propagandist purposes (which would be true of many which have informed the attempt to give a historical context in this volume). To rely on the objectivity of the archaeological evidence would be to overlook the extent to which such evidence needs to be interpreted. So the aim must be to use all the available evidence, aware of its strengths and weaknesses, to achieve as balanced a judgement as possible. The warning that it may be necessary to differentiate between the picture of a 'biblical' Israel created within the text, and the actuality of what was happening in the southern Levant in the first millennium BCE and the first century CE is a valid one. So the primary aim in this atlas is provide the reader with an awareness of the world in which the biblical narratives are set—the context against which the text is to be read.

There are a number of factors which need to be taken into account when considering apparently geographical statements in the Bible, not least the issue of the geographical awareness of those who made the statements and the extent to which the intention was to pass on information which was purely geographical. Brief mention will be made here of some of the relevant issues.

GEOGRAPHICAL ORIENTATION

In a society entirely accustomed to the use of maps and charts, atlases and gazetteers, it is difficult to imagine times when this would not have been the case. It has become so customary to view maps with north at the top that it is easy to assume that everyone shared this worldview. This particular question can be related specifically to the debate about whether Qumran, the site associated with the Dead Sea Scrolls, was a settlement of the group known as the Essenes. An ancient description of the Essenes (by Pliny the Elder in his *Natural History* 5) says that 'below the Essenes was the town of Engedi'. To the modern reader, this might naturally suggest that Engedi, on the western shore of the Dead Sea, was situated to the south of this Essene centre, a description which fits the site of Qumran. But the significance of Pliny's description could be that the Essene headquarters lay in the hills above Engedi. (It is highly likely that Qumran was an Essene centre, but whether Pliny's description proves this is more open to debate.) The Madaba Map (see p.10) has an east–west orientation.

VERBAL MAPS?

Within the biblical narrative, there are passages which might be said to provide verbal maps. The 'Table of the Nations' in Genesis 10 purports to be a list of the descendants of the sons of Noah after the Flood. But it soon becomes clear that many of the persons named are in fact nations or peoples, sometimes with an indication of where they lived (see for example the description of the extent of the territory of the Canaanites in verse 19). The whole chapter is an elaborate attempt to 'map' the ancient world into which the stories of Abraham and his descendants are about to be set. (A surprising feature of the 'Table of the Nations' is the fact that the sons of Cush, one of the sons of Ham and often thought to represent Ethiopia, are apparently located in Arabia rather than Africa.) Much of the latter part of the Book of Joshua comprises city lists and boundary lists, purporting to be the allocations of land to the various tribes by Joshua after the land had been taken. That these lists reflect some ancient attempt to define boundaries and possessions seems inherently likely, even if it is impossible to be certain of their origins. That they also reveal an awareness, either by the biblical narrators or those responsible for their sources, of how parts of the land may have related to others geographically is also probable. But above all, in their context, they serve a theological function. They demonstrate how God's promise to the ancestors (that they would have a land in which their descendants could dwell—for example, Genesis 17: 8) was fulfilled. Here were the details of the land whereby the promise was fulfilled.

Very different in nature is the verbal map presented at the end of the Book of Ezekiel. Chapter 48 envisages a future land of Israel, restored after the successive destructions of the northern kingdom of Israel by the Assyrians and the southern kingdom of Judah by the Babylonians, and the subsequent exile. The land is arranged in a highly stylized fashion. The tribes are assigned successive latitudinal ('from the east side to the west') strips of territory, from Dan in the north to Gad in the south. Between the territories allocated to Judah and Benjamin there is to be a 'sacred' or 'holy' portion, set apart from the rest of the land. At the heart of this would lie the Temple. The previous chapter has made a remarkable claim about the future Temple (Ezek. 47: 1–12). From its very threshold would flow a river whose waters would get deeper and deeper as they flowed eastwards until they reached the Dead Sea, giving life to its waters, enabling fish to live there and vegetation to grow around its shores. An awareness of the actual geography enables the reader to appreciate the significance of the theological claim being made here. God's Temple in Jerusalem will be at the heart of God's land and be a source of life in the most remarkable way.

THEOLOGICAL GEOGRAPHY

The clear theological significance of Ezekiel's presentation of a restored Israel raises the fact that there are a number of biblical statements and descriptions which purport to be geographical but whose primary purpose is theological. The wording of God's promise to Abraham, which included the statement that to his descendants would be given territory stretching from the Nile to the Euphrates (Gen. 15: 18) should be read as an expression of the idea of a Promised Land rather than an indication of land ever actually occupied by Israelites. Similarly in the New Testament, in the shaping of the Gospel narratives, some overtly geographical indications may have a deeper theological significance. In Mark, all of Jesus' early ministry is in Galilee. The pivotal point, halfway through Mark's account, is Peter's declaration that Jesus is the Messiah (Mark 8: 27–30). This declaration is set in Caesarea Philippi, in the northernmost part of the land. Then Jesus begins the journey from the far north to the religious heart of the land, Jerusalem, and to his death. Luke too presents the life of Jesus as a journey on which the disciples follow their master. This may be significant for the Lucan notion of Christianity as 'the Way', mentioned several times in the Acts of the Apostles (Acts 9: 2; 19: 9, 23; 24: 14, 22).

An awareness of the actual geography enables some apparently geographical statements about Jerusalem, and Mount Zion in particular, to be appreciated as theological. In Psalm 48: 1–3, reference seems to be made to Zion being located 'in the far north', but this does not make sense geographically. The Hebrew word for 'north' (ṣāpôn) is probably derived from the name of Mount Zaphon (modern Jebel el-Aqra in Syria) which, according to the texts from Ugarit, was the abode of the gods and where Baal had his palace. The psalmist is not locating Zion geographically, but claiming it as or likening it

Facing: The Dead Sea, with the Jordan flowing in from the north: a satellite image. A clearly visible feature is the Lisan (the word means 'tongue'), the promontory which juts out from the eastern shore towards the southern end of the sea. In biblical times the channel between the western shore and the Lisan was wider.

to the divine abode. In Psalm 46: 4, the probable association of Jerusalem (though the city is not named) with a river with streams, is more reminiscent of the picture of Ezekiel 47 (noted above) than of the actual situation. The small stream emerging from the Gihon spring hardly fits the description. But that the depiction may owe something to the tradition of the river which flowed out of the Garden of Eden and split into four branches, one of which is named as Gihon (Gen. 2: 10–14) is certainly a possibility. Jerusalem is perhaps being likened to Eden. The oracle preserved in Isaiah 2: 2 and Micah 4: 1, albeit speaking about the future, envisages 'the mountain of the LORD's house' (that is, Zion) as becoming 'the highest of the mountains' and 'raised above the hills'. Zion is in fact overlooked by higher hills such as the Mount of Olives. What is envisaged is not a geographical upheaval but a theological transformation.

The navel of the earth (omphalos)?

Mention should also be made in this context of the fact that, within the Bible, there are a few possible hints at a belief that Israel, or somewhere in Israel, particularly Jerusalem, was the 'navel' or very centre of the world. In the Book of Ezekiel, the Israelites are described as those 'who live at the centre of the earth' (Ezek. 38: 12). The Hebrew word translated 'centre' here is ṭabbûr, and in the Greek translation, the Septuagint, the word is rendered *omphalos* or 'navel'. (NRSV gives 'navel' as an alternative translation in a footnote to Ezek. 38: 12.) The word ṭabbûr is also used in Judges 9: 37 of a location in the vicinity of Shechem. NRSV and NAB treat it as part of a proper name (Tabbur-erez, Tabbur-Haares respectively), with no indication of the significance of the first element. REB retains the notion of 'centrality', translating 'central ridge' (see also RSV 'centre of the land'). But NJB proposes 'the Navel of the Earth'. (It has been suggested that the name of Mount Tabor may be associated with this word, and that this dome-shaped hill might have been considered as the navel of the land or the earth, but is highly unlikely that the two words are connected.)

Elsewhere in the Book of Ezekiel it is Jerusalem which is described as having been placed 'in the centre of the nations' (Ezek. 5: 5), and this idea is preserved in later sources (see, for example, Jubilees 8: 19). Josephus, in his *Jewish War* 3, says, with reference to Jerusalem, that 'some have quite appropriately called her the navel of the country'. (It is noteworthy that the placing of Jerusalem at the centre persisted in later map-making.)

AETIOLOGY (AND ETYMOLOGICAL AETIOLOGY)

Another feature of a number of biblical stories, not unrelated to the idea of theological geography, is that they seem to have been preserved principally to explain why a particular place was a *holy* place, and perhaps also to explain why it was called by its name. A story which combines both of those features, and perhaps adds a third, is that of Jacob's famous dream at Bethel (Gen. 28: 10–22). It accounts for why Bethel was an Israelite holy place, that is, because

God had revealed himself there to the ancestor Jacob/Israel; it explains the place's name as originating from Jacob's realization that it was 'none other than the house of God' (in Hebrew, Bethel means 'house of God', but it is likely that the place name reflects that originally it was a temple of El, the head of the Canaanite pantheon); and it may also explain a feature of the sanctuary at Bethel, a standing stone—Jacob's so-called pillow. The example of Bethel suggests that in part the purpose may be to bring much older sanctuaries into the sphere of Israelite worship. Archaeology suggests that the sanctuary at Shechem dates back to the Middle Bronze Age and that it was a feature of the Late Bronze Age city. But Genesis 12: 6–7 relates that God appeared there to Abra(ha)m, who marked the theophany by building an altar.

More generally, aetiologies are stories which explain how something came to be as it was, or (in the case of etymological aetiologies) why someone or somewhere was given a particular name, and there are many such in the Bible. In Joshua 4: 1–9, the setting up of twelve stones at Gilgal, to mark the crossing of the River Jordan, is described, ending with the type of phrase found in many aetiological stories, 'and they are there to this day'. The story explains the presence of a stone circle, and why the place was so-called (Gilgal may mean 'circle'). In the following chapter (Josh. 5: 1–7), the place name Gibeath-haaraloth ('hill of the foreskins') is explained by recounting how Joshua circumcised the sons of the generation that had come out of Egypt. This is followed by another explanation of the name Gilgal, this time relating the name to a verb meaning 'roll', because Joshua had 'rolled away . . . the disgrace of Egypt' (Josh. 5: 9). Another example of a double explanation of a place name is found in the story of the ownership of the wells at Beer-sheba (Gen. 21: 22–34). To mark the agreement (or covenant) between Abraham and Abimelech, confirming that Abraham had dug the wells, Abraham set aside seven lambs for Abimelech, and they swore an oath. The name Beer-sheba could mean 'well of seven' or 'well of an oath'. The preservation of this story may have had another aetiological function, that of establishing the ownership rights over an important oasis on the edge of the wilderness.

ANCIENT MAPPING

Ancient writers did not usually supply maps with the stories they told. But one possible exception is to be seen in a small tablet housed in the British Museum, which dates from about 600 BCE and depicts the known world, with the city of Babylon on the River Euphrates at its centre. The Persian Gulf is depicted as a river encircling the land, and beyond it are mysterious distant lands. The 'map' was drawn to illustrate an account of the campaigns of King Sargon of Akkad in the latter half of the 3rd millennium BCE. A relatively early attempt to map the lands of the Bible can be seen in the remarkable mosaic floor, discovered towards the end of the 19th century, in a Byzantine church at Madaba in Transjordan, probably dating from the 6th century CE. The map includes a representation of Jerusalem, and shows several details of

A map of the world (*c.*600 BCE) showing Babylon on the Euphrates at the centre.

The Madaba Map: detail of the 6th century CE mosaic map in the Church of St George at Madaba in Jordan, showing a plan of the city of Jerusalem. The piece of text (no longer completely preserved) above the city plan, reads 'The Holy City of Jerusalem'.

the city of Jerusalem as it was at the time, including the church of the Holy Sepulchre and other churches, streets lined with columns, the city walls and gates. It incorporates a number of biblical quotations, and the map has made a significant contribution to knowledge of the topography of the region.

MAPS: FROM ANCIENT TO MODERN

Many ancient stories are associated with places, and often these came to be marked in some way. An example of the associating of particular traditions with specific locations is seen in the Christian tradition of erecting churches to mark the sites of key events in the life of Jesus. These were visited by pilgrims, some of whom have left accounts of their travels which are also a valuable source. Another important ancient source is the *Onomasticon*, compiled by the historian Eusebius early in the 4th century CE. It was translated, with some revisions, by Jerome (*Liber de situ et nominibus locorum hebraicorum*) *c.*390 CE. The Crusades revived interest in the locations of holy places in Palestine, and in pilgrimages to such sites. Some such visitors have left accounts of their travels.

A real expansion of interest came about in the 19th century, and a particularly important contribution was made by the publication of Edward Robinson's accounts of his travels in Palestine and neighbouring regions in 1838–9 and in 1852. A new impetus was given to the study of the topography of the southern Levant by the establishment of the Palestine Exploration Fund in 1865. Under its auspices, Captain (later Field-Marshal) Kitchener and Captain Conder of the Royal Engineers were sent in 1871 to make a survey of the land with the intention of gathering geographical, archaeological, and natural–historical data relevant to the Bible. They mapped the whole of the region to the west of the Jordan, recorded the names of numerous ancient sites and described such remains as were visible, and succeeded in identifying many of them with places known from the biblical narrative.

The survey carried out by Kitchener and Conder was a surface exploration. An important step forward came in 1890 when Sir William Flinders Petrie applied his method (developed in Egypt) of excavation in order to understand the stratified formation of an ancient mound to a Palestinian site—Tel el-Ḥesi. Ever since those pioneering days, excavations have been carried out on numerous sites, providing new information relevant to the mapping of the land in which much of the biblical narrative is set.

Two particular factors relating to mapping should be mentioned. One

Sir William Flinders Petrie (1853–1942) arranging samples of pottery types.

relates to the actual lie of the land and, particularly important, to the availability of water. It is inherently likely that there would be a degree of continuity in the siting of settlements close to water sources or in areas where water storage and irrigation were possible. The location of the main roads and other routes was governed by the contours of the land and the presence of valleys. Towns would grow up sometimes at places where there was good access to roads and sometimes precisely to guard strategic points such as crossroads or passes. Again, there is likely to be an element of continuity in this.

Another issue of continuity relates to the extent to which modern place names, particularly those of Arabic origin, have preserved ancient names. Sometimes it is possible to relate the modern form of a name to the biblical form, for example, Beitin to Bethel, Seilun to Shiloh, Beisan to Beth-shan. Sometimes a modern name will preserve the sense of an ancient name, such as et-Tell and Ai ('ruin'). Sometimes modern names have 'moved' to another location in the vicinity of an ancient site. New Testament Jericho was not on the same site as the Jericho of the Hebrew Bible, and neither is in precisely the same place as the modern Eriha. The biblical Anathoth was thought not to be located at modern Anata, because of the lack of pre-Roman remains there. But recent excavations have revealed evidence of occupation in the Iron Age, making the identification possible. So caution is needed!

But some sites remain unidentified. Tel el-Ḥesi was thought by Flinders Petrie to be biblical Lachish, and subsequently it has been suggested that it was Eglon. Both suggestions were made on the basis of evidence from Eusebius' *Onomasticon*. The former suggestion is now discounted, and the latter remains uncertain. And it is perhaps not inappropriate that this introductory section should close on a note of uncertainty, since certainty about many of the details of what follows is impossible.

The Lands of the Bible

THE EXTENT OF THE LAND

The actual territory occupied by the ancient Hebrew / Jewish people varied from time to time. For the sake of comparison, its maximum extent covered an area a little larger than Wales in the United Kingdom or about the area of Vermont in the USA. A familiar biblical phrase describes the land as stretch-

Tel Dan: 'From Dan to Beer-sheba' was a traditional indication of the extent of the land (e.g. Judg. 20: 1).

13

ing 'from Dan to Beer-sheba' (for example, Judges 20: 1), a distance of some 150 miles (about 240 km). In 2 Kings 23: 8 the area occupied by the towns of Judah is said to stretch 'from Geba to Beer-sheba'. Elsewhere, the southern boundary is envisaged as extending as far as Kadesh-barnea (Num. 34: 4) some 45 miles (72 km) further south. The northern extent of territory occupied by Israelites is sometimes described as Lebo-hamath (for example, Num. 34: 8), a phrase which may mean 'Entrance to Hamath' and designate the area between the Orontes and Leontes rivers, or else a town (Lebweh) on

the Orontes. In 1 Kings 8: 65, a festival in the time of Solomon involving 'all Israel' is said to have involved people 'from Lebo-hamath to the Wadi of Egypt'. The biblical narrative also suggests that some Israelite tribes occupied territory in Transjordan. Deuteronomy 3: 8 mentions the territory from Mount Hermon in the north to the River Arnon in Moab. There are also suggestions that there were times when Israelite control included the whole of Moab and Edom (cf. 2 Sam. 8). The account of the reign of Solomon envisages the territory under his control as reaching as far south as Ezion-geber on the Gulf of Aqaba and thus including an important commercial outlet (1 Kgs. 9: 26); this territory would also have included the rich copper deposits of the Arabah. Even much later, the designation 'from Dan to Beer-sheba' conveys a reasonably accurate designation of the Kingdom of Herod, which stretched from the vicinity of Beer-sheba in the south and encompassed Judea, Samaria, and Galilee, reaching almost as far north as Paneas close to the site of Dan, and included land in Transjordan. The same is true of the time envisaged in the Gospels, when the Roman province of Judea and the tetrarchies of Herod Antipas and of Philip stretched from Beer-sheba to Paneas, renamed Caesarea Philippi.

THE FERTILE CRESCENT

The land formed part of the Fertile Crescent, a term coined to describe an approximately crescent-shaped area of territory which was comparatively fertile when compared with the desert regions which abutted it. The Fertile Crescent had at its eastern and western extremities the lands which were watered by the great rivers and their annual inundations, the Tigris and Euphrates in Lower Mesopotamia and the Nile in Egypt. The central part of the 'crescent', largely comprising Upper Mesopotamia and the eastern Mediterranean coastal strip, relied mainly on rain for its fertility. An awareness of the extent of the fertile land in the area is of paramount importance for an understanding of some of the traditions in the Bible and the background against which they are set. Travellers, whether engaged in trade or in seeking new areas in which to settle, would need to keep to the fertile land and avoid the deserts. Thus, those who told the story of Abraham would know that someone setting out from Ur (the addition of 'of the Chaldeans' shows that a southern Mesopotamian location was envisaged), with flocks and herds, and heading for what was to become Israel, would not travel to the west through the desert but would need to follow the Euphrates towards Haran before journeying south along the Mediterranean coast (Gen. 11: 31–12: 9). Similarly armies, heading for example from Mesopotamia towards Egypt or vice versa, would follow the Fertile Crescent. The east Mediterranean coastal strip was a land-bridge between Africa on the one hand and Asia and Europe on the other. So control of this territory was of great commercial and strategic importance. The death of the Judahite king Josiah is set in the context of an Egyptian pharaoh marching north to seek to assist the Assyrian king in warding off the rising threat of the Babylonians (2 Kgs 23: 28–30).

Lands of the Bible

GEOLOGY

The most striking feature of the lands of the east Mediterranean coast is the great Rift Valley, the result of a geological fault which begins in the Orontes Valley in northern Syria and continues south between the Lebanon and Antilebanon mountains, through the Jordan Valley, the Arabah, the Gulf of Aqaba, and the Red Sea proper and on into Africa. Because of the presence of this great rift, which runs parallel to the east Mediterranean coast, it has become customary to divide the area into four main longitudinal zones: the Coastal Plains, the Central Hill Country, the Rift Valley, and the Eastern Hills / Transjordan.

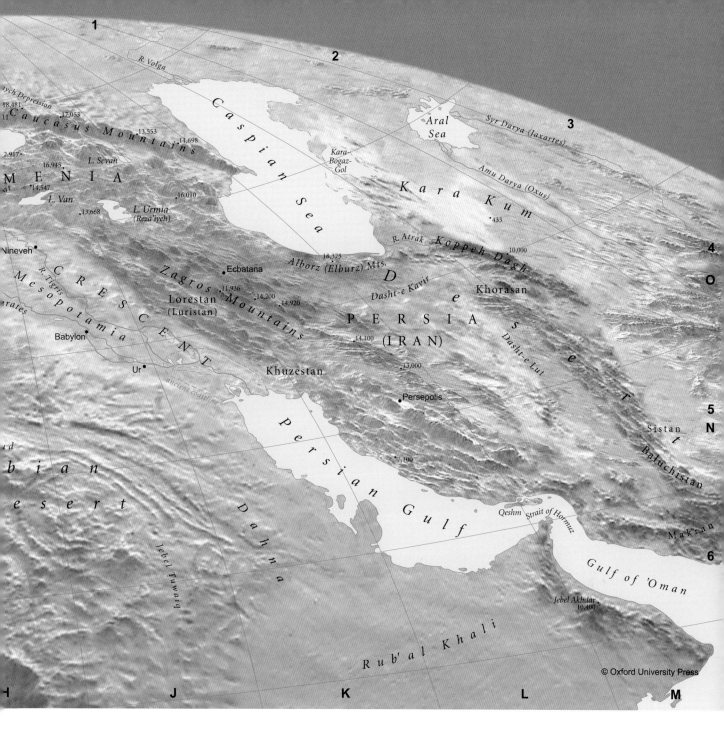

The rock which underlies the whole area is granite, and a split in the massive granite block led to the formation of the Rift Valley. The principal surface rocks are limestone, chalk and basalt. The limestone predominates in the hill country. It resists erosion, but does eventually weather into a reddish soil. The surface chalk is easily eroded and worn away to form valleys through which roads can pass. It accounts for important passes through the hills, including those across the Carmel Hills, and the so-called Judean 'moat' a valley separating the hills of Judah from the Shephelah. The basalt, a hard volcanic rock, occurs in Galilee and northern Transjordan.

MAIN GEOGRAPHICAL REGIONS OF PALESTINE

The coastal plains

The cliffs of Ras an-Naqura, also known as the 'Ladder of Tyre', which divide the Plain of Phoenicia to the north from the Plain of Acco to the south, form an appropriate northern boundary. The Plain of Acco reaches to the point where the limestone Carmel Promontory juts out into the Mediterranean and the plain is reduced to an extremely narrow coastal strip before it broadens somewhat to form the Plain of Dor which stretches down to the Croco-

dile River (Wadi Zerqa), around whose mouth was an area of marshland. South of this is the much broader Plain of Sharon, once thickly forested. The southern limit of Sharon was the Valley of Aijalon, through which ran the road to the port of Joppa.

One of the apparently surprising facts about the ancient Hebrews is that, despite dwelling along the coastline, they were not seafarers, unlike their northern neighbours the Phoenicians. The reason is probably that there were few natural harbours. Another feature of the coastal plains, particularly in the south, is the sand dunes which sometimes stretch inland for some

The Nile delta and the Sinai peninsula: a satellite image. The green colouring reveals agriculture amidst the surrounding desert regions. The Dead Sea is clearly visible (top right).

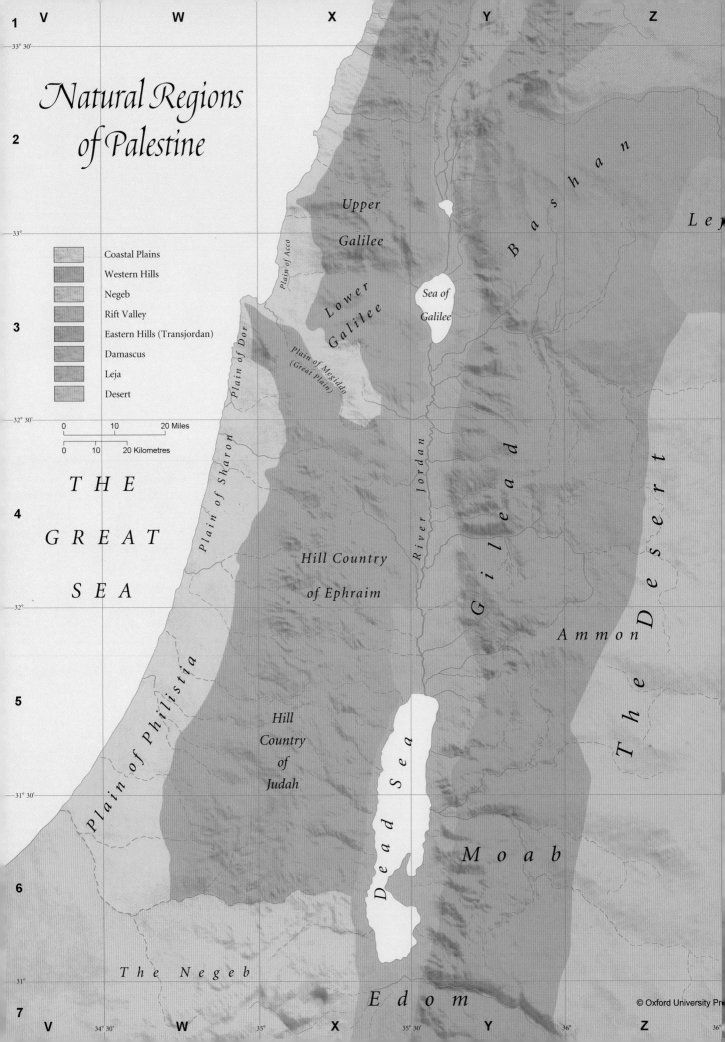

Natural Regions
of Palestine

Legend
- Coastal Plains
- Western Hills
- Negeb
- Rift Valley
- Eastern Hills (Transjordan)
- Damascus
- Leja
- Desert

0   10   20 Miles
0   10   20 Kilometres

V W X Y Z

33° 30'
33°
32° 30'
32°
31° 30'
31°

34° 30'   35°   35° 30'   36°

THE

GREAT

SEA

Upper
Galilee

Lower
Galilee

Plain of Acco

Plain of Dor

Plain of Megiddo
(Great Plain)

Sea of
Galilee

Bashan

Le

Plain of Sharon

Hill Country

of Ephraim

River Jordan

Gilead

The Desert

Plain of Philistia

Hill
Country
of
Judah

Dead Sea

Ammon

Moab

The Negeb

Edom

© Oxford University Pr

distance. But there was a port at Joppa, mentioned in the story of Jonah as the point of his embarkation on his ill-fated sea journey (Jon. 1: 3); its existence is implied in 2 Chronicles 2: 16 and Ezra 3: 7. Ultimately Herod the Great had a harbour constructed at Caesarea (Maritima).

South of the Plain of Sharon lies the Plain of Philistia, so-called because it was where the Philistines had settled.

The central hill country

Galilee, the northernmost section of the hill country, is a continuation of the Lebanon range. It is usually subdivided into Upper Galilee, whose highest mountain, Jebel Jermaq, rises to 3,962 ft (*c.*1300 m), and the gentler slopes and wider fertile valleys of Lower Galilee. To the south, the line of hills is inter-

The Coastal Plain: the road between Tel Aviv and Haifa.

The hills of northern Galilee, with Mount Hermon in the background.

Above: The Judean hill country between Bethlehem and Hebron. The construction of terraces created more cultivable land on the slopes of the hills.

Facing, above: The Judean hills: a barren landscape near the Wadi Qilt.

Facing, below: The Wadi Qilt: the old road from Jerusalem to Jericho, the setting of the parable of the Good Samaritan, ran through this area.

rupted by the Plain of Megiddo or Esdraelon, an approximately triangular shaped area which linked the Plain of Acco to the Valley of Jezreel and the Jordan Valley. The apex of the triangle is marked by the conspicuous limestone dome of Mount Tabor, and the base is formed by the Carmel hills which link the promontory to the region of Ephraim. The hill country of Ephraim (sometimes subdivided into Ephraim and Manasseh) is an area of rolling limestone hills and valleys, but east of the water-parting the land is largely wilderness. The successive capitals of the northern Kingdom of Israel (Shechem, Tirzah, and Samaria) were situated in this area. To the south is the hill country of Judah, separated from the coastal plains by the foothills of the Shephelah; the name means 'lowland' so it must have been given from the perspective of the higher hill country. On the whole the region is more rugged than Ephraim, and it falls away in the west into an area known as the Wilderness of Judah, even more desolate than that further north. The southern capitals, Hebron and Jerusalem, lay in the heart of the hill country of Judah. Further south, beyond the Valley of Beer-sheba and the Valley of Salt, the hills continue into the Negeb, a largely inhospitable region of steppeland but where some pasturing of crops and limited agriculture was possible. The

The Negeb: shepherds seek pasture for their flocks in an arid area with little vegetation.

Negeb extends from the Mediterranean coast in the west to the Arabah in the east, merging with the Sinai peninsula to the south-west.

The Rift Valley

In the vicinity of Dan are the springs which form the sources of the River Jordan, fed by water from the snow-capped Mount Hermon to the north-east. From these springs, the waters flow into the Huleh basin where, in biblical times, there was a lake whose Greek name was Lake Semechonitis. From Huleh, 223 ft (68 m) above sea level, the Jordan drops rapidly to the Sea (or Lake) of Galilee (or Chinnereth), which is already 695 ft (212 m) below sea level. The name 'Jordan' is probably connected with a root which means 'go down', so the name is very appropriate. The descent continues south of the Sea of Galilee, as the river continues to drop towards the Dead (or Salt) Sea whose surface is nearly 1,300 feet (400 m) below sea level, and whose deepest point is another 1,300 ft lower still. Between the Sea of Galilee and the Dead Sea, the Jordan flows though a valley known as the Ghor, in which it has formed a lower flood plain, the Zor, an area of thick vegetation and probably that which is described in Jeremiah 12: 5 as the 'jungle [NRSV thickets] of the Jordan'. A feature of this stretch of the river is its meandering. The distance 'as the crow flies' between the Sea of Galilee and the Dead Sea is about 65 miles (105 km); but the river flows nearly 200 miles (about 320 km) to cover the distance. The most noteworthy feature of the Dead Sea is the extremely high level of saltiness of its water, some six times the salt content of the oceans, so high that no marine life can survive in it. This is due almost entirely to evap-

Facing: The River Jordan at Paneas (Banias): a picture of the river close to one of its sources taken in winter.

oration, since the Jordan does not wash down appreciably more chemicals than other rivers. South of the Dead Sea, the Rift Valley continues some 100 miles (160 km) until it reaches the Gulf of Aqaba. This region is known as the Arabah, although sometimes that designation is used with reference to the whole of the Rift Valley south of the Sea of Galilee.

Transjordan

Much of the territory to the east of the Jordan comprises relatively high tableland, divided by four major rivers. Because of its height it receives a significant amount of rainfall, though this decreases further east and the land becomes desert. To the north of the River Yarmuk, which joins the Jordan just south of the Sea of Galilee, Bashan is the broadest part of the fertile strip, known for its produce and cattle (Deut. 32: 14; Amos 4: 1). East of Bashan is the Leja (whose Greek name was Trachonitis), a rugged area of basalt hills. South of the Yarmuk is the territory of Gilead, divided by the River Jabbok. This region too was noted for its cattle (for example, Num. 32: 1; S. of Sol. 4: 1; 6: 5) and is mentioned alongside Bashan in Micah 7: 14 in a context which suggests they were noted for their fertility. Further south are regions which, in the period reflected in the Hebrew Bible, were separate kingdoms. To the east and south of Gilead is the territory of Ammon. Further south again, and to the east of the Dead Sea, lies Moab, through which flows the River Arnon. The biblical narrative records that Moab was known as a sheep-breeding centre (2 Kgs. 3: 4), and the Book of Ruth opens with a reference to people of Judah seeking refuge there in time of famine (Ruth 1: 1). Separated from Moab by the valley of the Zered and south of the Dead Sea is the rugged region of Edom.

MAIN ROADS

It has already been noted that the region forms part of a land-bridge between Africa and Arabia on the one hand, and Anatolia and Mesopotamia on the other. Through the region passed important roads, whose route was determined by the lie of the land. The most important road was the 'Way of the Sea' (Isa. 9: 1). From Egypt it made for Gaza and then passed through the Plain of Philistia, following the line of the coast then moving further inland skirting the edge of the hill country. The hills eventually formed a barrier as they came closer to the coastline at the Carmel promontory, so the road cut through the Megiddo pass to enter the Plain of Megiddo or Esdraelon. Thence it made its way towards the northern end of the Sea of Galilee, crossed the Jordan in the vicinity of Hazor, south of Lake Huleh, and headed towards Damascus, skirting the foothills of Mount Hermon.

The other major south–north route of the region was the 'King's Highway' (Num. 20: 17; 21: 22), which led from the Gulf of Aqaba, though the hill country of Edom, Moab, and Ammon into Gilead, and thence towards Damascus.

There was also another road which ran through the central hills, linking a

Facing, above: The River Jordan at Paneas (Banias): a picture of the river close to one of its sources taken in summer.

Facing, below: The Sea (or Lake) of Galilee.

number of important cities: Beer-sheba, Hebron, Jerusalem, Bethel, and Shechem. It then formed two branches, one heading via Samaria and Ibleam into the Plain of Megiddo (Esdraelon), the other heading into the Jordan Valley via Beth-shan. Linking these north–south routes and the coast were a number of east–west roads, often following the lines of valleys through the hill country. Many important towns were established at crossroads or at strategic points controlling valley routes into the hills.

Climate, Flora, and Fauna

The latitude of Palestine is roughly that of southern Spain in Europe or Georgia in the USA. Its climate is also influenced by the configurations of the land and its proximity to the sea on the west and the desert on the east. Although it possesses a variety of climate, in general it has two main seasons: a 'winter' (including also the autumn and the spring), which is the cooler rainy season, and a summer which is rainless, sunny, and often very hot. The dryness of the summer is relieved by dew, important for the ripening of the summer fruits. (On the occurrence of dew, see Judges 6: 36–40.)

RAINFALL

Prevailing winds are from the west, that is, from the sea, and so the rains tend to come from a westerly direction. The rainclouds drop most of their moisture on the western slopes of the hills, with a considerably decreased amount falling on the eastern slopes. In general the rainfall tends to become less from west to east, although this may be counteracted by the fact that rainfall may increase with altitude. The average annual rainfall near Acco on the coast and at Jerusalem up in the hills is about 24–6 inches (61–6 cm). This is similar to the annual rainfall in the London area (23.5 inches, 60 cm), Edinburgh (25 inches, 64 cm) or Victoria, British Columbia (27 inches, 69 cm). The important difference is that the rains do not fall throughout the year but are restricted to the 'winter'; the summers are rainless. Inland, on the plain north of Megiddo, where the elevation is slight, annual rainfall is a little less than 16 inches (about 40 cm). The high hills of Upper Galilee receive about 47 inches (120 cm) of rain (compare New York City with about 42 inches or 107 cm). South of Hebron only about 12 inches (30.5 cm) falls. This illustrates how in general there is tendency for the rainfall to decrease as one goes from north to south.

The biblical text refers to early (or former) rains and later rains (see for example Deut. 11: 14). The early rains come in the autumn and with them begins the agricultural year because ploughing can now be done on the rain-

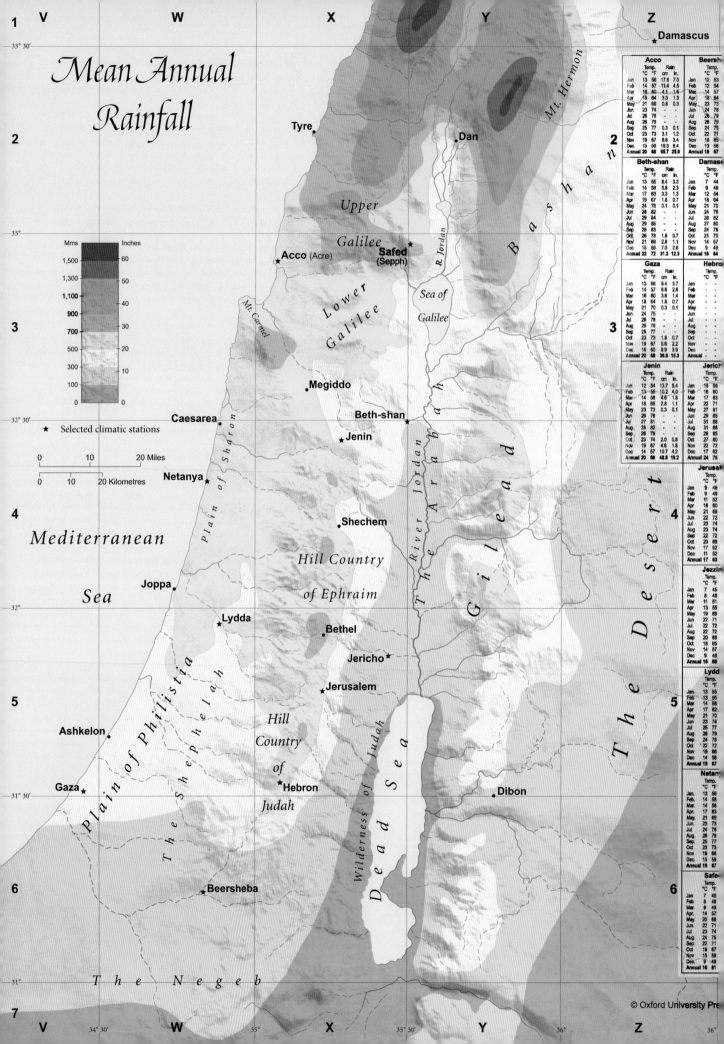

Jerusalem covered in snow. The picture was taken on an unusually snowy day in 1992. The Church of the Dormition is in the background.

softened ground. It is quite understandable that the Israelites had an autumnal calendar; as in the modern Jewish calendar, the New Year occurred in the autumn, near the autumnal equinox. The heaviest rainfall occurs from December to March. The later or spring rains are those of April and May, so important for the ripening of the crops (see Prov. 16: 15; Jer. 3: 3; Amos 4: 7). Proverbs 26: 1 alludes to the problem of rains which come at the wrong time. The verse also mentions snow, which is relatively rare but not unknown in the hills. Frost also occurs from time to time in the winter.

MAIN CROPS

Agriculture in Palestine was dependent on rainfall rather than on irrigation (as in Egypt and Mesopotamia). This had the advantage of not requiring human effort to water the land (see Deut. 11: 10-12), but if either the early or the late rains failed the result could be disastrous for the farmer. The three main crops were grain, wine, and oil (Joel 2: 19), but in a summary description of the land in Deuteronomy 8: 8, a somewhat fuller indication of the principal products of the land is given.

The most important of the field crops were the various types of cereal (including wheat and barley) grown in particular for the making of bread and (in the case of barley) for the brewing of beer. The most important fruits were the grape, cultivated principally for the production of wine, and the olive which was grown for its oil. Other fruits included figs and pomegranates. The final commodity mentioned in Deuteronomy 8: 8, often translated

31

An olive press from Maresha (biblical Mareshah): this example dates from about the 5th century CE.

The 'Gezer Calendar': inscribed on limestone, this is possibly the oldest known piece of Hebrew writing, dating from about the 10th century BCE.

as 'honey', may be something produced from dates. Other vegetables, especially pulses, herbs, and spices, were also grown, as were pistachios and almonds.

Interesting light is shed on the agricultural year by the 'Gezer Calendar', dating from about the 10th century BCE, so-called because it was found at Gezer and listed farming activities for successive months (or two-month periods) of the year. It suggests the following sequence, though the actual crops are not always specified: two months for gathering (olives?), two months for sowing (grain?), two months of late sowing (vegetables?), one month for hoeing, one month for harvesting barley, one month for harvesting (wheat?) and measuring, two months for harvesting grapes, and one month for gathering summer fruit.

ANIMALS

There are numerous references to animal life in the Bible. The account of creation in the first chapter of Genesis speaks of the creation of winged creatures and aquatic creatures on the fifth day (Gen. 1: 20–3) and of the land animals on the sixth day (Gen. 1: 24–5). The land animals are subdivided into wild animals, cattle (domesticated animals), and creeping things. Evidence of an awareness of a considerable variety of species of animal comes not only

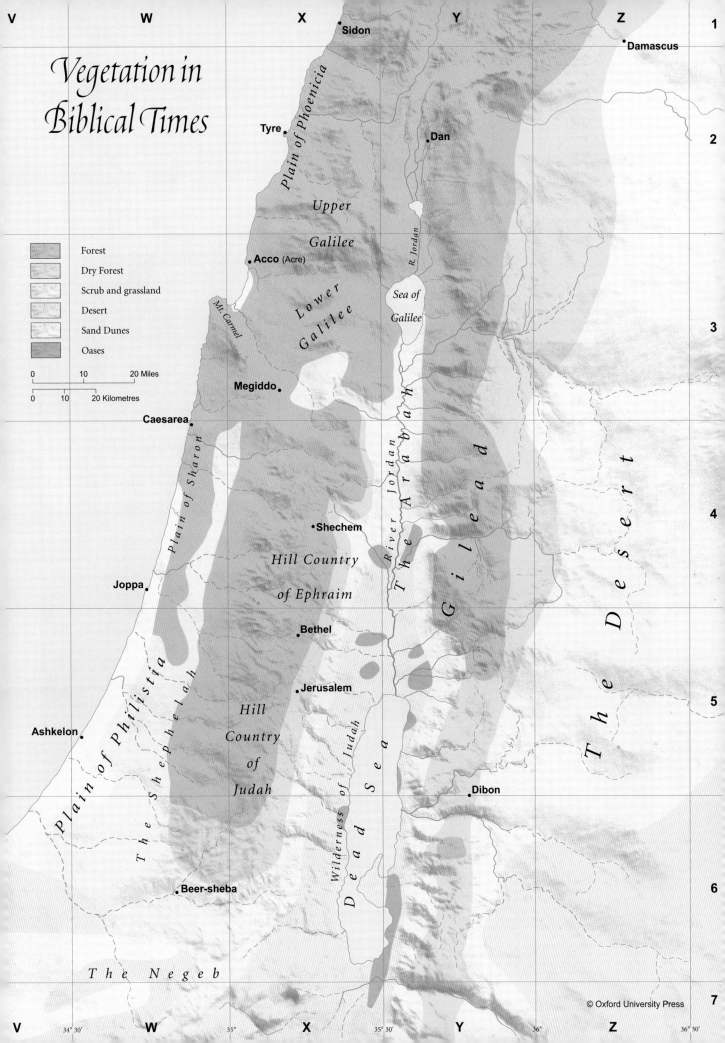

Vegetation in Biblical Times

V W X Y Z

1

• Sidon

• Damascus

Plain of Phoenicia

Tyre •

2

• Dan

Upper

Galilee

Forest

Dry Forest

Scrub and grassland

Desert

Sand Dunes

Oases

Acco (Acre)

R. Jordan

Lower

Galilee

Sea of Galilee

Mt. Carmel

3

0   10   20 Miles

0   10   20 Kilometres

Megiddo •

Caesarea •

Plain of Sharon

The Arabah

River Jordan

G i l e a d

4

• Shechem

Hill Country

of Ephraim

T h e   D e s e r t

Joppa •

• Bethel

Jerusalem •

5

Plain of Philistia

The Shephelah

Hill

Country

of

Judah

Wilderness of Judah

Dead Sea

Ashkelon •

• Dibon

• Beer-sheba

6

T h e   N e g e b

© Oxford University Press

7

V W X Y Z

34° 30'   35°   35° 30'   36°   36° 30'

from narrative passages, but from different types of biblical material including poetry and prophecy, legal and wisdom material. The regulations concerning clean and unclean animals in Leviticus 11 and the references to various creatures in God's responses to Job (Job 38: 39–39: 30; 40: 15–41: 34) are but two examples, and more will be given below. (The precise identification of some of the creatures mentioned in such passages is uncertain.)

Domesticated animals

The herding of animals was an important part of the way of life in rural communities, not only among true nomads and semi-nomads, but also in settled communities around which shepherds would lead their flocks from pasture to pasture. And the raising of other domesticated animals was a vital part of the rural economy. Particularly important were sheep and goats, kept as a source of meat and of milk (and thence various dairy products). They also provided wool and goats' hair and their skins could be used for a number of purposes, not least as containers for liquids. Larger cattle were also raised. Oxen were primarily draft animals, and their hides were a useful commodity. They were probably little used for meat, but the cows were a source of milk. Donkeys and mules were beasts of burden and also used for riding, sometimes in prestigious circumstances. Solomon rode on a mule to his anointing at Gihon (1 Kgs. 1: 38; see also Zech. 9: 9 where a king is envisaged as riding on a donkey). Horses were predominantly used for military purposes, for riding

Sheep and goats are guided along a road with pillars from the Roman period at Sebasṭiyeh (ancient Samaria).

or drawing chariots. The widespread use of the camel was probably relatively late (see the final chapter, on 'Archaeology and the Bible'). Evidence for the domestication of fowls is limited, but chickens appear to have been used in the Levant from the Persian period, and perhaps earlier.

Wild creatures

There is frequent reference to wild animals in the Bible, particularly the Hebrew Bible. Some familiar stories speak of the encounter between humans and wild animals. An example of Samson's strength is seen in his ability to tear apart a young lion which roared at him (Judg. 14: 5–6). In the story of David and Goliath, part of David's justification of his claim to be able to confront the Philistine warrior is that he has in the past killed lions and bears (1 Sam. 17: 34-6). When Joseph's torn and bloodstained coat is shown to Jacob, his immediate reaction is that a wild animal must have killed his son (Gen. 37: 33). Lions seem to have been particularly associated with the thick vegetation of the Jordan Valley (see Jer. 49: 19; Zech. 11: 3).

References to wild animals are frequent in imagery. For example, God's coming to punish his people is likened to the activity of animals (see Hos. 5: 14; 13: 7–8). The roaring lion is a simile of the devil in 1 Peter 5: 8. The officials and judges of Jerusalem are described as lions and wolves respectively in Zephaniah 3: 3. Amos's graphic description of the 'Day of the Lord' as something from which there will be no escape suggests that it will be as if someone succeeds in escaping from a lion only to encounter a bear, or manages to reach the apparent safety of the house only to be bitten by a snake (Amos 5: 19).

That the people of Israel were observant of the ways of animals and birds is suggested in numerous passages, of which the following are a few examples. The migration of birds is mentioned in Jeremiah 8: 7, and the soaring flight of the hawk and nesting habits of the eagle are referred to in Job 39: 26–7. A psalmist in distress likens his situation to that of an owl of the wilderness and waste places, or a lonely bird on a housetop (Ps. 102: 6–7). Jesus is presented as making allusion to the raven (Luke 12: 24) and the commonness of the sparrow (Matt. 10: 29, 31; Luke 12: 6–7). The abodes of various birds and animals are mentioned in Psalms 104: 17–18. And even the smallest of creatures, such as ants, badgers, locusts, and lizards (or perhaps spiders) could be used to teach a lesson (Prov. 30: 24–8).

Knowledge of some animals may have come from further afield. The account of the wealth of Solomon includes a statement that, every three years, ships of Tarshish would come, bringing not only gold, silver, and ivory, but also apes and what have traditionally been though of as peacocks, but the word may refer to baboons or to another type of monkey (1 Kgs. 10: 22). It has been suggested that the 'Behemoth' of Job 40: 15–24 was probably the hippopotamus, and known from Egypt, but there is now evidence that the hippopotamus may have lived in the Palestine area prior to the 8th century BCE. That the 'Leviathan' of Job 41 is the crocodile, known from Egypt, rather than the mythological monster, is widely accepted. But it is noteworthy that part of the description moves beyond what might reflect actual observation to suggest that it breathed fire and smoke (Job 41: 19–21). This raises the possibility that, in the popular imagination, there were creatures which lived on the fringes of the inhabited world which had strange and mysterious features. In Numbers 21: 6 and Deuteronomy 8: 15 there are references to the 'fiery serpent' (the translation reflects the fact that the word is probably associated with the verb 'to burn', and this is perhaps an allusion to the effect of its venom rather than to any literal fire). But in Isaiah 30: 6, at the beginning of an oracle concerning the animals of the Negeb, there is mention, among other creatures, of a winged fiery serpent (NRSV 'flying serpent'). In the ocean depths there were thought to be great sea-monsters, but they too came to be envisaged as part of God's creation (Gen. 1: 21).

Israel and the Nations

THE CRADLE OF CIVILIZATION

The story of Israel and of Judah and of the beginnings of Christianity, as recounted in the Bible, is set in the ancient Near East, an area to which later civilizations owe an immense debt. Here were the beginnings of agriculture and village life, and of literature, law, and science. This was the area from which three major world religions, Judaism, Christianity, and Islam, were to develop and spread, and where the sacred texts of those religions emerged.

All this was due in no small measure to the emergence in the ancient Near East of systems of writing (see on 'Writing Systems'). Thanks to the Sumerians' development of the cuneiform script to record their language, it is possible to know something of their stories of creation and flood which seem to have provided the pattern for other later accounts from widely scattered areas of the ancient Near East. Tablets from Erech, probably dating from the latter half of the 4th millennium BCE, seem to give groupings of birds, fish, animals, plants, personal names, etc. These can with some justification be thought of as scientific records; it is possible that they were intended to be a teachers' handbook. Among the Sumerians and their successors, the Assyrians and the Babylonians, are to be found the beginnings of medicine, mathematics, astronomy, geology, and metallurgy. To them is to be credited the sexagesimal system (counting by sixties, or multiples or fractions of 60) reflected in the division of the hour into 60 minutes and the circle into 360 degrees.

The development of the alphabetic system of writing can also be traced to the ancient Near East. The importance of this cannot be overstated, not least because it simplified considerably the process of writing. The Hebrew, Greek, Roman, and Arabic alphabets among others can be traced back to this development.

High levels of cultural achievement were reached not only in the field of literature but in crafts, such as pottery manufacture and metal working, in art, architecture, and music. Sumerian musical instruments have been found, dating from the 3rd millennium BCE. From Ugarit comes evidence of musical

Illustration of the method of writing the cuneiform script using a wooden stylus. (See on 'Writing Systems'.)

activity, including a text which is thought to record musical notation. Canaanite musicians seem to have been popular in Egypt, and the Hebrews may owe part of their musical heritage to the Canaanites.

In what follows, brief consideration will be given to the great civilizations of the ancient Near East which form the backdrop to the stories preserved in the Bible. Further information will also be given in appropriate sections later in this atlas.

EGYPT

The presence of the River Nile, and more particularly the phenomenon of its annual flooding, made it possible for human civilization to develop along a relatively narrow strip of fertile land, surrounded by desert, in north-east Africa. The annual inundations of the Nile brought down deposits of rich soil, making agriculture possible in a rainless and otherwise desert region. This also accounts for the development of human society, and ultimately the state, in Egypt, because the control of irrigation, the draining of swamps, the construction of dams, drainage channels, and canals required cooperation and an authority to oversee such vital tasks. The Nile also provided the principal means of travel and communication. The vegetation along its banks was the habitat for game and fowl and, particularly noteworthy, included the papyrus reed from which material on which to write was manufactured. Knowledge of the importance of the resources supplied by the Nile is graphically reflected in Isaiah 19: 4–10. Egypt was divided into Lower Egypt, predominantly the area of the Nile Delta, with its marshes, canals, and channels running into the Mediterranean (see Exod. 7: 19), and Upper Egypt which stretched south to the First Cataract of the Nile at Syene.

To some extent Egypt was geographically isolated from the rest of the ancient Near East, with desert on either side, and a land journey across the Sinai peninsula or a sea journey around the coast needed for contact with neighbours to the east. Nevertheless it was essential for Egypt not to become isolated but to maintain access to or control over the land and sea routes along the Levantine coast, for commercial and strategic reasons, so Egyptian armies were often in those regions. But Egypt's control over the Levant fluctuated. Unusual circumstances prevailed from the 18th to 16th centuries BCE when a group known as the Hyksos, probably including Indo-European and Asiatic elements, moved south along the east Mediterranean coast, and gained control in Egypt, establishing their capital at Avaris; but they were ultimately expelled. Subsequently, Pharaoh Thutmose I (1504–1492) passed through the area and reached as far as the Euphrates where he erected a stele by its banks. Pharaoh Thutmose III (1479–1425) claims to have conquered numerous cities in the area, including Megiddo whose capture was 'the capture of 1000 towns'. The letters discovered at Tell el-'Amarna (ancient Akhetaten), dating from the 14th century, include some written from the southern Levant by vassals of Pharaoh Akhenaten (1352–1336), imploring his assistance against trouble-makers: this suggests that Egyptian control over the area was

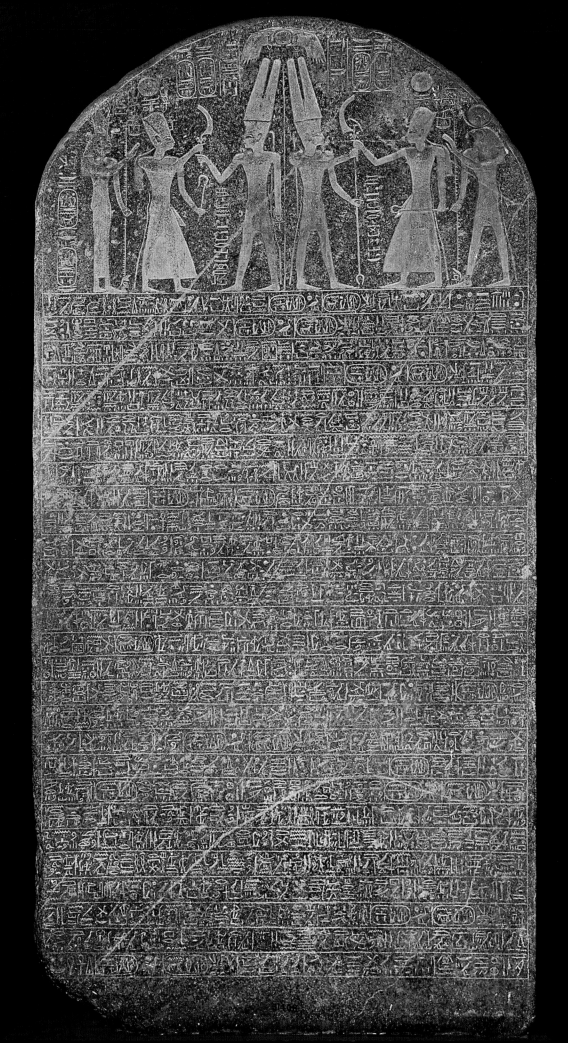

relatively weak at that time. (See 'The Setting of the Genesis Stories'.) It is in a stele recording the victories of Pharaoh Merneptah (1213–1203) that the earliest allusion to a people called Israel is to be found. The stele contains the statement, 'Israel is laid waste and his seed is not'.

The biblical narrative contains a number of allusions to contacts with Egypt and Egyptians, some of which suggest that the writers were familiar with Egyptian customs and practices (for example, mummification; Gen. 50: 1–3), and possibly also Egyptian stories such as the 'Tale of the Two Brothers'. Abraham is said to have visited Egypt (Gen. 12: 10–20), and much of the Joseph story is set there (Gen. 30–50). (It has been suggested that the Joseph story may reflect an awareness of the Hyksos period, a time when a non-Egyptian from Asia might have held a position of authority.) The Israelite bondage is set in Egypt (Exod. 1), as is the birth of Moses (Exod. 2: 1–10; the biblical writer provides a Hebrew etymology for what is in fact an Egyptian name). Solomon married an Egyptian princess in order to establish an alliance with the Pharaoh (1 Kgs. 3: 1; 9: 16), and engaged in trade with Egypt (1 Kgs. 10: 28–9). Before taking the throne of the northern kingdom of Israel, Jeroboam fled to Egypt to take refuge with Pharaoh Shishak I (Shoshenq) (1 Kgs. 11: 40). There is an allusion to Shishak's campaigns in Judah and Israel in 1 Kings 14: 25. It is likely that various subsequent revolts by Israel and Judah against the Assyrians were instigated or encouraged by Egypt. 2 Kings 18: 19–25 presents an Assyrian official warning Hezekiah of Judah of the futility of relying on Egypt. Later Pharaoh Neco, seeking to support the Assyrians against the rising power of the Babylonians, marched north and killed King Josiah of Judah, who was attempting to prevent him, at Megiddo in 609 (2 Kgs. 23: 29). Neco's subsequent defeat by Nebuchadrezzar at Carchemish is recalled in Jeremiah 46: 2–12. Neco placed Jehoahaz on the throne of Judah briefly, but then removed him and took him to Egypt, replacing him with Jehoiakim who taxed the land in order to pay tribute to Egypt (2 Kgs. 23: 33–5). According to Jeremiah 37: 5–12, an Egyptian army did try to come to the help of the besieged city of Jerusalem, causing the withdrawal of the Babylonian for a while and making it possible for people to leave the city. (Mention will be made in the section on 'The Greeks' of other contacts with Egypt.)

The above outline has concentrated on narrative passages in the Hebrew Bible, but there are also prophetic oracles directed against Egypt in Isaiah, Jeremiah, and Ezekiel.

Did Egypt have any significant religious influence on Israel? A theory which must now be considered very doubtful concerns the possibility that the attempt to inaugurate something approaching monotheism by Pharaoh Akhenaten in the 14th century BCE might have influenced Moses and thence the faith of Israel. But there are a number of difficulties, not least the fundamental fact that Akhenaten's worship was directed to a natural object, the solar disc (the Aten). However, there are some affinities between the famous 'Hymn to the Aten', thought by some to have been written by the pharaoh himself, and parts of Psalm 104; these have suggested the possibility that the

Hymn was known in Israel, perhaps in translation, but it is also possible that the writers were drawing upon similar traditions rather than there being direct literary dependence. It was perhaps in the area of Wisdom literature that Egypt had an influence, although Wisdom literature is also known from Mesopotamia. (See 1 Kings 4: 30, where there is an allusion to the wisdom of Egypt but also to the wisdom of the East.) Wisdom books known as 'Instructions' were used in Egypt in the training of officials and administrators and, since Israel's court officials seem to have been modelled on those of Egypt, it is not impossible that the accompanying Wisdom literature had an influence. Part of one of these Egyptian documents, the 'Instruction (or Wisdom) of Amenemope' seems to be quoted in Proverbs 22: 17–23: 11.

The River Euphrates in Syria.

MESOPOTAMIA

The name 'Mesopotamia' means '(the land) between the rivers' and reflects the Greek rendering of the Hebrew *Aram-naharaim* (Aram of the two rivers), the area of the upper and middle Tigris and Euphrates, the location of places associated with the Patriarchal traditions such as Haran (for example, Gen. 11: 31) and Nahor (Gen. 24: 10). The term came to refer to the whole of the Tigris–Euphrates region, including the area where the rivers join and become one before reaching the Persian Gulf. Although rain does fall in the

41

Facing: Obelisk of Shalmaneser III (858–824). The second panel from the top shows the Israelite King Jehu paying homage to Shalmaneser.

area, fertility depended to a considerable extent on the waters of the rivers (see below). The Tigris and Euphrates have changed their courses through the Mesopotamian plains over the years, but the pattern of ancient settlement can be seen in the presence of numerous mounds containing buried cities which were once located near a river or on a canal. The Tigris and Euphrates have their origins in the high mountain regions of Armenia (Urartu). Two important tributaries of the upper Euphrates were the Balikh and the Habor. Two major tributaries of the upper Tigris were the Upper (or Great) Zab and the Lower (or Little) Zab. Further south were the Adhaim and the Diyala. The Tigris and Euphrates share with the Nile the feature of an annual inundation which would begin in the spring and, as it receded, leave behind rich deposits of fertile soil. So, as with Egypt, the origins of ordered society are to be connected with the need to cooperate in the preparation and upkeep of irrigation channels, dams, canals, etc. Sometimes these inundations would occur with such destructive force that the surrounding countryside would be laid waste. This phenomenon doubtless lies behind the stories of a great deluge which had their origin in this area. Evidence of the effects of flooding have been found in a number of excavations, including Kish, Ur, and Shuruppak, the last of which is recorded as the home of the hero of the Mesopotamian flood traditions. A Sumerian flood tablet found at Nippur calls the hero Ziusudra. Later stories call him Atrahasis and, in the famous Epic of Gilgamesh, Utnapishtim. These graphic flood descriptions may well have been based on personal experience.

Water control was a continuing necessity in the economy of the region. The area from the vicinity of ancient Eshnunna and modern Baghdad as far south as ancient Ur and Eridu, a distance of over 200 miles (320 km), could be irrigated. Further north, one of the most impressive of public water works was the aqueduct and associated canal built to supply the city of Nineveh with water by Sennacherib, king of Assyria—just one of a number of hydraulic works constructed at his instigation.

The regions of Sumer and Akkad lay in the alluvial plain of Mesopotamia, Sumer to the south and Akkad to the north. Excavations suggest that the early cities in Akkad were relatively small and the region rather sparsely settled, in contrast with Sumer which was politically and culturally prominent earlier than Akkad. The more extensive cultivation of Akkad did not begin until after 2000 BCE, with the construction of extensive irrigation channels. The terms Sumer and Akkad continued to be used long after the periods of Sumerian and Akkadian domination. So, for example, Cyrus the Persian called himself 'king of Sumer and Akkad'. Subsequently, Babylonia in the southern plains covered largely the area of the former Sumer and Akkad, and Assyria lay to the north in a more mountainous region. Further north still, from the 16th to 14th centuries, was the Hurrian kingdom of Mitanni.

Biblical allusions to Mesopotamia are numerous, and include some of the first stories encountered in the Book of Genesis. The Tigris and Euphrates are said to have been two of the four branches of the river which flowed out of the Garden of Eden (Gen. 2: 14). The biblical flood traditions (Gen. 6–9) are clearly related to the Mesopotamian flood stories. (A later version of the Mesopotamian story, reported by Berossos, has the Ark coming to rest in Armenia which is identical with the mountains of Ararat (Urartu) of the biblical account.) The 'land of Shinar' (Gen. 11: 1) is probably the region of Sumer and Akkad, and Babel (Gen. 11: 9) is Babylon, and the story may owe its origins to reminiscences of the construction of ziggurats or temple-towers by the Sumerians. Abraham and his family are said to have travelled from Ur in southern Mesopotamia to Haran in the north (Gen. 11: 31). There is a reference in Genesis 14: 1 to a King Amraphel of Shinar (see the chapter on 'The Patriarchs in Canaan'). Isaac's wife, Rebekah, is said to have come from Aram-naharaim, more specifically Paddan-aram (Gen. 24: 10, 25: 20), and it was there that Jacob went to find a wife (Gen. 28: 6).

The biblical narrative suggests that the first of the judges, Othniel, delivered the Israelites from a certain King Cushan-rishathaim of Aram-naharaim (Judg. 3: 7–12). It has been suggested that the element 'Aram' here is a corruption of the name 'Edom', and that *naharaim* is a later gloss. Another possibility is suggested by the fact that *rishathaim* means 'of double wickedness'. Perhaps this was a story to illustrate the activity of the 'judges', presenting an archetypal evil king said to come from the region of the enemies *par excellence* of the people of Israel and Judah, the Assyrians and the Babylonians.

Information about contacts between the Assyrian kings and the lands of the east Mediterranean coast, and with the kings of Israel and Judah in particular, often comes from Assyrian records and includes incidents not mentioned in the Bible. (This is not surprising since the purpose of the biblical writers was not to provide complete annals of the Assyrian contacts with Israel and Judah.) Noteworthy examples include the fact that King Ahab of Israel was part of a coalition which fought against Shalmaneser III in the battle of Qarqar, on the River Orontes, in 853, and that King Jehu submitted to Shalmaneser in *c.*841. The latter episode is recorded on the 'Black Obelisk', which depicts Jehu kneeling before Shalmaneser, while behind him stand Israelites bearing tribute. Sometimes the biblical writer may refer to an episode without providing the details which the modern reader might expect. In 2 Kings 13: 5, what matters to the writer is to claim that God provided a 'saviour', giving the credit to God rather than to the person who may lie behind the epithet, Adad-nirari III. His records say that he campaigned against Damascus and Philistia, and that various terri-

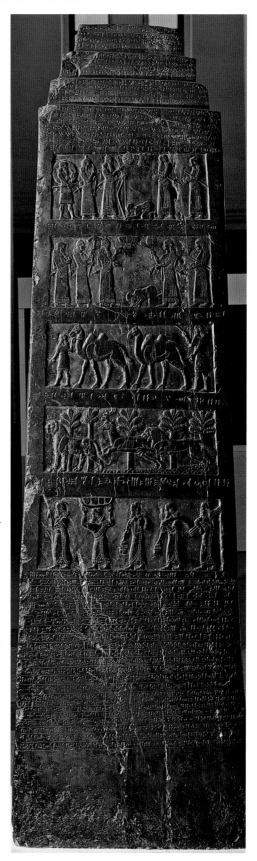

tories, including the 'land of Omri' (that is, Israel), recognized his overlord-ship.

The biblical account has a number of references to contacts with Assyria during the latter half of the 8th century BCE, the period which included the fall of the northern kingdom to Assyria. 2 Kings 15: 19–20 records that King Menahem had to submit to the authority of, and pay tribute to, King Pul of Assyria. This was the great Tiglath-pileser III, whose own records report how Menahem fled but how he returned him to the throne and imposed tribute on him. The narrative also tells how Ahaz of Judah purchased the help of Tiglath-pileser against King Rezin of Damascus and King Pekah of Israel, prompting an Assyrian attack on Damascus (2 Kgs. 16). This paved the way for a subsequent invasion of Israel, culminating in the capture of Samaria, which the biblical account credits to King Shalmaneser V (2 Kgs. 17: 1–6). This may accord with a reference in the Babylonian Chronicle, but the reading of the relevant place name as 'Samaria' has been disputed. Shalmaneser's successor, Sargon II, who campaigned in the Mediterranean coastlands, certainly claimed the credit for this feat. A later campaign of Sargon in which Ashdod was captured is mentioned in Isaiah 20.

The activity of Sargon's successor, Sennacherib, is also mentioned in the biblical account. He is said to have captured all the fortified cities of Judah (2 Kgs. 18: 13); his own annals record the taking of 46 cities and the besieging of Jerusalem. Sennacherib's siege of Lachish, where Hezekiah of Judah is said to have visited him (2 Kgs. 18: 14), is commemorated in a set of reliefs which decorated his palace at Nineveh (see on 'Lachish'). The biblical account records a miraculous delivery of Jerusalem when 'the angel of the LORD set out and struck down one hundred and eighty-five thousand in the camp of the Assyrians' (2 Kgs. 19: 35). The fact that this is not mentioned in Sennacherib's own account has led to the suggestion that it belonged to a later campaign or else that the account was legendary or fictional. But Sennacherib's account does not say that he actually *captured* Jerusalem, and states that the tribute which Hezekiah paid was sent later to Nineveh. It is therefore possible that he was forced to withdraw from Jerusalem, perhaps because of an outbreak of plague, something which it is perhaps not surprising that he would not want to record in his annals, and that Hezekiah paid tribute to forestall another invasion. The biblical writer may have placed the paying of tribute *before* the siege of Jerusalem in order to present a more theologically significant account, highlighting God's deliverance of the city.

Other references to contacts with Assyria in the biblical narrative are in 2 Chronicles 33: 10–13 which suggest that Manasseh was taken captive to Babylon by the 'commander of the army of the king of Assyria'; the king is not named, but the reference may be to Esarhaddon. King Ashurbanipal is mentioned as 'Osnappar' in Ezra 4: 10.

Just as Assyria was responsible for the downfall of Israel, so in turn Babylon was to be Judah's nemesis. In the days of Sennacherib of Assyria, King Merodach-baladan of Babylon is recorded as having made approaches to

Hezekiah of Judah (2 Kgs. 20: 12–19; Isa. 39). The account of Josiah's ill-fated attempt to stop Pharaoh Neco's advance to bolster the forces of the king of Assyria (2 Kgs. 23: 28–30) does not mention that the context was the growing threat of Babylon. But Nebuchadrezzar's advance south along the east Mediterranean coastlands, mentioned in his own chronicles, is reflected in the biblical accounts (2 Kgs. 24: 1; see also Jer. 35: 11). Jehoiakim's revolt is perhaps to be associated with an unsuccessful attack on Egypt by the Babylonians. Nebuchadrezzar besieged Jerusalem, and took the young king Jehoiachin, the queen mother, and other leading citizens into exile, along with treasures from the Temple, and placed Zedekiah on the throne of Judah (2 Kgs. 24: 10–17). When Judah subsequently revolted, probably inspired by Egypt, Jerusalem was again besieged and captured, and the Temple destroyed. Zedekiah was taken in chains to Babylon, with another group of exiles and yet more plunder from the Temple (2 Kgs. 24: 20b–25: 21; Jer. 52: 3b–27). Gedaliah was placed in charge in what remained of Judah (2 Kgs. 25: 22–6). Jeremiah 52: 30 mentions a third deportation five years later. Nebuchadrezzar's son, Amel-marduk (called Evil-merodach in the biblical account) elevated Jehoiachin above other captive kings (2 Kgs. 25: 27–30; Jer.

Section of the reliefs from the Palace of Sennacherib at Nineveh, depicting the siege of Lachish. Here Sennacherib is shown seated on a throne, receiving the surrender of the city. (See on 'Lachish'.)

52: 31–4). The territory which had belonged to Judah remained under Babylonian control until the Persians became the dominant power in the Near East.

The exile in Babylon was the context of the activity of the prophet Ezekiel, and part of the Book of Isaiah (chapters 40–55) is widely held to have originated in Babylon and been primarily addressed to the Jewish exiles there.

Mention has already been made of the likelihood that Mesopotamian traditions influenced certain biblical stories such as the Flood and the Tower of Babel. This is also true of other accounts, including the first creation story in Genesis 1: 1–2: 4a, which has certain affinities with (and certain fundamental differences from) the Babylonian creation story, *Enuma Elish*. In considering how similarities between some Hebrew and Babylonian ideas might have arisen, a number of possibilities might be suggested. One would be that they reflect common ancestry. The biblical writers are at pains to claim that their ancestors came from Mesopotamia and, if there is truth in that claim, then it might be surprising if they did not have some ideas in common, even though they may have developed differently. But it is also possible that the Jews in exile in Babylon came into contact with Babylonian traditions and were tempted by Babylonian religion, given the apparent failure of their own God to protect them. It may have been important for the biblical writers to stress that it was their God who created the universe, sent the flood, and confounded Babel.

PERSIA

The territory of the Medes and the Persians lies to the east of Mesopotamia (although at the height of the Persian Empire they occupied lands further west). It is a huge plateau between the Tigris and Euphrates in the west and the Indus in the east. On the north are the Alborz (Elburz) Mountains, south of the Caspian Sea, and further east are the mountains of Koppeh Dagh. On the south-west lie the Zagros Mountains and their extension, running parallel to the Tigris–Euphrates and the Persian Gulf and then turning eastward. The Persian plateau is a region of mountains, deserts, and some fertile areas. There are swamps and dry saline areas in it, such as the major depression, the Dasht-e Kavir. The average height of the plateau has been estimated at about 4,000 feet (1,220 m) with the greater elevation towards the rim. There is little rainfall, except in the Alborz Mountains, and the region experiences wide extremes of climate.

It was not until the time of Cyrus the Great that the Persians had an impact on the story of the Jews. It seems that it was the meteoric rise of Cyrus and his conquests that raised hopes among the Jewish exiles in Babylon that deliverance was at hand (Isa. 44: 24–45: 7). The biblical account records that it was in the very first year of his reign over Babylon (538), that Cyrus issued a decree permitting the Jewish exiles to return to Judah and authorizing the rebuilding of the Temple in Jerusalem (Ezra 1: 1–4; 6: 3–5). The first group of Jews presumably returned soon afterwards. The Hebrew Bible hints at the possibility that, during the period of rebellion and instability which followed the accession to the throne of Darius I (522–486), whilst he was seeking to establish his position, there was intrigue in Judah, planning to throw off the Persian yoke and make Zerubbabel, Jehoiachin's grandson, king, alongside the high priest Joshua (Hag. 2: 23; Zech. 4; 6: 9–14). But such plots must have come to nothing, and Zerubbabel disappears from the scene; it is possible that he was removed by the Persian authorities if they got wind of the plans associated with his name. Tattenai, the governor of the province Beyond the River (Trans-Euphrates), and his associates reported to Darius that the Jerusalem Temple was being rebuilt, perhaps suspecting that this was an act of revolt. But confirmation of Cyrus's decree was found at Ecbatana, and a new directive was issued that the work should proceed (Ezra 5: 3–6: 12).

The Book of Ezra also suggests that there had been an attempt to rebuild the walls of Jerusalem in the earlier years of the reign of Artaxerxes I (465–424), but that this too was viewed with suspicion by the officials in Samaria and the rest of the province Beyond the River. They sent a letter to Artaxerxes, as a result of which instructions were given that the work should cease (Ezra 4: 7–23). The completion of the rebuilding of the walls is credited to Nehemiah, a Jew serving in the Persian court who, in the twentieth year of Artaxerxes I, sought and was granted permission to travel to Jerusalem to rebuild the walls (Neh. 2: 1–9). Despite opposition, the task was completed (Neh. 3–4). It seems that it was also in the twentieth year of Artaxerxes that Nehemiah was appointed governor (Neh. 5: 14). He returned to Persia in the thirty-second year of Artaxerxes but was subsequently given permission to return to Judah (Neh. 13: 6–7).

The biblical account suggests that Ezra came to Jerusalem in the seventh year of Artaxerxes, in order to 'study the law of the Lord and to do it, and to teach the statutes and ordinances in Israel' (Ezra 7: 1–10). But the writer does not make it clear to which Artaxerxes reference is being made. There are grounds for believing that the reference is to Artaxerxes II (405–359) and the year 398, and that Ezra was envisaged as supplementing and reinforcing the reforms made by Nehemiah.

Although biblical references to contacts with the Persians are relatively limited, it has increasingly been thought likely that the Persian period may have been a highly formative one for the Jewish people. While the time of the Exile in Babylon may have seen some literary activity, as attempts were made to preserve traditions in danger of being lost and to reflect on what might have brought such a disaster upon Judah and Jerusalem, it was perhaps in the Persian period that the newly restored community needed to establish the story of its past and the criteria for its future life.

THE GREEKS

There is very limited direct reference to Greece and Greeks in the Hebrew Bible, but there are allusions to events in the Hellenistic period, and of course

Athens: the Acropolis.

the New Testament makes many references to Greece and Greeks, albeit in the context of the Roman Empire. Nor is there much, if any, clear evidence of the influence of Greek thought on the Hebrew Bible, though some of the ideas in Qoheleth (Ecclesiastes) have been suggested as having affinities with Greek ideas.

There is a reference to 'Greece' (Javan) in Zechariah 9: 13 but it is not clear precisely to which entity reference is being made. Elsewhere 'Javan' sometimes seems to refer to the Ionian coastland of Asia Minor or the adjacent islands. Ezekiel 27: 13 associates Javan with Tubal and Meshech, regions in Asia Minor, as being involved in trade with Tyre. In Isaiah 66: 19, mention of

Javan follows a reference to Tubal and to Lud (Lydia). In a passage in the Book of Joel (Joel 3: 4–8), 'Tyre, Sidon and all the regions of Philistia' are upbraided for selling people from Judah and Jerusalem as slaves to the Greeks (Javan). In the Book of Daniel there are somewhat oblique allusions to the rise of Alexander, the subsequent division of his empire after his death, and the rivalry among his generals, in particular the Ptolemies in Egypt and the Seleucids in Syria. (See, for example, Daniel 10: 18–11: 9.)

The spread of Hellenism and the vicissitudes of the Hellenistic Period must have made their impact on the Jews of Palestine, though direct references in the Bible itself are limited. They do, as already noted, help to explain the context from which it is now widely believed that the Book of Daniel emerged and sought to address. So a brief outline of some key events is not inappropriate here.

After Alexander had defeated Darius III at Issus in 332, he captured Damascus, laid siege to the island city of Tyre, and eventually took it after a seven-month siege. He then pressed on south and took Gaza on the way to Egypt. On his return, he destroyed Samaria to avenge the murder of one of his officials. In a cave in the Wadi Daliyeh in the wilderness of Judah were found papyrus documents brought there by refugees from Samaria. The presence of a non-Palestinian type of fortification, the round tower, at Samaria has given rise to the suggestion that, after it had been destroyed by Alexander, it was resettled by Macedonians. The rebuilding of Shechem in the late 4th century, after a long period when it was not occupied, raises the possibility that the Samaritans returned there and established it as their capital.

Alexander's death was followed by a period of confusion and warfare. Ultimately his empire was divided among his generals (see Dan. 8: 8, 22; 11: 4). Ptolemy I assumed the kingship of Egypt and initially took possession of Palestine and Phoenicia. But he lost these territories to Antigonus, ruler of Phrygia, who besieged and captured Tyre and left his son, Demetrius, in command at Gaza. Three years later, Ptolemy defeated Demetrius at Gaza and, according to a tradition preserved by the Jewish historian Flavius Josephus, Ptolemy then entered Jerusalem with his troops on the Sabbath day, when the inhabitants refused to fight. The exile of many Jews into Egypt by Ptolemy at this time is recorded in the Letter of Aristeas. Antigonus subsequently sought to invade Egypt, but was unsuccessful and many of his ships were wrecked in a storm at Raphia.

Seleucus, another of Alexander's generals, established his control over Babylonia by about 312–311, and so began the Seleucid era. After the defeat of Antigonus in the battle of Ipsus in Phrygia in *c*.301, Seleucus was given Coele-Syria (Palestine). He took possession of the northern part of Syria, making Antioch his capital, but in fact Palestine was to remain under the control of the Ptolemies of Egypt until the reign of Antiochus III (the Great), after a series of wars between Ptolemies and Seleucids. (Daniel 11 reflects the troubled events of this period; the term 'the king of the south' refers to the various Ptolemaic rulers, and 'the king of the north' to the Seleucid kings.)

Antiochus was initially unsuccessful in his attempts to invade Palestine. However, when the child-king Ptolemy V came to the throne in Egypt, Antiochus was presented with another opportunity, and this time he was successful in taking over Palestine from Egypt (Dan. 11: 15–16). In fear of Rome, Antiochus III married his daughter Cleopatra to Ptolemy at Raphia (Dan. 11: 17). An attempted foray into Greece was thwarted by Rome, and he was defeated at Magnesia 'ad Sipylum' (in Asia Minor) by the Roman general Scipio (Dan. 11: 18–19).

During the reign of Antiochus III (223–187), the Jews in Palestine were treated favourably. He remitted certain taxes and made contributions to the costs of sacrifices. But his reign, and that of his successors, was a time of feuding over the rights to the collection of taxes and over the high priesthood. Onias II, the high priest, had refused to pay taxes, 20 talents of silver, to Ptolemy V. Tax-collecting rights for the whole of Palestine were given to a certain Joseph, of the family of Tobias. When Palestine came under the control of Antiochus III, the tax-collecting rights remained with the Tobiad family, which became powerful and wealthy, and there was bitter rivalry between the house of Onias and the house of Tobias. Antiochus III was succeeded by Seleucus IV, whose chief minister, Heliodorus, went to Jerusalem to seize the Temple treasury (Dan. 11: 20). Onias III went to Seleucus to secure assistance in quieting riots in Jerusalem, but Seleucus was murdered by Heliodorus, and Antiochus IV (Epiphanes) became king in 175 (Dan. 11: 21). In the absence of Onias, his brother Jason bribed Antiochus to grant him the high priesthood. As his name suggests, he was a Hellenist, in favour of accommodating the Jewish faith to Greek religion and culture. But after three years a larger bribe was offered to Antiochus by Menelaus, who was not of a priestly family, but who now became high priest. He was an even more avid Hellenist, who encouraged his own brother to steal vessels from the Temple and who secured the murder of Onias at the sanctuary of Daphne, near Antioch.

In his first campaign in Egypt Antiochus won some significant victories, and it was while returning in triumph that he stopped in Jerusalem in 169 in order to raid the Temple treasury. In the following year he again campaigned in Egypt, but in a suburb of Alexandria he was ordered from Egypt by a Roman official. On his way home, humiliated, he again intervened in affairs in Jerusalem, to put down a rebellion which may have been sparked by rumours that he had died in Egypt. In 167 he sent his general, Apollonius, to maintain order in Jerusalem. This led to the creation of a fortress (the Akra), and the imposition of heavy taxation. Subsequently a decree was issued which virtually proscribed the practice of Judaism. The Temple was desecrated, an altar to Zeus was constructed, and a pig was sacrificed. This was the 'desolating sacrilege' (often known more archaically as the 'abomination of desolation') in December 167 (1 Macc. 1: 54).

This led to the outbreak of the Maccabean revolt under Mattathias and his sons. (See chapter on 'Judah, Yehud, and Judea'.) The detailed story is recounted in 1 Maccabees. As a result of the victories of Mattathias's son,

Judas, the Temple was rededicated three years later in December 165, and, according to 1 Maccabees 4: 54, on the very same day on which it had been profaned. Another of Mattathias's sons, Simon, became independent ruler, and the high priesthood was vested in him and his descendants. (His brother Jonathan had earlier been made high priest by the Seleucid Demetrius II.) Judas and his successors are known as 'the Hasmoneans' after an ancestor named Hasmon.

In its account of the early days of the Maccabean revolt, 1 Maccabees 2: 42 records that Mattathias and his followers were joined by a company of Hasidim. This was a group, which emerged or became prominent at this time, of faithful Jews who were opposed to Hellenization. It is possible that both the Pharisees and the Essenes emerged from among the number of the Hasidim. It was during the period of Hasmonean rule that a person known as the 'Teacher of Righteousness' may have led a group of people, probably Essenes, into the Judean desert and established the community at Qumran— on the north-west shore of the Dead Sea—which is associated with the 'Dead Sea Scrolls'. Simon's son, John Hyrcanus (135–104) was succeeded in turn by his son, Aristobulus I (104–103), who may have been the first of the Hasmoneans to assume the title 'king'. Another view is that Alexander Jannaeus

The Dead Sea: the barren landscape of the western shore. Salt deposits are clearly visible. (See on 'The Rift Valley'.)

(103–76) was the first to take the title 'king'. Hasmonean rule ultimately came to an end when Jerusalem was conquered by Rome in 63 BCE.

THE ROMANS

The New Testament's accounts of the birth, ministry, and death of Jesus set the events clearly in the context of Roman occupation. The Gospel of Luke associates the birth with a registration of the population in the time of the Emperor Augustus (Luke 2: 1), and all the canonical Gospels refer to the involvement of the Roman governor, Pontius Pilate, in the events leading up to the crucifixion (for example, Matt. 27: 2; Mark 15: 1; Luke 23: 3; John 18: 28). The story of the early spread of Christianity is set in the context of the Roman Empire. Therefore an awareness of some of the key events, particularly those which impinged on Judea, is important for understanding the setting of the New Testament.

In 63 BCE, Pompey besieged the Temple in Jerusalem, eventually breaking in on the Day of Atonement. It is said that some 12,000 Jews fell at that time. Jerusalem and Judea came under the power of Rome and a number of free cities were established: Gadara, Hippos, Scythopolis, Gaza, Joppa, Dor, and Strato's Tower. In the aftermath of a revolt led by Alexander, the son of Aristobulus II, Judea was divided into five districts (Jerusalem, Gadara, Amathus, Jericho, and Sepphoris) under Gabinius, the proconsul of Syria. Hyrcanus II, who had been made high priest and ethnarch of the Jews, was under the con-

Model of Herodian Jerusalem in the grounds of the Holy Land Hotel. The city is dominated by the Temple on its specially constructed platform.

trol of Antipater, the governor of Idumea. Antipater was an astute politician, who first supported Pompey and then, after Pompey's death, Julius Caesar. When Caesar invaded Egypt, Antipater assisted him by providing a Jewish army, 3,000-strong. He also persuaded the Arabs and the Syrians to support Caesar, and he himself assisted in the capture of Pelusium. As a result, Caesar appointed Antipater procurator of Judea. He became virtually the ruler of the whole of the Palestine area, and he made one of his sons, Phasael, prefect of Judah, and another, Herod, prefect of Galilee.

Antipater was poisoned in 43 BCE. Antigonus, the son of the last of the Hasmonean rulers (Aristobulus II) was prevented from conquering Judea by Herod. Mark Antony made Phasael and Herod tetrarchs of the Jews. But subsequently Antigonus, with the help of the Parthians who had invaded Syria, was successful in taking control of Judea. Phasael was imprisoned and then committed suicide, and Hyrcanus was exiled to Babylon. Antigonus ruled and served as high priest from 40 to 37. But Herod, having first placed his family at Masada, travelled to Rome to secure the help of Mark Antony and the Roman Senate appointed him king of the Jews. He returned from Rome to Ptolemais, took Joppa, and recovered control of Galilee of which he had been prefect. Three years later he married Mariamme, granddaughter of Aristobulus II and Hyrcanus II. In 37 BCE he took Jerusalem, with the assistance of the Roman legions, and ruled as king until 4 BCE. Matthew's Gospel mentions King Herod in the story of the visit of the Magi after the birth of Jesus, and blames Herod for the instigation of the 'massacre of the innocents' (Matt. 2: 1–18).

Herod's status was that of client king. There were many such rulers in the Roman Empire, including Cleopatra who ruled in Egypt as a client queen. Such rulers reigned with Rome's approval, and they were appointed or replaced and their territories enlarged or reduced at Rome's pleasure. Herod's appointment marked a change in the policy replacing such rulers by others in the same royal line. Herod, an Idumean, replaced the last of the Hasmonean kings, Antigonus. Client kings were personally bound to the emperor, often through marriage alliances, and sometimes the emperor brought up their children with his own family or else appointed guardians for their children. They were relatively independent within their own kingdoms and might issue coins, as did Herod, albeit that he was only permitted to issue copper coinage. They were expected to provide military assistance to the emperor, if required, and in many cases their primary function seems to have been to maintain order on the boundaries of the empire. Herod was bitterly disliked by the Jews. He despoiled them for his own gain and was prepared to put to death not only his enemies but even members of his own family.

In 31 BCE, Mark Antony was defeated by Octavian in the battle of Actium and, in the following year, Antony and Cleopatra committed suicide. Herod went in haste to Rhodes to meet Octavian, now ruler of the Roman Empire, to pledge the support he had formerly given to Antony. Octavian was impressed, and replaced on Herod's head the crown which Herod himself had removed, thereby reconfirming his kingship. In 27 BCE the Roman Senate conferred upon Octavian the title Augustus. He reigned until 14 CE, when he was suceeded by Tiberius (14–37) who was followed in turn by Caligula (37–41).

A feature of Herod's reign was his building activity, ordering the construction of temples, palaces, and other public buildings in places such as Nicopolis in Greece, Antioch in Syria, Rhodes, Tyre, Sidon, and Damascus. In Palestine, notable among his activities were the rebuilding of Samaria, the construction of the port of Caesarea, and the transformation of Jerusalem. (On his building activity in Palestine, see 'The Kingdom of Herod and his Successors' and 'Jerusalem in New Testament Times'.)

As noted above, the New Testament places the birth of Jesus in the reign of Herod. The reigns of Herod's successors provide the context of the life and ministry of Jesus, and some knowledge of these often turbulent times is of relevance to readers of the Bible, although direct references to the events are limited in number. After Herod's death, and in accordance with his will, the rule passed to his three sons; Archelaus became king of Judea, Antipas was designated tetrarch of Galilee and Perea, and Philip became tetrarch of Trachonitis, Batanaea, and Gaulanitis. The Jews of Judea did not welcome Archaelaus as their ruler, and there was a disturbance at the time of the Passover, following the death of Herod, in which some 3,000 Jews were reputed to have been killed by the horsemen of Archelaus. Subsequently, while Archelaus was away visiting Rome, a revolt broke out in Judea and spread to Galilee, Idumea, and Perea. The revolt was quelled by Varus, the governor of Syria, and Josephus reports that 2,000 Jews were put to death at this time. In the end, Archelaus was designated ethnarch—not king—of Judea by Augustus, and he ruled from 4 BCE to 6 CE. Then he was sent into exile and his kingdom, Judea, was made part of a Roman province which included Samaria, Judea, and Idumea.

Herod Antipas ruled as tetrarch of Galilee and Perea from 4 BCE to 39 CE. He built the city of Tiberias on the shores of Sea of Galilee, and made it the capital of Galilee. It was Herod Antipas to whom Jesus referred as 'that fox' (cf. Luke 13: 32). He seems to have been a capable ruler who kept the balance between maintaining his friendship with Rome and attempting not to offend the religious scruples of the Jews. He did however suffer a defeat at the hands of the Nabataean king Aretas, and he was eventually exiled to Gaul, having been accused of rebellion against the Roman emperor Caligula by Agrippa I (who had been made king over what had previously been the tetrarchy of Philip).

Philip ruled from 4 BCE to 34 CE as tetrarch of Trachonitis, Batanaea, Gaulanitis, Auranitis, and Ituraea. He built Caesarea Philippi (Paneas) as his capital, and enlarged and developed the city of Bethsaida on the Sea of Galilee, calling it Julias in honour of Augustus's daughter Julia. He seems to have been a moderate and just ruler. Because he died without heir, the territory he had ruled was added to the province of Syria.

In Judea, after Archelaus was exiled in 6 CE, rule passed into the hands of Roman governors, the first of whom was named Coponius (6–9). There seems to have been a census, taken for taxation purposes at the time of the establishment of the province, conducted by Quirinius, the governor of Syria. This census may be alluded to in Luke 2: 1–2, where it is mentioned as the context for Joseph and Mary's journey to Bethlehem and the birth of Jesus. But Matthew's Gospel places the birth of Jesus earlier, in the time of Herod. Acts 5: 37 suggests that the census provoked protest, led by one Judas the Galilean, who was put to death. The best known of the Roman governors of Judea was Pontius Pilate (26–36 CE), under whom Jesus was crucified (for example, Matt. 27: 24–6; Mark 15: 6–15; Luke 23: 20–5; John 19: 13–16). He was not a good administrator, and he angered the Jews by setting up votive shields in Herod's palace. He also put to death many Samaritans, as a result of which an embassy was sent to Vitellius, the Roman legate, complaining of his actions. Pilate was ordered to go to Rome to answer before the emperor, and he was removed from his governorship.

When Caligula, who had the reputation of being insane, succeeded Tiberius as emperor in 37 CE, he appointed Herod Agrippa I, a grandson of Herod the Great, as king over the former tetrarchy of Philip. Agrippa succeeded in persuading Caligula to give up a project to set up a statue of himself as a god in the Jerusalem Temple. When Claudius (41–54) succeeded Caligula, who was murdered, Judea and Samaria were added to Agrippa's territory. Thus he came to rule all the territory that had formerly belonged to his grandfather, Herod the Great. Agrippa began to build a wall around the north suburb (Bezetha) of Jerusalem, probably in the vicinity of the present northern wall, but he was instructed by Claudius to cease this project. It was Herod Agrippa who, according to Acts 12: 1–19, had James, the brother of John, put to death, and who was responsible for having Peter arrested and imprisoned. It was under Claudius that Jews were expelled from Rome, including Aquila and Priscilla (Acts 18: 2).

When Herod Agrippa died unexpectedly in 44, his kingdom was again made a province ruled by Roman governors. The first of these, Cuspius Fadus (44–6), angered the Jews by ordering that the robes of the high priest should be placed in the Antonia Tower under Roman charge. The matter was referred to the emperor, Claudius, who decided in favour of the Jews. Herod Agrippa I's only son, also named Agrippa, had remained in Rome after his father's death. In 49 he was appointed king (Herod Agrippa II) of Chalcis. After the death of Claudius, Nero (54–68) gave him territory in Galilee and in Perea. His capital was at Caesarea (Paneas) which he temporarily renamed Neronias in honour of the emperor. He was granted the authority to appoint the high priest at Jerusalem and to supervise the Temple and its funds.

M. Antonius Felix was Roman governor of Judea, from 52–60. He married Drusilla, the sister of Herod Agrippa II (Acts 24: 24). During his period of office a group known as Sicarii (after the daggers they carried) or 'Assassins' arose among the Zealots, to campaign against Roman authority. They laid the groundwork for the rebellion which was to break out in 66 (see below). It was before Felix that Paul was tried (Acts 24: 1–23). When Felix was recalled by Nero, he was succeeded by Porcius Festus (60–2). Paul was brought from prison at Caesarea to appear before Festus (Acts 25: 1–12), who proposed that he should be tried in Jerusalem, but Paul made his appeal to the emperor. So the matter was laid before Herod Agrippa II, who asked to hear Paul and, as a result, Paul made his famous address to Agrippa and his sister Bernice (Acts 25: 13–26: 32).

Later, when Gessius Florus (64–6) became governor, Bernice appealed to him on behalf of the Jews, urging that he adopt a more conciliatory attitude towards them. There had been protests and demonstrations against Florus in Jerusalem which Florus had put down violently, with many Jews being killed. Herod Agrippa II, who investigated the situation, urged the Jews to submit to Roman authority and, at his suggestion, arrears in tribute were collected and repairs were made to the Temple precincts. But the Jews in Jerusalem soon turned against Agrippa; he was attacked with stones and left the city.

The deterioration in the relationship between the Roman government and the Jews of Judea led ultimately to the outbreak of a revolt against Rome in 66. The priests, led by one Eleazar, stopped the practice of offering sacrifices on behalf of the emperor, thereby signalling the rejection of Roman authority. Nero chose Vespasian to put down the revolt. Vespasian overcame Galilee, forcing the resistance leader, John of Gischala, and his Zealot supporters to flee to Jerusalem. Vespasian became emperor in 69. In the April the following year his son Titus arrived at Jerusalem with a force of Roman legionaries and laid siege to the city. The siege lasted from April to September. On the 9th of Ab (in August) the gates were burnt, and the Temple was also burnt, despite the fact that Titus had given orders to the contrary. John of Gischala held out for a time in Herod's palace on the western hill, but the

The Arch of Titus, Rome. The detail shows Roman soldiers carrying the Menorah and other objects looted from the Jerusalem Temple prior to its destruction.

whole city was in Titus' hands on the 8th of Elul (in September). The war dragged on until 73, when the fortress of Masada finally fell. Titus commemorated his victory by the erection of a triumphal arch in Rome, with pictures of the Temple treasures being carried off in procession. Titus succeeded his father Vespasian as emperor in 79, and he in turn was succeeded by Domitian (81–96). Under Domitian there occurred the persecution of Christians which provides the context for the writing of the Book of Revelation.

THE DIASPORA AND THE SPREAD OF CHRISTIANITY

The origins of the movement which was to become known as Christianity were centred on Jerusalem but it quickly spread throughout Judea and beyond. After the death of Stephen, there was persecution, and 'all except the apostles were scattered throughout the countryside of Judea and Samaria' (Acts 8: 1). Acts 8–10 recount how Philip travelled to Samaria, Gaza, Azotus, and Caesarea, and how Peter visited Lydda, Joppa, and Caesarea. Those who had been scattered by the persecutions took news of their faith to Phoenicia, Cyprus, and Antioch, apparently initially speaking only to Jews (Acts 11: 19). But at Antioch, some of their number from Cyprus and Cyrene began to speak to Greeks (Acts 11: 20). And it was at Antioch that the disciples were first called 'Christians' (Acts 11: 26). The gospel also reached Rome, and it is possible that this was as a result of those who had heard Peter's preaching at Pentecost. Certainly tradition came to associate Peter with the church at Rome. Paul was able to build on these foundations as he, along with various companions, undertook his missionary travels. (See 'Paul's Journeys'.)

To understand the early spread of Christianity, and in particular the successes of Paul, it is important to set this movement within the context of the Jewish Diaspora (or 'Dispersion'). There were many Jewish communities in the Roman Empire. In Acts 2: 5–13 there is a description of those who heard the apostles' preaching at Pentecost which includes a list of 'devout Jews from every nation under heaven' who were in Jerusalem at the time. Whether or not the list gives an accurate account of those actually present on that day, it is likely that it does provide an indication of places where there were known to have been Jewish communities, whose members might have visited Jerusalem: Parthia, Media, Elam, Mesopotamia, Cappadocia, Pontus, Asia, Phrygia, Pamphylia, Egypt, the part of Libya belonging to Cyrene, Rome, Crete, and Arabia. Another list which may give an indication of the presence of Jewish communities comes in 1 Maccabees 15, where there are references to a number of rulers and countries to whom letters were sent from Rome on behalf of the high priest Simon and the Jewish people. The contents of the letter sent to king Ptolemy (verses 16–21) are given, and then it is indicated that the same message was sent to Demetrius (of Syria), Attalus (of Pergamum), Ariarthes (of Cappadocia), Arsaces (of Parthia), and to Sampsames, Sparta, Delos, Myndos, Sicyon, Caria, Samos, Pamphylia, Lycia, Halicarnassus, Rhodes, Phaselis, Cos, Side, Aradus, Gortyna, Cnidus, Cyprus, and Cyrene.

The origins of the Jewish Diaspora were, of course, centuries earlier. Exiles were taken from Judah to Babylon by Nebuchadrezzar at the beginning of the 6th century BCE. Some Jews had fled to Egypt after the fall of Jerusalem to Babylon (Jer. 43: 4–7, and see Jer. 44: 1 where mention is made of Jews living at Migdol, Tahpanhes, Memphis, and in the land of Pathros). Aramaic papyri from Elephantine at Syene (Aswan) in Upper Egypt provide insights into the life and religion of a Jewish community of the Egyptian Diaspora of the 5th and early 4th centuries BCE. After the time of Alexander there developed a large Jewish community at Alexandria. For the benefit of its Greek-speaking Jewish citizens, the Hebrew Bible was translated into Greek. The Letter of Aristeas preserves the legend that 72 Jewish elders were commissioned to produce a translation of the Torah by Ptolemy Philadelphus in the 3rd century BCE, and hence the translation came to be known as the 'Septuagint' ('Seventy', often abbreviated to LXX). The Prologue to Ben Sira (Sirach or Ecclesiasticus) mentions the translation from Hebrew of 'the Law itself, the Prophecies, and the rest of the books'. Philo of Alexandria perhaps represents the finest example of 1st century CE Hellenistic Jewish scholarship.

Although some Jewish exiles to Babylon and their descendants returned to Judah, there continued to be a considerable Jewish presence in Babylonia. In New Testament times there were some important Jewish communities, including the one at Nisibis on the Euphrates. That there were Jews in the 1st century CE in Adiabene, an area to the east of the Tigris, is clear from the

Depiction of Mordecai and Esther: a wall painting from the Dura Europus synagogue in Syria, *c*.3rd century CE.

59

account of the conversion of the royal house of Adiabene to Judaism. There King Izates, his sister Helena, and his mother Helena became proselytes to Judaism. Queen Helena made a pilgrimage to Jerusalem and lived there for many years. Izates sent five of his sons there to be educated. Queen Helena was buried north of the city in what is known popularly as 'the tomb of the kings'. It is reasonable to suppose that the adoption of Judaism by the royal family encouraged the growth of Jewish settlements there, and Josephus records that Adiabene was one of the places where his work *The Jewish War* was read in Aramaic before it was put into Greek. The language of the area was Syriac, a dialect of Aramaic, and it was perhaps in Adiabene, during the time of its first Jewish kings, that the Hebrew Bible began to be translated into Syriac. There were also Jews in Edessa in Mesopotamia, and Christianity appears to have reached Edessa at an early stage, the local Syriac-speaking Christians claiming that their origins were in the 1st century. Josephus also records that his work was read in Aramaic by Parthians, Babylonians, and Arabians, presumably within Jewish communities.

There were also many Jews in Syria, Asia Minor, Greece, and the islands of the east Mediterranean. When Jason was deposed from the high priesthood in 168 BCE, he fled to Sparta where he knew he would find a Jewish community. Paul was a native of Tarsus, the chief city of Cilicia, where he belonged to the Jewish community and where he later preached to the Jews.

The above reference to the royal family of Adiabene prompts further mention of proselytism which seems to have been a not uncommon phenomenon in the Hellenistic period and the 1st century. There is a reference in Matthew 23: 15 to the fact that the scribes and Pharisees would 'cross land and sea to make a single convert'. It is possible that the spread of Judaism was in part due to the activities of Jewish merchants and travellers. The Phoenician colonies around the Mediterranean provided ground for new converts. The kind of enlightened religion represented by Judaism was appealing to those who were tired of and disillusioned by the old gods. Josephus recalls that, in the time of the emperor Nero and the governor Florus, the men of Damascus distrusted their own wives 'who, with few exceptions, had all become converts to the Jewish religion'. But it must also be remembered that, in addition to those who converted of their own accord, there were some forcible conversions of Gentiles, as when a mixed population of northern Galilee and the Ituraeans were converted to Judaism by Aristobulus I, and when John Hyrcanus forced the Idumeans to be circumcised.

In addition to proselytes, there were those who were attracted to Judaism but who were reluctant to take on the full rigour of the Jewish law. Those described in the New Testament as 'God-fearers' (see Acts 10: 2; 13: 16, 26) or the 'devout' (see Acts 13: 43; 17: 4, 17) probably belonged to this category. They believed in the God of the Jews and attended the synagogues. The Hellenized Jews of the Diaspora, the proselytes, and the God-fearers were regarded by Paul as the most likely to be converted to Christianity, and it is likely that the proselytes and in particular the God-fearers were most responsive, since they welcomed release from what they regarded as the burden of the Jewish law. In the synagogue at Thessalonica, Paul is reported to have argued about the scriptures on three successive sabbaths, persuading some of the Jews, along with 'a great many of the devout Greeks, and not a few of the leading women' to join him and Silas (Acts 17: 1–4). The summary statement of Paul's activities in Corinth probably reflect his typical policy, 'Every Sabbath he would argue in the synagogue and would try to convince Jews and Greeks' (Acts 18: 4).

It is, then, clear that the phenomenon of the Jewish Diaspora was of the utmost importance in the early expansion of the Church. But although Paul made it his practice to preach first in the synagogues, when rejected by the Jewish communities he turned to the Gentiles. This policy is summed up in the words placed in the mouths of Paul and Barnabas, addressing the Jews in Pisidian Antioch; 'It was necessary that the word of God should be spoken first to you. Since you reject it and judge yourselves to be unworthy of eternal life, we are now turning to the Gentiles' (Acts 13: 46). So increasing numbers of Gentiles, converts from paganism (see, for example, Gal. 4: 8), became Christians. The Christians shared the monotheistic faith of the Jews and revered the Jewish scriptures. The opening address of the First Letter of Peter suggests virtually a Christian Diaspora; 'To the exiles of the Dispersion in Pontus, Galatia, Cappadocia, Asia and Bythinia . . .' (1 Pet. 1: 1).

The sack of Jerusalem by the Romans, and the destruction of the Temple in 70 CE (with its aftermath at Masada), marked the end of an era. Later, in 132–5, there was a second Jewish revolt, led by Bar Kochba, but this too was unsuccessful. It was elsewhere, in the Diaspora, that Jewish communities and the expanding Christian Church flourished. Early Christian meetings for worship doubtless took place primarily in private homes, so have left little trace. But evidence has survived of Christian burial places, most notably the catacombs in Rome. Excavations during the 1940s beneath St Peter's in the Vatican have yielded remarkable finds, including a memorial monument, dating from the 2nd century, purporting to mark the last resting-place of the body of Peter, reputed to have been martyred in Rome during the persecutions in 64–5, during the time of Nero.

As noted above, the scriptures of the early Church were those of the Hebrew Bible, often its Greek translation. But gradually Christian writings emerged, and the New Testament witnesses to the importance of letter-writing as a means of teaching, encouraging, and sometimes admonishing the early Christian communities. It also gives evidence of the preparation of accounts of the activities and the teaching of Jesus. Some evidence of early Christian literary activity has survived, in particular in papyrus documents from Egypt. Particularly noteworthy is a small fragment of the Gospel of John, now housed in the John Rylands University Library of Manchester, which has been dated to the first half of the 2nd century, making it in all probability the earliest surviving Gospel fragment. Other important early manuscripts date from the late 2nd or early 3rd centuries, including the Bodmer

Papyri from Egypt which contain, among other things, segments of the Hebrew Bible and of the New Testament, including sections of the Gospels of Luke and John. Some non-biblical documents are also of great significance, for example, the papyri written in Coptic found in 1947 at Nag Hammadi. These have been dated to the early 4th century, but go back to Greek originals from the 2nd and 3rd centuries. They include the famous 'Gospel of Thomas' which has been thought to have originated in the Christian community of Edessa in the mid-2nd century. The Nag Hammadi texts have been particularly important in shedding light on the origin and nature of Gnosticism, an issue which is of relevance for the study of some Christian (for example, the Gospel of John) and Jewish (for example, the Qumran scrolls) texts.

The study of the Bible brings its readers into contact with the ancient Near Eastern and Mediterranean worlds, sometimes its great empires and rulers and sometimes its small communities and individuals. This overview is intended to help the reader to see the text in context.

A page from the Nag Hammadi codex of the Gospel of Thomas. The two indented lines near the foot of the page identify it as the Gospel of Thomas.

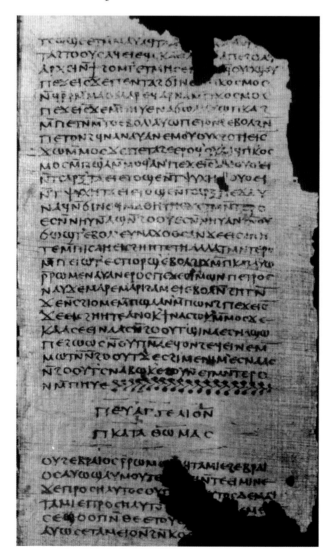

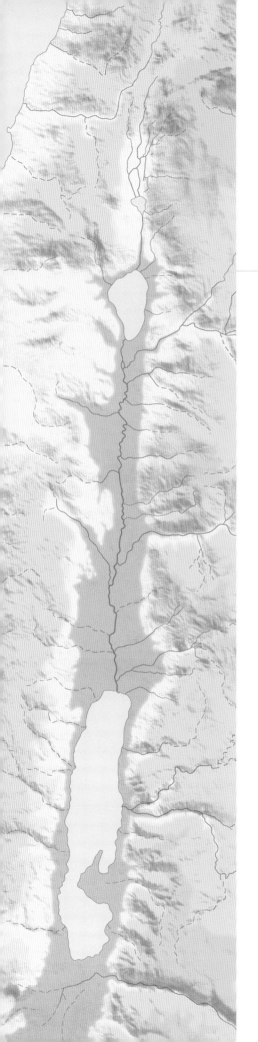

The Hebrew Bible

The Setting of the Genesis Stories

The Book of Genesis is set against a wide geographical background. At first, the setting is Mesopotamia. The story of the Garden of Eden mentions a river flowing from the garden which divided into four rivers branches, two of which are the great rivers which gave Mesopotamia its name ('between the rivers'), the Tigris and the Euphrates (Gen. 2: 14). The other rivers mentioned there cannot be identified with certainty. The story of the Tower of Babel (Gen. 11: 1–9) is doubtless based on the memory of the great ziggurat or temple-tower of Babylon. It was from Ur in southern Mesopotamia that Abraham is said to have set out and travelled via Haran in north Mesopotamia to Canaan (Gen. 11: 31–12: 9). The wives of both Isaac (Gen. 25: 20) and Jacob (Gen. 28: 5) are said to have come from Paddan-aram in Aram-naharaim, the Hebrew equivalent of Mesopotamia (meaning Aram-of-the-two-rivers) but often referring to Upper Mesopotamia in particular. Although Abraham is said to have travelled as far as Egypt (Gen. 12: 10–20) it is primarily with Joseph that the scene shifts to Egypt (Gen. 39–50). Joseph is said to have married the daughter of the priest of On, that is, Heliopolis (Gen. 41: 45). The story ends with a reference to his mummification (Gen. 50: 26). Abraham is also said to have encountered Hittites, albeit in Canaan, and to have purchased from one of them—Ephron—a piece of land with a cave in it in which to bury Sarah (Gen. 23).

It is therefore appropriate for readers of the Bible to have some knowledge of the wider ancient Near Eastern context in which the writers set the stories, and a brief overview of the earliest history of the region follows. The accompanying map reflects approximately the middle of the 2nd millennium BCE.

MESOPOTAMIA

The Sumerians, a non-Semitic people who perhaps came from the east (see Gen. 11: 2) in about 3300 BCE, flourished in the lower Tigris–Euphrates valley from Nippur to Ur and Eridu. They were responsible for one of the early forms of writing (see 'Writing Systems'). Before the end of the 4th millennium a type of picture-writing which was later to develop into the

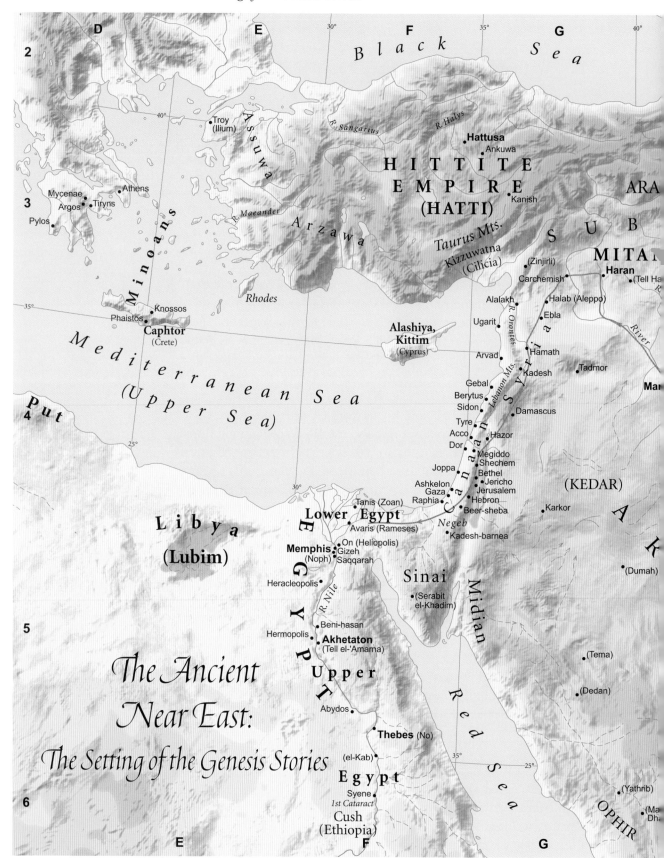

The Ancient Near East: The Setting of the Genesis Stories

The city

Knowledge of the Canaanites was initially derived largely from the Hebrew Bible. However in 1929 an important advance came about, with the discovery on the site of Ras Shamra in Syria of the remains of the ancient city of Ugarit. Excavations have revealed a cosmopolitan city with an impressive royal palace and temples dedicated to the gods Baal, Dagan and perhaps El. Numerous artefacts have been found revealing that a sophisticated culture developed. Texts in several languages were discovered, but particularly important were those inscribed using the cuneiform method of writing but in a hitherto unknown language. This language was surmised to be the local language and has come to be known as Ugaritic. To write it the scribes used an alphabetic script (see 'Writing Systems'). Excavations demonstrate that Ugarit was a very ancient city, dating back to the Neolithic period, but whose 'golden age' was in the Late Bronze Age (*c.*1550–1200 BCE), the period during which the texts were produced.

Was Ugarit Canaanite?

A difficulty in answering this question lies in the fact that it is impossible to be certain of the extent of a land known as Canaan. It has been suggested on the basis of some descriptions that Ugarit lies too far to the north. Gen. 10: 15–19 suggests that Canaan was thought to stretch from Gaza in the south, beyond Sidon, as far north as Hamath, i.e. almost as far north as Ugarit. But another description of the boundaries of Canaan (Num. 34: 2–12) places its northern limit considerably further south at Lebo-Hamath (Lebweh). Texts in the Ugaritic

language have been found in other locations, some near Ras Shamra, but others much further afield; tablets were found at Taanach and Beth-shemesh and an inscribed dagger near Mount Tabor. This suggests that the beliefs and practices reflected in the texts from Ugarit may represent a more widespread phenomenon, and it can be argued that it belonged to the same cultural sphere as the rest of Canaan. So in all probability Ugarit offers us the best picture we have of the Canaanites and their religion.

Baal

On the city's acropolis was the temple dedicated to the god Baal. It was identified as such thanks to the discovery of a dedicatory stele which had been presented by an Egyptian ambassador and, nearby, another stele bearing what has become the most familiar of the representations of Baal. He is depicted wearing a helmet decorated with horns, probably symbolizing his divinity (though there may also be a fertility connection), a skirt and a scabbard. In his right hand, raised above his head, is a club, and in his left hand he holds an object which is pointed like a spear. These have been interpreted as symbols of thunder and lightning respectively. Thus Baal appears as a warrior, armed with the weapons associated with the storm god. Some of the important myths discovered describe his defeat of Yam, the god of the seas, the building of a palace for Baal on Mount Zaphon, and his periodic conflicts with Mot, the god of death and the underworld. This cycle of myths has been thought to reflect the pattern of the seasons.

Tablet from Ugarit inscribed with the letters of the Ugaritic alphabet.

Remains of the royal palace at Ugarit.

Left: Stele from Ugarit depicting the god Baal armed with club and spear.

Right: Seated figure from Ugarit, thought to represent the god El.

copies of this list, plus an Akkadian translation, have been found. Other texts are associated with the sacrificial cult, describing or prescribing the rituals for various regular or special sacrifices or series of sacrificial rites. Material has also been found relating to funerary practices, as well as non-sacrificial liturgies, oaths, incantations, and prayers. One of the tablets may include what may be the only known example of a prayer to Baal. There are also a number of texts in which mythological and more practical or magical elements are juxtaposed, for example, two stories which involve spells against snakebite and perhaps the ridding of the land of serpents. There is a text which describes El at a banquet, and may include a recipe for hangover! El is described as being in his *mrzḥ*, a term which has been understood as referring to a feasting house or drinking club. The Hebrew prophets criticized the behaviour associated with such institutions (Jer 16: 5; Amos 6: 7).

Among the longer texts in Ugaritic are two groups which tell the stories of two figures, Keret and Danel, who were probably thought of as kings, although this is not explicitly stated of the latter. They seem to have been envisaged as human beings, though there is constant interplay between the divine and human participants. But these stories are perhaps better described as epics or legends rather than myths. They suggest certain beliefs about the king and his role, showing him for example in the role of judge and as the protector of the vulnerable members of society.

The Canaanites, their practices, and their gods, especially Baal, are roundly condemned in the Hebrew Bible. But the discoveries at Ugarit help to provide a more balanced picture of these ancient people and of the god Baal.

Ugaritic religion

The Ugaritic texts mention many other deities, including El, the head of the pantheon, and Athirat his consort (the Asherah of the Bible). Among the discoveries have been what are often described as 'Pantheon lists'. There may have been what amounted to an 'official' pantheon list with carefully arranged groupings of deities. Two

The ziggurat of Ur, constructed towards the end of the 3rd millennium BCE by King Ur-Nammu.

Statuette from Ur, dating from the 3rd millennium BCE, probably depicting a goat and a tree, but at one time associated with the 'ram caught in a thicket' (Gen. 22:13).

wedge-shaped (cuneiform) script appears on clay tablets found at Erech. At Erech, too, was one of the earliest ziggurats, an artificial mountain on which the god was believed to dwell. A Sumerian list of long-lived kings before the flood suggests that kingship appeared first at Eridu. The same list places the first dynasty after the flood at Kish, the second at Erech, and the third at Ur. Sumerian culture flourished through the first half of the 3rd millennium and beyond. A high point of the material culture is illustrated by objects found in the royal tombs at Ur. One of the kings of Lagash, Urukagina, instituted social reforms and tax revisions. Lugal-zaggisi, who conquered Lagash and ruled as king of Erech and Ur, claimed to have gained control of the whole area from the Lower Sea (the Persian Gulf) to the Upper Sea (the Mediterranean). He was defeated by Sargon of Akkad, who established an Akkadian dynasty and whose power extended to Syria, southern Asia Minor, and the Mediterranean Sea. In about the 23rd century BCE, Akkadian domination was brought to an end by the barbarian Gutians from the Zagros Mountains. But towards the end of the 3rd millennium there was a revival of Sumerian power and culture. Gudea ruled at Lagash, and Ur-Nammu, who made the earliest known code of laws, established the 3rd Dynasty of Ur. This was a time when literature and art flourished.

In the 20th century BCE Ur fell to the Elamites. Late in the same century King Lipit-Ishtar of Isin issued a Sumerian code of laws. Perhaps contemporary in origin are the Akkadian laws of Eshnunna. In the 1st Dynasty of Babylon ruled the greatest lawgiver of them all, King Hammurabi (c.1792–1750), who was both conqueror and administrator. A contemporary of his was Zimri-lim, king of Mari.

ASIA MINOR AND BEYOND

The 17th century BCE saw the rise to power of the Hittites, who ruled Anatolia (Asia Minor) and part of upper Mesopotamia from their capital Hattusa. This was followed by the rise of Mitanni, a kingdom dominated by Hurrians, which controlled a large territory in northern Mesopotamia by the early 15th century. The period of the supremacy of the New Hittite Empire in the 14th and 13th centuries was initiated by King Suppiluliumas, whose campaigns led him to the borders of Babylonia and to the Lebanon mountains. The kingdom of Ugarit on the Mediterranean coast was flourishing at this time. It is notable in particular for the texts in the local language which provide what is perhaps the best available evidence to shed light on Canaanite religion. The Egyptians and Hittites sought to maintain good relationships with the kings of Ugarit, doubtless because of its commercial and strategic potential.

EGYPT

During the Proto-dynastic period (*c.*3100–2650 BCE) Upper and Lower Egypt were united by Menes of the 1st Dynasty. Already the hieroglyphic script was in use. In the Old Kingdom period, in the middle of the 3rd millennium, particularly in the 3rd and 4th Dynasties, Egypt rose to great power. To the 3rd Dynasty belongs Djoser's step pyramid at Saqqarah, and the great pyramids at Gizeh to the 4th Dynasty. From the 5th and 6th Dynasties come the pyramid texts, which shed considerable light on Egyptian religion. After a period of decline during the 1st Intermediate Period, Egypt revived at the beginning of the 2nd millennium (the Middle Kingdom), and its control over much of Syria–Palestine was reasserted. A large and varied literature comes from this period. But there was then another period of weakness, and during the 15th and 16th Dynasties Egypt was under the Hyksos, who, towards the end of the 18th century BCE swept along the Levantine coast and infiltrated Egypt. Memphis was their capital at first, but Avaris became the centre of their rule.

The New Kingdom (18th and 19th Dynasties) was the golden age of Egyptian expansion and power. Thutmose III (1479–1425), at the battle of Megiddo, defeated a revolt headed by the prince of Kadesh, and his armies reached the Euphrates. Evidence that Egyptian power in the Levant weakened in the 13th century is found in the Tell el-ʿAmarna letters. These were found at Tell el-ʿAmarna, ancient Akhetaten, the capital of the so-called heretic pharaoh Akhenaten (1352–1336), who sought to institute a new form of religion involving the worship of the solar disc. Correspondence was found from the kings of Babylonia, Assyria, the Hittites, Mitanni, Cyprus, Cilicia, Syria. There were also other letters from many places including Ugarit, Gebal, Berytus, Sidon, Tyre, Acco, Damascus, Megiddo, Ashkelon, Jerusalem, Shechem.

Pharaoh Rameses II (1279–1213) of the 19th Dynasty has been associated with the oppression of the Hebrews in Egypt. From the time of his successor, Merneptah (1213–1203), comes an inscription containing the earliest reference to a people called Israel.

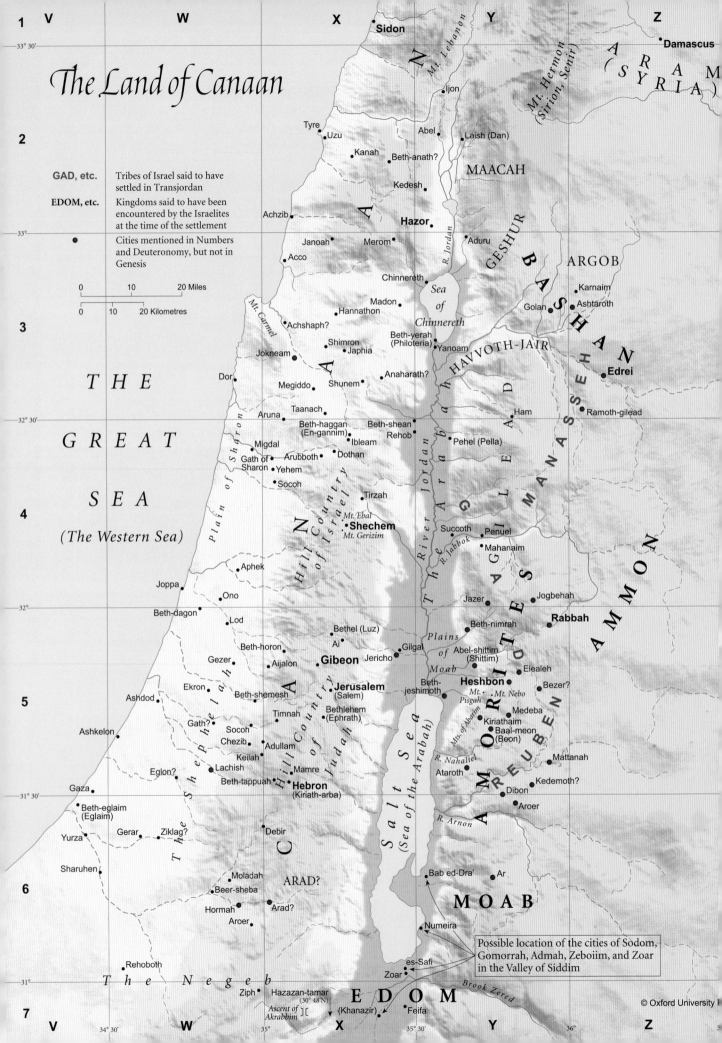

The Land of Canaan

GAD, etc.   Tribes of Israel said to have settled in Transjordan

EDOM, etc.   Kingdoms said to have been encountered by the Israelites at the time of the settlement

•   Cities mentioned in Numbers and Deuteronomy, but not in Genesis

0   10   20 Miles

0   10   20 Kilometres

Sidon
Damascus

A R A M
(A S Y R I A)

Tyre
Uzu

Kanah
Abel
Laish (Dan)

Beth-anath?

Kedesh

MAACAH

Achzib

Hazor

Janoah
Merom
Aduru

Acco

GESHUR
BASHAN
ARGOB

Chinnereth
Karnaim
Golan
Ashtaroth

Madon
Sea of Chinnereth

Hannathon

Mt. Carmel
Achshaph?
Shimron
Beth-yerah (Philoteria)
Japhia
Yanoam
HAVVOTH-JAIR

Joined
Anaharath?

Edrei

Dor
Shunem
Ham
Ramoth-gilead

Megiddo

Taanach

T H E
Aruna
Beth-haggan
(En-gannim)
Beth-shean
Rehob
Pehel (Pella)

Migdal
Ibleam
Gath of Sharon
Arubboth
Dothan
Succoth
Penuel

G R E A T
Yehem
Mahanaim

Socoh

Tirzah

Mt. Ebal
Shechem
Mt. Gerizim

S E A

(The Western Sea)

Aphek
Jazer
Jogbehah

Joppa
Ono

Beth-dagon
Lod
Jericho
Gilgal
Abel-shittim (Shittim)
Rabbah

Beth-horon
Bethel (Luz)
Ai
Beth-nimrah

Gezer
Aijalon
Gibeon
Jericho
Elealeh

Ekron
Heshbon
Bezer?

Ashdod
Beth-shemesh
Jerusalem
(Salem)
Beth-jeshimoth
Mt. Pisgah
Mt. Nebo
Medeba

Timnah
Bethlehem
(Ephrath)
Kiriathaim
Baal-meon (Beon)

Ashkelon
Gath?
Socoh
Adullam

Chezib

Keilah
Mamre
Ataroth
Mattanah

Gaza
Eglon?
Lachish
Beth-tappuah
Hebron
(Kiriath-arba)

Beth-eglaim
(Eglaim)
Kedemoth?

Gerar
Ziklag?
Debir
Dibon

Yurza
Aroer

Sharuhen
Bab ed-Dra'
Ar

Moladah
ARAD?
MOAB

Rehoboth
Beer-sheba

Hormah
Aroer
Arad?
Numeira

Ziph
Hazazan-tamar
(30° 48'N)
E D O M
es-Safi
Zoar

Ascent of Akrabbim
(Khanazir)
Feifa

Possible location of the cities of Sodom, Gomorrah, Admah, Zeboiim, and Zoar in the Valley of Siddim

Salt Sea
(Sea of the Arabah)

River Jordan
The Arabah

GILEAD
MANASSEH
GAD
AMMON
REUBEN
AMORITES
Plains of Moab
Brook Zered

The Negeb

The Shephelah
Hill Country of Israel
Hill Country of Judah
Plain of Sharon

Mt. Lebanon
Mt. Hermon
(Sirion, Senir)
Ijon

© Oxford University P

The Patriarchs in Canaan

The term 'Canaan' is here used loosely to refer particularly to the southern Levant. There are several biblical allusions to its extent, but these do not coincide precisely. The 'Table of Nations' (Gen. 10: 15–19) suggests that its compiler understood Canaan to stretch from Gaza in the south, beyond Sidon, as far north as Hamath. But another description of the boundaries of Canaan (Num. 34: 2–12) puts the northern limit at Lebo-Hamath (Lebweh), considerably further south. Numbers 33: 51 suggests that Canaan covered the whole area west of the Jordan, whereas Numbers 13: 29 suggests that the Canaanites inhabited the coastal area and land along the Jordan only. Evidence from Egyptian sources suggests that the Egyptian province of Canaan comprised the territory north of Gaza, between the Mediterranean to the west and the Jordan valley to the east; unfortunately the northern limits are rather less clear.

ABRAHAM

As already noted (see 'The Lands of the Bible' and 'The Setting of the Genesis Stories') the biblical narrative presents Abraham (originally called Abram) as having set out from Ur in southern Mesopotamia and having travelled via Haran to the land of Canaan. (It is worthy of note at the outset that a number of the stories of the Patriarchs make reference to the construction of altars and the digging of wells, suggesting that part of their significance lies in the authentication of holy places and the establishment of rights over important water supplies.) Abraham is presented as having arrived at Shechem where he built an altar (Gen. 12: 6–7), then moving on to a point between Bethel and Ai where he erected another altar (Gen. 12: 8). Thereafter he headed south for the Negeb (Gen. 12: 9) and on into Egypt (Gen. 12: 10–20), before returning via the same route to the spot between Bethel and Ai (Gen. 13: 1–4). It is in this context that the biblical narrative sets the decision of Abraham and Lot (his nephew) to separate; Lot chose the Jordan valley and settled at

The River Jordan, meandering south of the Sea of Galilee. The hills of Gilead are in the background. (See on 'The Rift Valley'.)

Sodom, while Abraham remained to the west of the Jordan, moving his encampment to Mamre near Hebron (Gen. 13).

Gen. 14 presents an account of an episode which it sets in the days of King Amraphel of Shinar. Attempts to identify the named characters with those known from other sources (for example, Amraphel with Hammurabi of Babylon) or to place the events in a historical context have not generally been found convincing. The chapter describes how a group of kings of the so-called Cities of the Plain (Sodom, Gomorrah, Admah, Zeboiim, and Zoar) had rebelled against King Chedorlaomer of Elam, and gathered in the Valley of Siddim (which the biblical narrative identifies with the 'Salt [that is, Dead] Sea'). Chedorlaomer and his allies subdued Ashtoreth-karnaim, Ham, Shaveh-kiriathaim, the Horites in the hill country of Seir, the territory of the Amalekites, and the Amorites who lived in Hazazon-tamar. They put to flight the kings of Sodom and Gomorrah and plundered their cities, taking Lot captive. When Abraham heard of his nephew's capture, he and his allies pursued the enemy north to Dan, and on to the north of Damascus, and recovered Lot and the plundered goods. It was after his return that he received the blessing of King Melchizedek of Salem (that is, Jerusalem). Later, Abraham is described as leaving Mamre and journeying through the Negeb to Gerar, where he encountered King Abimelech with whom he entered into a treaty over the ownership of the well at Beer-sheba (Gen. 20; 21: 22–34). It was while in the Negeb that Sarah bore Abraham a son, Isaac (Gen. 20: 1–8). The narrative also records God's testing of Abraham by instructing him to take Isaac to 'the land of Moriah' (Gen. 22: 2; probably Jerusalem—see 2 Chr. 3: 1) and to offer him as a sacrifice, and the provision of a substitute in the form of 'a ram caught in a thicket' (Gen. 22: 13). Abraham is also described as purchasing the cave of Machpelah, to the east of Mamre, in which to bury Sarah (Gen. 23); subsequently he too was buried there (Gen. 25: 7–10).

ISAAC

Isaac in fact plays a rather limited role in the biblical narrative, being recalled in particular in the contexts of the testing of Abraham (see above) and Jacob's deceit (see below). But it is noteworthy that he too settled in Gerar and encountered Abimelech, and that he also is associated with the digging (or redigging) of the well at Beer-sheba and other wells in the neighbourhood (Gen. 26). These traditions underline the importance of water-supplies such

The tell of Beer-sheba, traditionally the southern limit of Israelite territory (Judg. 20:1).

as that of Beer-sheba to those who lived in or journeyed through the arid region of the Negeb.

JACOB

The story of Jacob, like that of Abraham, associates the ancestor with a number of sanctuaries. According to the biblical account, Jacob deceitfully obtained his father Isaac's blessing, thereby doing his brother Esau out of his birthright (Gen. 27). He then set out from Beer-sheba for Paddan-aram (Upper Mesopotamia) in search of a wife, and it was on the way that he stopped at Bethel overnight and had his famous dream of the ladder joining heaven and earth, setting up a stone to mark the place (Gen. 28). He ultimately returned with his wives Leah and Rachel. Genesis 32 describes his encounters with 'the angels of God' at Mahanaim (verse 1) and his wrestling with an unknown assailant, probably to be understood as God (verse 28), near the River Jabbok at Penuel / Peniel (verses 30–1). The narrative also tells of his meeting with his brother Esau, after which he went by way of Succoth to Shechem, where he erected an altar, while Esau returned to Seir (Edom) (Gen. 33: 16–20). Subsequently Jacob went again to Bethel and built an altar (Gen. 35: 1–7). Rachel died and was buried near Bethlehem (Gen. 35: 19). Jacob then came to his father Isaac at Mamre; there Isaac died and was buried by his sons (Gen. 35: 27–9).

JOSEPH

Joseph's story centres on Egypt, but begins in Canaan and in a sense ends there. He was sent by his father Jacob to visit his brothers who had been pasturing their flocks near Shechem but who had moved on to Dothan (Gen. 37: 12–17). They sold him to a caravan of Ishmaelites who took him down to Egypt where, after initial setbacks, he is said to have achieved a position of prominence in the land, and to have been joined by his brothers and his father Jacob (Gen. 39–49). Jacob died in Egypt, his body was embalmed and taken back to Canaan where it was buried in the cave of Machpelah (Gen. 49: 33–50: 13). Joseph, having buried his father, returned to Egypt where he died and his body was embalmed (Gen. 50: 14, 22–6). But the narrative also says that Moses took Joseph's bones with him when he led the Israelites out of Egypt (Exod. 13: 19) and Joshua 24: 32 records that they were ultimately buried at Shechem.

JUDAH

Set within the wider context of the Joseph story is an episode relating to the eponymous ancestor of the tribe of Judah. It tells how Judah failed to fulfil his duty to Tamar, the widow of his eldest son Er, by ensuring that she was able to bear a son by one of Er's brothers, and how she succeeded in seducing him. As a result of this she bore twins, Perez and Zerah (Gen. 38), whose names are recorded in Numbers 26: 20–1 as the heads of two important Judahite families (NRSV 'clans').

The Exodus and Wilderness Traditions

OUT OF EGYPT

The biblical narrative tells of how the Hebrews lived in the Goshen area, in the Nile Delta region in Egypt, and worked as slaves on the store cities of Pithom and Rameses (Exod. 1: 1–11). Since the latter was named after Pharaoh Rameses II, those who have sought a historical context for these events have suggested that Rameses II was the pharaoh of the oppression. According to the biblical account, Moses was found floating in a basket by the daughter of the pharaoh (a similar tale is told about the Mesopotamian king Sargon) and brought up in Egypt, but when he had grown up he fled to the land of Midian (Exod. 2). (The Midianites were a nomadic people so their 'land' is difficult to locate on a map.) While looking after the sheep of his father-in-law Jethro, a Midianite priest, he is described as having his encounter with God who called him to return to Egypt to rescue his people (Exod. 3). After a series of plagues which afflicted Egypt (Exod. 7–12), Moses led the people via Succoth and Etham 'on the edge of the wilderness' (Exod. 13: 20) until they encamped 'in front of Pi-hahiroth, between Migdol and the sea' (Exod. 14: 2). This was the setting of the remarkable deliverance described in Exodus 14: 15–30.

Attempts have been made to pinpoint geographically the place of the crossing of the sea as envisaged in the story, but the places mentioned cannot be located with certainty. The stretch of water has traditionally been referred to as the Red Sea, but the Hebrew phrase *yam sûp* is perhaps more accurately translated Reed Sea (though the word *sûp* also seems to refer to underwater vegetation in Jonah 2: 5). A suggested location for the Reed Sea has been Lake Sirbonis on the shore of the Mediterranean, but the biblical account stresses that 'God did not lead them by the way of the land of the Philistines' (Exod. 13: 17), a route which would have passed close to Lake Sirbonis. In 1 Kings 9: 26, the term clearly refers to the eastern arm of the Red Sea, the Gulf of Aqaba, but it is highly unlikely that this location is envisaged in the Exodus story which sees the crossing of the sea as the precursor of the entry into the wilderness. It is perhaps more likely that the story presupposes a location in

77

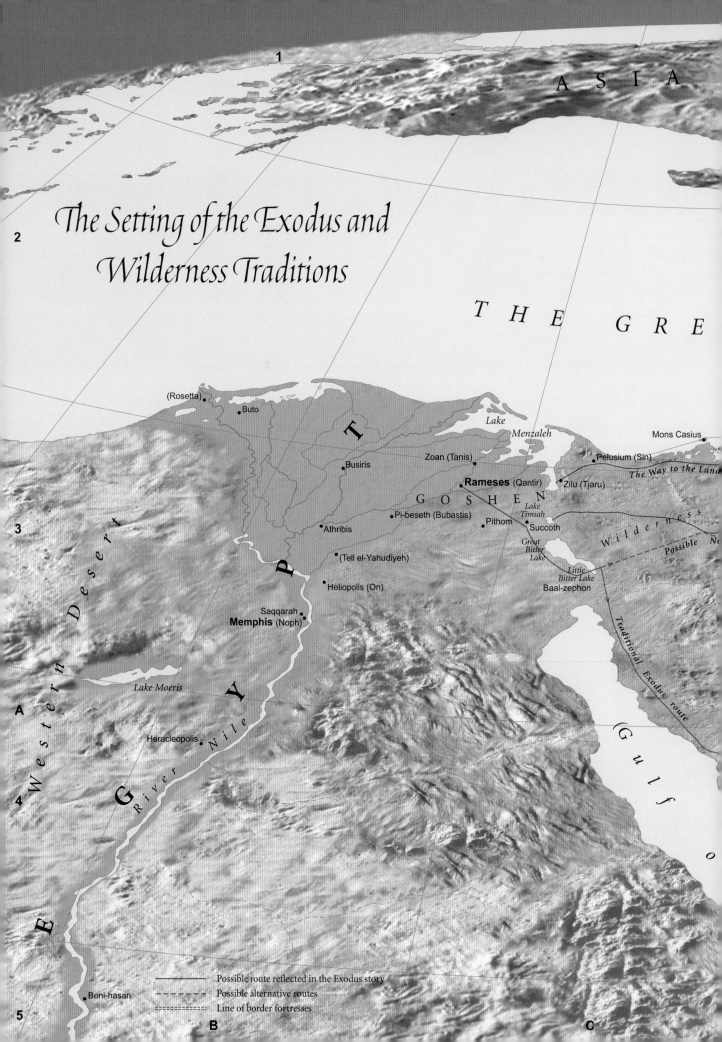

The Setting of the Exodus and Wilderness Traditions

A S I A

T H E G R E

(Rosetta)

Buto

Lake
Menzaleh

Mons Casius

T

Zoan (Tanis)

Pelusium (Sin)

Busiris

Rameses (Qantir)

Zilu (Tjaru)

The Way to the Land

G O S H E N

Pi-beseth (Bubastis)

Pithom

Lake
Timsah

Athribis

Succoth

Wilderness

Western Desert

P

(Tell el-Yahudiyeh)

Great
Bitter
Lake

Possible No

Heliopolis (On)

Little
Bitter
Lake

Baal-zephon

Saqqarah

Memphis (Noph)

Lake Moeris

Y

Traditional Exodus route

Heracleopolis

G

River Nile

(G u l f

o

E

Beni-hasan

	Possible route reflected in the Exodus story
- - -	Possible alternative routes
▫▫▫	Line of border fortresses

B   C

1

River Euphrates

2

MINOR

Cyprus

SEA

_Sea of
Chinnereth_

Bethel
Ai
Jericho

Gezer

Jerusalem
Azekah

Ashdod

Libnah?   Lachish

Gaza

Hebron

Juttah

ARAD?

Raphia

Gerar

Debir

Beer-sheba

Arad?

Hormah

_Salt
Sea_

R. Arnon

Rabbah

Shittim

Heshbon

Mt. Nebo

Medeba

Dibon

Kir-hareseth

Plain of

Philistia

_C A N A A N_

The Negeb

_Wilderness
of Zin_

Bene-jaakan
(Beeroth)

Azmon

Hazar-addar

_Mt. Sinai? (Horeb)
(Jebel Helal)_

Hazazon-tamar

Oboth

Kadesh-barnea
(Meribah)

Sela
Punon

Bozrah

_M O A B_

_E D O M_

The Arabah

The King's Highway

Alternative Exodus route

_A r a b i a n_

_D e s e r t_

Ezion-geber

_S I N A I_

_Wilderness
of Sin?_

_Mt. Sinai (Horeb)?
(Jebel Musa)_

(Gulf of 'Aqaba)

_M I D I A N_

Brook of Egypt

The Way to Shur

Wilderness of Paran

ines

ur

route

_z)_

Red Sea

D

E

3

4

5

© Oxford University Press

the vicinity of the Bitter Lakes, north of the Gulf of Suez. But in any event it is the theological significance which matters to the biblical writer more than the geography, a point often overlooked by those who seek to find natural explanations for the phenomena described in the story.

THE WAY OF THE WILDERNESS

The traditional reconstruction of the route taken by Moses and the Israelites heads towards the southern part of the Sinai peninsula, doubtless as a result of the equation of biblical Sinai (also called Horeb) with Jebel Musa ('Mountain of Moses'). But this equation can only be traced back to the 4th century CE, though it may rest on earlier traditions. Such a location would fit statements which suggest that Sinai / Horeb was some distance from Kadesh-barnea (for example, Deut. 1: 2 and also Num. 33: 15–36). But there is other biblical evidence which points to a more northerly location in the region of Edom / Seir, notably in some poetic passages widely believed to be relatively early, for example, Judges 5: 4 and Deuteronomy 33: 2, the latter of which may also suggest it was close to Kadesh if the awkward 'With him were myriads of holy ones' is emended to read 'he came from Meribath-Kadesh'. The stories in Exodus also support this view, since Exodus 17: 6 mentions Horeb in the same context as the Amalekites (another nomadic people who seem to have lived close to the Negeb) and as Meribah, which may well be another name for (Meribath-)Kadesh / Kadesh-barnea. Thus, a more northerly route may be envisaged, heading east from the area of the Bitter Lakes towards Sinai in the vicinity of Kadesh and Edom. Attempts to locate Sinai in an area of volcanic activity on the basis of such passages as Exodus 19: 16–19 fail to appreciate the significance of the theophany language being employed.

FROM KADESH TO NEBO

According to the biblical traditions, the Israelites journeyed from Kadesh to Mount Hor (whose location is unknown), where Aaron died, and they then defeated the king of Arad at Hormah (Num. 20: 22–21: 3). Thereafter, it is difficult to be clear what route is envisaged by those who recounted the traditions. A summary account of the route (Num. 33: 41–9) describes them as heading relatively directly for Moab, via Zalmonah, Punon, and Oboth. However, Numbers 21: 4 suggests a detour via the Re(e)d Sea, that is, probably Ezion-geber and the Gulf of Aqaba (see Deut. 2: 8), and an avoidance of the land of Edom. They subsequently encamped in the Wadi Zered, and then crossed the River Arnon and continued on to the vicinity of Mount Pisgah (Num. 21: 10–20).

The biblical account suggests that, in their travels, the Israelites encountered hostility, in particular from two kings who seem to have become almost archetypal opponents—King Sihon of the Amorites, and King Og of Bashan (see, for example, Deut. 1: 4; Josh. 12: 2, 4; Ps. 135: 11; 136: 19–20). Sihon refused the Israelites permission to pass through his territory via the King's Highway (see 'Main Roads'), but he was defeated in a battle at Jahaz and Israel captured his territory from the River Arnon to the River Jabbok, including Sihon's capital Heshbon (Num. 21: 21–6). Then the Israelites headed north towards Bashan, the kingdom of Og (who was defeated at Edrei, Num. 21: 33–5). They then returned to camp in the Plains of Moab, and it is in this context that the biblical account tells how Balak, the king of Moab, called upon Balaam to curse Israel but how Balaam uttered oracles on behalf of Israel's God (Num. 22–4).

The tribes of Reuben and Gad and the half-tribe of Manasseh are recorded as having chosen to remain to the east of the Jordan and to have been given the former territories of Sihon and Og (Num. 32: 33). The Gadites rebuilt Dibon, Ataroth, Aroer, Atroth-shophan, Jazer, Jogbehah, Beth-nimrah, and Beth-haran (Num. 32: 34–6). The Reubenites rebuilt Heshbon, Elealeh, Kiriathaim, Nebo, Baal-meon, and Sibmah (Num. 32: 37–8). Deuteronomy 3:

Grapes on a vine. (See on 'Main Crops'.)

16–17 suggests that Reuben and Gad occupied part of Gilead as well as territory further south between the Jabbok and the Arnon, with the Dead Sea and the Jordan valley as the western boundary. The remainder of Gilead, along with all Bashan including the region of Argob and the villages of Havvoth-jair, became the possession of the half-tribe of Manasseh (Num. 32: 39–41; Deut. 3: 13–14). Bezer in Reuben, Ramoth-gilead in Gad, and Golan in Manasseh were designated cities of refuge (Deut. 4: 43).

Moses is credited with establishing the boundaries of the land of Canaan which the remainder of the Israelites were to occupy (Num. 34: 1–12). But the biblical account suggests that Moses did not enter that land. He is depicted as having climbed up from the Plains of Moab to 'Mount Nebo, to the top of Pisgah' from where he was able to view the whole of the land, summarized as including Gilead and as far as Dan, Naphtali, the land of Ephraim and Manasseh, Judah as far as the Mediterranean (the 'Western Sea'), the Negeb, and the Valley of Jericho (that is, the Jordan valley) as far as Zoar (Deut. 34: 1–3).

The Stories of Joshua and the Judges, Samuel and Saul

CONQUEST, INFILTRATION, OR EMERGENCE?

One of the most debated topics in the study of the Hebrew Bible in recent years has been whether the traditional view of an Israelite conquest of the land of Canaan is historically reliable. The traditional picture owes much to the general sweep of the stories in the Book of Joshua, recounting the tumbling down of the walls of Jericho (Josh. 5–6), the destruction of the city of Ai (Josh. 8), the defeat of a coalition of the five kings of Jerusalem, Hebron, Jarmuth, Lachish, and Eglon who made war on the Gibeonites (Josh. 9–10), and the defeat of a northern coalition led by King Jabin of Hazor, and the destruction of his great city (Josh. 11: 1–15). In a summary statement, a biblical writer claims, 'So Joshua took all that land: the hill country and all the Negeb and all the land of Goshen and the lowland and the Arabah and the hill country of Israel and its lowland, from Mount Halak, which rises toward Seir, as far as Baal-gad in the valley of Lebanon below Mount Hermon' (Josh. 11: 16–17a). But the biblical narrative itself raises questions about this picture of an overall conquest of the land. Even within the Book of Joshua, there are suggestions that much land remained to be possessed, including some territory ostensibly within the boundaries of what Joshua had taken, notably the five cities of the Philistines (Josh.13: 1–7). And the opening chapter of the Book of Judges presents a very different picture. What it describes is apparently the situation after the death of Joshua (Judg. 1: 1), but in fact Joshua is again described as alive in Judges 2: 6 and his death is recalled in the subsequent verses. The likelihood is that Judges 1 is an alternative account of the taking of the land, perhaps set after Joshua's death by an editor who wanted to avoid apparent contradiction with the general impression given by the Book of Joshua. The presentation in Judges 1 is stylized, commencing with Judah and some of its subgroups in the south, and then dealing with some of the other tribes in an approximately south-to-north sequence; but it is frequently noted that the previous inhabitants were not driven out but continued to live alongside the Israelites, albeit sometimes reduced to forced labour.

In part because of the biblical hints at a more complex picture, and in part

The Setting of the Stories of Joshua, the Judges, Samuel and Saul

ASHER, etc.   Tribes of Israel
●   Cities of refuge
■   Philistine Cities

0   5   10   15 Miles

0   5   10   15 Kilometres

Damascus

Sidon

Tyre

Mt. Lebanon

Valley of Lebanon

Mt. Hermon

Baal-gad?

Ahlab

Beth-anath?

Yiron

Kedesh

Dan (Laish)

Beth-rehob

Hazor

R. Jordan

Waters of Merom

Merom

Madon

Rimmon

Hammath

Chinnereth

Sea of Chinnereth

Lakkum

Golan

Ashtaroth

Edrei

Tob

Ramoth-gilead

Kamon?

Jabesh-gilead

Tabbath?

Abel-meholah

Beth-shean

Beer

Mt. Gilboa

En-dor

Shunem

V. of Jezreel

Jezreel

En-gannim (Beth-haggan)

Ibleam

Bezek

Thebez

Socoh

Hepher?

Taanach

Megiddo

Jokneam

Harosheth-ha-goiim

Mt. Tabor

Hill of Moreh

R. Kishon

Shimron

Hannathon

Achshaph?

Bethlehem

Nahalol

Aphik

Cabul

Rehob

Acco

Achzib

Abdon

Misrephoth-maim

Mt. Carmel

Naphath-Dor

Dor

NAPHTALI

DAN

ASHER

ZEBULUN

ISSACHAR

HAVVOTH-JAIR

BASHAN

MANASSEH

GAD

Gilead

Jordan

ISSACHAR

Country of Israel

MANASSEH

THE GREAT SEA

Damascus

33° 30'
34° 30'
35°
35° 30'
36°
33°
32° 30'

V W X Y Z

1 2 3

Hazor: remains of a Canaanite temple from the 14th century BCE. Josh. 11:10 suggests that Hazor was renowned as having been the most important city in the area.

because archaeology does not present such a clear-cut picture of a conquest as was once claimed to be the case, other models were put forward to explain the process whereby the Israelites came to control their territory. One was that of 'nomadic infiltration', a largely peaceful process of nomads moving into and settling in unpopulated areas, perhaps occasionally coming into conflict with the local inhabitants. This view was particularly associated with Martin Noth, but was also espoused by others. A more radical alternative proposal, put forward by George Mendenhall, has come to be known as the 'peasants' revolt' model. This suggested that there was no 'statistically significant' invasion but a relatively small group of incomers entered the land, bringing with them a religion whose characteristics appealed to those already in the land who felt themselves oppressed by what were envisaged as feudal-type overlords. These oppressed people withdrew from an existing Canaanite city-state system to make common cause with the newcomers. This model underwent a number of refinements, including that associated with Norman Gottwald, who argued for a process of retribalization as a more egalitarian form of organization developed. Such variations on the traditional 'conquest' model have attempted to account not only for the Bible's own suggestions that there was not a complete conquest and that Israelites and Canaanites continued to live alongside each other but also for the very limited evidence for major destructions or a significant change of population. The recent trend has been to think more of the 'emergence' of Israel from among the previous inhabitants.

CITIES AND BOUNDARIES

It is necessary to return to the Book of Joshua because much of the latter part of the book describes the distribution of the land among the tribes, first in Transjordan (Josh. 13: 8–33) and then to the west of the Jordan (Josh. 14–19). Special arrangements are made for cities of refuge (Josh. 20) and for cities to be allocated to the Levites (Josh. 21). In addition to lists of cities there are details of the boundaries of the various tribal territories. There has been much debate, but no real agreement, as to the origins of these city and boundary lists. What is clear is that such lists existed and that there was a concern as to which territory and which cities belonged to which group. In the broad sweep of the Bible's account of Israel's story, the promises made to the ancestors that they would eventually possess a land in which to dwell are seen as fulfilled by the events described in the Book of Joshua. So the interest is doubtless in part geographical but it is also to a great extent theological.

THE JUDGES

The Book of Judges tells the stories of a number of major 'judges' and gives brief details of some minor 'judges'. The term 'judge' is misleading, certainly as a description of the major 'judges' since, with one exception (Deborah, see Judg. 4: 4–5), they are not described as administering justice. It is possible that the so-called minor 'judges' (Judg. 10: 1–5; 12: 8–15) were envisaged as having some sort of administrative role, and it has been suggested that the term 'ruler' might be more appropriate. They are each said to have 'judged Israel', but they are associated with different places and it is not clear whether they were thought to have had some sort of responsibility for the whole land. Even the term 'ruler' is hardly appropriate for the major 'judges'. A better description is a term used within the stories, that is, 'deliverer' (Judg. 3: 9, 15).

They are presented as charismatic leaders, raised up by God to confront particular enemies who threatened different parts of the land at different times. Othniel is associated with the defeat of Cushan-rishathaim, said to be from Aram Naharaim, that is, Mesopotamia, but 'Aram' may be a corruption of 'Edom', with Naharaim subsequently having been added in error (Judg. 3: 8). Ehud, a Benjaminite (there is irony here because Benjamin means literally 'son of the right hand' yet his left-handedness contributes to his success) kills the Moabite king, Eglon (Judg. 3: 12–30). There is a passing reference to Shamgar whom the text describes as 'son of Anath', possibly implying that he was from Beth-anath, and his slaying of 600 Philistines (Judg. 3: 31). Deborah summoned Barak to gather an army from Naphtali and Zebulun on Mount Tabor and fight against Sisera in the Plain of Esdraelon/Jezreel. The understanding of this episode is helped by an awareness of geographical factors. There are two accounts of the victory over Sisera; one in prose in Judges 4, and the other in the ancient 'Song of Deborah' in Judges 5. It is the latter

Examples of weapons from Mesopotamia, dating from about the middle of the 2nd millennium BCE. A two-edged sword or dagger is mentioned in the story of Ehud (Judg. 3:16).

which enables the reader to appreciate how Israelite infantry were able to defeat Sisera's chariotry despite having left the security of Mount Tabor for the plain where chariots would have supremacy. Torrential rain turned the River Kishon into a raging torrent, sweeping some chariots away (Judg. 5: 4, 21), while the surrounding land doubtless became waterlogged so that the chariots could not function, accounting for Sisera's flight on foot (Judg. 4: 15).

Gideon is recorded as having summoned an army from Manasseh, Asher, and Zebulun, and achieved victories over the Midianites and the Amalekites (Judg. 6–8). Jephthah led the men of Gilead against the Amalekites (Judg. 11). And the mighty Samson is described as engaging in various exploits against the Philistines, before being blinded and then dying when he brought down the building in which he had been forced to entertain his captors (Judg. 12–16).

The general picture of tumultuous times presented by the Book of Judges is completed with a description of how the tribe of Dan found a new home in the far north (Judg. 17–18) and of conflict between Benjamin and the other tribes (Judg. 19–21).

The opening verse of the Book of Ruth states that the events it describes took place 'in the days when the judges ruled'. Hence it has been placed after the Book of Judges in the Christian canonical order, although in the Hebrew Bible it is included among the Writings. The book tells how Ruth, a Moabite, accompanied her mother-in-law Naomi back to Bethlehem, married Boaz, and was an ancestor of King David.

SAMUEL

Facing: Mount Gilboa: the setting of Saul's battle with the Philistines (1 Sam. 31).

The exploits of Samuel are recounted in the first book that bears his name. His early years are associated with the sanctuary at Shiloh (1 Sam. 1–3) and the narrator reports that he became known from Dan to Beer-sheba as a 'trust-

worthy prophet of the LORD' (1 Sam. 3: 20). But his main sphere of activity is presented as more local, in the central hill country where, we are told, he would make an annual circuit from his home at Ramah visiting Bethel, Gilgal, and Mizpah (1 Sam. 7: 16–17). Samuel's career is set in the context of conflict between Israelites and Philistines. 1 Samuel 4 tells of the capture of the Ark of the Covenant from Shiloh by the Philistines, and the destruction of Shiloh is probably to be associated with Philistine activity, though the biblical narrator does not mention this explicitly. (See also Jeremiah 7: 12–14 where the destruction is credited to God, with no mention of the means of execution.) The story concentrates on the fate of the Ark in Philistine hands, and the outbreak of plagues at two of the Philistine cities, Ashdod and Ekron (1 Sam. 5), and its subsequent return into Israelite hands via Beth Shemesh to Kiriath-jearim (1 Sam. 6: 1–7: 2). Samuel is credited with the anointing of Israel's first king, Saul, although the biblical account leaves the reader unsure as to whether Samuel was reluctant to take this step or welcomed it (compare 1 Sam. 8 with 1 Sam. 9–10). Subsequently he was also to anoint David at Bethlehem (1 Sam. 16. 1–13).

SAUL

The stories of Saul stress that he was a Benjaminite (for example, 1 Sam. 9: 1–2) and that his home was Gibeah (for example, 1 Sam. 10: 26). The geographical significance of this information may lie in an attempt to underline that he came from a town in the heart of the land but that he did not belong to one of the more powerful tribes to the south or north. He is presented as demonstrating his leadership abilities by defeating Ammonites who were besieging Jabesh-gilead, prior to the setting of the seal on his kingship at Gilgal (1 Sam. 11). Thereafter the story tells of his attempts to defeat the Philistines, and becomes inextricably bound with the accounts of the rise of David. Initially the account is one of success, thanks in no small measure to Saul's son Jonathan, with a victory over a Philistine garrison at Michmash and their pursuit to Aijalon (1 Sam. 14). Indeed, a summary statement claims numerous successes against 'all his enemies on every side' including the Philistines (1 Sam. 14: 47–8). But as the story unfolds he is unable to defeat the Philistines or to cope with the rise to power of David. Ultimately, after consulting the dead Samuel via a medium, the so-called 'Witch of Endor' (1 Sam. 28: 3–25), he died in battle, taking his own life, against the Philistines on Mount Gilboa (1 Sam. 31). This location relatively far north and a considerable distance from their heartlands in the coastal plains shows the extent of Philistine power and highlights the task facing David.

The Stories of David and Solomon

The stories of David and Solomon, and also of the later kings of Israel and Judah, are told in the Books of Samuel and Kings, and also in the Books of Chronicles. There is a great deal of similarity in the accounts but there are also important differences, not least in the rather rosier picture of David presented in the latter. In what follows, references will predominantly be given to the Samuel–Kings account.

DAVID

The early stories of David tell of the handsome shepherd-boy anointed by Samuel at Bethlehem (1 Sam. 16: 1–13), who played the lyre for Saul (1 Sam. 16: 14-23). He famously and remarkably succeeded in defeating the Philistine 'giant' Goliath, armed only with a sling and stone (1 Sam. 17: 1–51). The narrator in 1 Samuel is at pains to set the scene of this exploit precisely: the Philistines were encamped between Socoh and Azekah at a place (whose exact location is not known) called Ephes-dammim, and the Israelites in the Valley of Elah (1 Sam. 17: 1–2). After David's victory the Israelites pursued the Philistines to two of their cities, Ekron and Gath (1 Sam. 17: 52). Thereafter, David, having become Saul's rival, is described as pursuing an unsettled existence in the hill country of Judah, spending time with the priest at Nob (1 Sam. 21: 1-9), going to the Philistine king, Achish of Gath (1 Sam. 21: 10–15), fleeing to the cave of Adullam (1 Sam. 22: 1), and even journeying as far as Moab (1 Sam. 22: 3) before returning to Judah. He defeated the Philistines at Keilah (1 Sam. 23: 1–12), then fled to the wilderness of Ziph (1 Sam. 23: 14), and thence to the wilderness of Maon (1 Sam. 23: 24), of Engedi (1 Sam. 24: 1), and of Paran (1 Sam. 25: 1). He married Abigail, the widow of Nabal of Maon, who had refused to pay 'protection' to him (1 Sam. 25: 2–42). Subsequently he is described as going over to the Philistines, and being given the city of Ziklag by Achish of Gath (1 Sam. 27: 6).

When Saul died, the biblical narrative suggests that at first there were rival claims to the succession. At Hebron, David was anointed king of Judah by the people of Judah (2 Sam. 2: 4) but at Mahanaim in Transjordan, Saul's son

The Setting of the Stories of David and Solomon

SYRIA, etc.   Non-Israelite peoples
■   Places fortified by Solomon
I–XII   Solomon's administrative
                  districts (1 Kgs. 4. 7-19)

0   10   20 Miles
0   10   20 Kilometres

V **W** **X** **Y** **Z**

1

33° 30'

Sidon

Tyre

Abel-beth-maacah   Dan
                    Beth-rehob

2

S I D O N I A N S   **S Y R I A (ARAM)**

ZOBAH

Damascus

Mt. Lebanon   BETH-REHOB   Mt. Hermon

M A A C A H   **A R G O B**

G E S H U R

33°

Hazor ■

IX   Merom   VIII

Acco

Cabul

Sea of Chinnereth

Helam

3

T H E

Mt. Carmel   R. Kishon

Jokneam (Jokmeam)   X

Dor   IV

Megiddo ■

Jezreel

Taanach

V. of Jezreel

Mt. Gilboa   Beth-shean

HAVVOTH-JAIR

VI

Rogelim   Ramoth-gilead   Tob

32° 30'

G R E A T

III

Hepher?   Socoh   Arubboth

Thebez

V

Jabesh-gilead

Abel-meholah

VII

4

S E A

Plain of Sharon

Mt. Ebal   Shechem

Pirathon   *Mt. Gerizim*

I

Lo-debar?   R. Jabbok

Succoth

Zarethan?   Mahanaim

G I L E A D

A M M O N

32°

Joppa

Gath-rimmon

Zeredah

∴ Shiloh

Baal-hazor

Ephraim

Jazer

Rabbah (Rabbath-ammon)

Beth-hanan   Bethel
Lower Beth-horon   Upper Beth-horon
Shaalbim   Gibeon   Geba
Gezer ■   II   Elon   Beeroth?
Makaz   Kiriath-jearim   Gibeah?   Anathoth
Baalath? ■   Sorek

Gilgal

Jericho

XI   XII

5

Ashdod   Ekron

Beth-shemesh

Jerusalem

Bethlehem

Netophah

Heshbon

Medeba

Gath?

Timnah

Ashkelon

Libnah?   Adullam

Giloh

Tekoa

P H I L I S T I N E S

The Shephelah (Lowland)

Hebron

Wilderness of Judah

Salt Sea (Sea of the Arabah)

R. Nahaliel

M O A B

31° 30'

Gaza

Gerar   Ziklag?   Debir

Carmel

Dibon
Aroer

R. Arnon

6

Brook Besor

Kabzeel?   Arad

Beer-sheba

Valley of Salt

T h e   N e g e b

A M A L E K I T E S

Brook Zered

31°

7

E D O M

© Oxford University P

Tamar ■
(30° 48'N)

V **W** **X** **Y** **Z**

34° 30'   35°   35° 30'   36°

Ish-bosheth (Ish-baal) was declared king by Abner, Saul's commander-in-chief (2 Sam. 2: 8–9). Their armies came into conflict at the pool of Gibeon (2 Sam. 2: 12–32). Abner planned to defect to David, but he was killed by Joab, David's commander (2 Sam. 3). Ish-bosheth was assassinated and his head was brought to David at Hebron (2 Sam. 4). David was declared king of all Israel (2 Sam. 5: 1–5), the beginning of what came to be known as the 'United Monarchy'.

The first act with which David is credited after being made king of all Israel was the establishment of a new capital city, taking from its previous inhabitants the stronghold of Jerusalem (2 Sam. 5: 6–10). For a discussion of the capture of the city, see 'Jerusalem in the 1st Millennium BCE'. He subsequently established it as a religious centre by transferring the Ark of the Covenant there from Kiriath-jearim (2 Sam. 6). David is also credited with a succession of victories, securing and expanding his kingdom. The victories were achieved thanks to the existence of a standing army, at whose core were

Jerusalem: aerial view from the south. The City of David was on the hill to the south of the Temple Mount, with the Kidron Valley to the east.

93

mercenary soldiers whose designations suggest that they may have been Philistines—Cherethites, Pelethites, and Gittites (2 Sam. 8: 18; 15: 18). He removed the Philistine threat, driving them from the hill country and pursuing them from Geba to Gezer (2 Sam. 5: 17–25). He is accorded victories over neighbouring kingdoms to the south and in Transjordan. The Edomites were defeated in the Valley of Salt and garrisons placed throughout Edom (2 Sam. 8: 13–14). The Moabites too were defeated and placed under tribute (2 Sam. 8: 2). A victory was won over the cavalry and chariotry of the Aramean (Syrian) king Hadadezer of Zobah, and an army from Damascus who came to Hadadezer's assistance, and tribute was exacted and plunder taken (2 Sam. 8: 3–8). The Ammonites sought the assistance of the Arameans of Beth-rehob, the Arameans of Zobah, the king of Maacah, and the people of Tob (2 Sam. 10: 6), but the Aramean forces were defeated and the alliance with the Ammonites broken (2 Sam. 10: 6–19). Subsequently Ammon was attacked, its capital city Rabbah besieged, and the Ammonites set to hard labour (2 Sam. 11: 1; 12: 26–31). It is in the context of the fighting against the Ammonites that the story of David's liaison with Bath-sheba, and the death of her husband, Uriah the Hittite, is set (2 Sam. 11: 2–27). It is also suggested that, as David's strength increased, kings of territory further to the north sought to establish friendly relationships with him—King Hiram of Tyre (2 Sam. 5: 11) and King Toi of Hamath (2 Sam. 8: 9–11). The territory presented as coming under David's control, from the borders of Hamath in the north down to the territory of Edom in the south, seems to reflect an ideal view of the totality of the Promised Land. Ezekiel's vision of the restored land (Ezek. 48) envisages the tribes as occupying very much this extent of land. A slightly smaller area is reflected in the description of the territory included in David's census (2 Sam. 24). This is described as beginning in Transjordan, from Aroer, just north of the River Arnon, going northward through Gad and Gilead and on to Dan and the region of Tyre and Sidon, and thence southward through the territory to the west of the Jordan, as far south as Beer-sheba.

The latter part of the account of the reign of David given in 2 Samuel and 1 Kings suggests a time of dissension and uncertainty over who was to succeed. (The account in 1 Chronicles omits this and suggests a smooth transition from David to Solomon.) First his son Absalom had himself declared king in Hebron (2 Sam. 15: 10), forcing David to flee to Mahanaim in Transjordan where he was befriended by people from Rabbah, Lo-debar, and Roge-lim (2 Sam. 17: 27–9). After Absalom was killed in battle in the 'forest of Ephraim' (2 Sam. 18: 6), the people of Judah were persuaded to bring David back to Jerusalem (2 Sam. 19). But this is presented as having led to dissension with the northern tribes, who revolted at the instigation of a Benjaminite named Sheba, who declared, 'We have no portion in David, no share in the son of Jesse! Everyone to your tents, O Israel!' (2 Sam. 20: 1). The revolt was put down by Joab, who besieged Sheba in Abel-beth-maacah in the far north (2 Sam. 20: 14). Then when David was on his very deathbed, another of his sons, Adonijah, sought to take the kingship but was frustrated by the protagonists of Solomon who, according to the account in 1 Kings 1, finally persuaded David to declare Solomon his successor. (Contrast the brief statement in 1 Chronicles 23: 1: 'When David was old and full of days, he made his son Solomon king over Israel.') Solomon was anointed king at the spring Gihon (1 Kgs. 1: 38–9).

SOLOMON

The account of Solomon's reign suggests that his first steps were to remove any potential rivals to his position (1 Kgs. 2). This piece of political 'wisdom' precedes the account of his famous prayer for wisdom at the high place of Gibeon (1 Kgs. 3). Solomon is presented as having brought about peace, wealth, and prestige. He set up an administrative system for his kingdom, established a policy of forced labour for his building projects, exploited his land's strategic position for the purposes of trade, and made a number of political marriages. The bulk of the kingdom was divided into twelve administrative districts over which twelve officials were placed (1 Kgs. 4: 7–19). The districts are listed as: (I) the hill country of Ephraim; (II) Makaz, Shaalbim, Beth-shemesh, Elon, Beth-hanan; (III) Arubboth, including Socoh and the land of Hepher; (IV) Naphath-dor—the coastal region around Dor; (V) Taanach, Megiddo, Beth-shean, Abel-meholah, Jokmeam; (VI) Ramoth-gilead, including Havvoth-jair, Argob (in Bashan); (VII) Mahanaim; (VIII) Naphtali; (IX) Asher, Bealoth; (X) Issachar; (XI) Benjamin; (XII) Gilead and the land of Sihon and Og between the Arnon and the Jabbok. (See numbers on the accompanying map; apart from the description of the districts in 1 Kgs. 4, there is no information as to the extent of each of these districts.) It is noteworthy that Judah seems to have been excluded, although there is an additional comment that 'there was one official in the land of Judah' (1 Kgs. 4: 19b).

To Solomon are credited a number of major building activities, notably the construction in Jerusalem of a temple and a royal palace (1 Kgs. 6–7). He also used forced labour to rebuild or fortify several key strategic cities, Hazor, Megiddo, Gezer, Lower Beth-horon, Baalath, and Tamar (1 Kgs. 9: 15–18). Excavations at some of these sites have provided evidence of the extent of these activities, though it is not always possible to be certain which structures are to be assigned to Solomon. The fortified gateways at Gezer, Hazor, and Megiddo, built very much to the same design, have been thought to reflect activity of Solomon's instigation. Store cities and cities for his chariots, horses, and cavalry were also established (1 Kgs. 4: 26; 9: 19). He is recorded as having been involved in the importation of horses and chariots from Egypt and Kue (1 Kgs. 10: 26-9). Extensive installations at Megiddo were at one time confidently described as 'Solomon's Stables', but subsequent excavations have suggested a later date, perhaps the time of Ahab, and the debate continues as to whether they are to be identified as stables or storehouses (see 'Megiddo'). (Further mention of Solomon's trading activities will be made in the brief discussion of 'Ancient Trade Routes' which follows.)

Although the presentation of Solomon's reign is largely one of a time of

Megiddo (Tell el-Muteselim) was an ancient city and a strategically important city. It was situated at a point where it guarded the 'Way of the Sea' (see on 'The Lands of the Bible: Main Roads') as it passed through the hills into the Plain of Megiddo or Esdraelon, and was the site of battles past and future. A famous battle was fought there in the time of Thutmose III (1479– 1425), and it was there that king Josiah of Judah met his death in 609, trying to prevent the march northwards of another pharaoh, Neco II (610–595). The Book of Revelation (16: 16) places the forthcoming conflict between the forces of good and evil at Megiddo (Armageddon—'Mount Megiddo'). It is not surprising that it is listed as one of the key strategic cities fortified by Solomon, along with Hazor and Gezer (1 Kgs. 9: 15). Excavations reveal that there were buildings on the site from the earliest phase of the Early Bronze Age. Probably from EBA II comes a stone built circular 'high place', some 7.5 m (25 ft) in diameter and 1.5 m (5 ft) high, approached by steps. It was surrounded by a wall, inside which pottery and bones were found, the latter probably the remains of sacrifices.

Solomon's stables?

Evidence that Megiddo was indeed fortified in the time of Solomon was found in the discovery of a casemate wall and a six-chambered gate. Similar gates were found at Hazor and Gezer, places also mentioned in 1 Kgs. 9: 15. Structures comprising rooms with two rows of pillars lining passageways down the centre, sometimes with stone troughs or perhaps mangers between the pillars, were identified as stable complexes and linked with the reference to the statement that Solomon established 'cities for his chariots' in 1 Kgs. 9: 19. Further study of the stratigraphy suggested that the complexes belonged to a stratum later than that of the Solomonic gate, and that it was more likely that they came from the time of King Ahab. A text of Shalmaneser

Aerial view of Tell el-Muteselim, the site of Megiddo. The gate area is in the foreground, and the shaft giving access to the water tunnel is at the far right.

III records that Ahab supplied 2,000 chariots to fight in the battle of Qarqar in 853 BCE, so he too would have needed stables! (It has been suggested that the construction may have begun in the time of Solomon, but that there was further development in the time of Ahab.) But were they stables? Similar structures elsewhere, for example, Hazor and Beersheba, have been identified as storehouses, and 1 Kgs. 9: 19 also mentions that Solomon built 'storage cities'. The water troughs or mangers might have been for the benefit of donkeys which had transported the goods for storage. (Recent study has revealed evidence of 'cribbing', suggesting the presence of equids.) The debate still continues as to whether they were stables, but the dating of the finished complexes to the time of Solomon is no longer tenable. The question must be asked as to the extent to which the original identification was influenced by a biblical text.

Important strategic sites needed a secure water-supply. The water system at Megiddo may have been begun in the time of Solomon, but was probably completed in the time of Ahab. A gallery leading to an underground spring was blocked off, a shaft was dug inside the city walls and then a tunnel about 64 m (70 yds) long was hewn out of the rock to give access to the water.

Top: Circular altar or 'high place' at Megiddo.
Right: The rock-cut tunnel at Megiddo, providing access to a regular water-supply.

prosperity and peace, there are references to adversaries. Those named are Hadad the Edomite, Rezon from Zobah and, most significantly, Jeroboam, an Ephraimite who was encouraged to revolt by Ahijah, a prophet from Shiloh, but who was forced to flee to Egypt, taking refuge with Pharaoh Shishak until Solomon's death (1 Kgs. 11: 14–40). It was Jeroboam who was to become the king of the northern tribes when, after Solomon's demise, the 'United Monarchy' could not be maintained. But descendants of David continued to rule over Judah, beginning with Solomon's son, Rehoboam, until the Babylonian exile. And thereafter, prophets looked forward to a restoration of the United Monarchy under a king of David's line.

Ancient Trade Routes

Mention has already been made of the fact that the territory occupied by the Israelites formed a land-bridge through which routes from Africa and Arabia to Mesopotamia and Asia Minor (and vice versa) must have passed, and of its consequent strategic and commercial significance. So merchandise carried over land must have passed through this narrow coastal strip. Solomon's exploitation of this geographical location has also been alluded to. It is therefore appropriate to make some brief comments on ancient trade routes in so far as that is possible.

THE BIBLE AND TRADE

It is not surprising that the biblical writers have little to say directly about trade, since this was not something in which they were particularly interested and it was often incidental. For example, the reference to a caravan of Ishmaelite or Midianite traders 'coming from Gilead, with their camels carrying gum, balm, and resin, on their way to carry it down to Egypt' (Gen. 37: 25) explains how Joseph was taken down to Egypt. It is possible that such marriages as that of Ahab to Jezebel, the daughter of the king of Sidon (1 Kgs. 16: 31), were undertaken for commercial reasons, but this is not stated explicitly.

It is not possible to reconstruct a precise picture of the ancient Israelites' trading relations, to distinguish clearly between times when trade flourished or was slack. So the accompanying map is not related to any specific period or any particular book of the Bible. It represents an attempt to show what trade routes may have been in use at approximately the time of the Hebrew monarchy, and the principal towns or peoples with which the Israelites or their neighbours may have had trade relations. Some of the names, especially in Arabia, appear as personal names in the Bible. Genesis 25: 1–6 purports to list the descendants of Abraham as a result of his taking Keturah as a wife. But when it is remembered that Keturah means 'incense', and that Arabian incense was an important source of wealth in ancient times, it becomes likely that that the names of Keturah's sons and grandsons represent not individual persons but well-known peoples or places connected with the incense

Ancient Trade Routes

Approximate line of principal trade route

| 0 | 100 | 200 Miles |

| 0 | 100 | 200 Kilometres |

© Oxford University Pr

Map labels:

Pergamum
Sardis
Smyrna
LYDIA
(LUD)
Iconium
Rhodes
Crete
35°

HITTITES
Kanish
F
Meshech
Tubal
Markasi
Kue
Tarsus
Sam'al
Adana
Ya'udi
Alalakh
Posidium
Ugarit
Enkomi
Kittim
(Alashiya)

The Great Sea

Melid
Gurgum
Kummukhu
G
Haran
Carchemish
Halab
Tiphsah
Hamath
Qatna
Homs
Gebal
Berytus
Sidon
Lebo-Hamath
Tadmor
Tyre
Acco
Dor
Megiddo
Samaria
Shechem
Joppa
Ashkelon
Gaza
Judah
Kenites
Seir
Sela
Edom
Sinai

ARARAT
(URARTU)
L. Van
Van
Amida
HURRIANS
Gozan
Singara
ASSYRIA
Asshur
Tirqa
Mari
Damascus
Hazor
Bashan
Bozrah
Gilead
Rabbah
Ammon
Jerusalem
Moab
Nebaioth

J
Tabriz
L. Urmia
Nineveh
Calah
Arbela
Arrapkha
Nuzi
MEDIA
Ecbatana
KASSITES
ELAM
BABYLONIA
Eshnunna
Babylon
Nippur
Susa
Ur
ancient coastline
Sealand
Persian G

K
Caspian Sea

Pharos
Naucratis
Heliopolis (On)
Memphis
(Noph)
Shur
Ezion-geber
Midian
Dumah
Buz
EGYPT
Akhetaton
(T.el-'Amarna)
Oasis
Thebes
(No)
Syene
Berenike
Abu Simbel
Buhen
ETHIOPIA
(CUSH)
Napata
Meroe
R. Nile

KEDAR
ARABIA
Ephah
Tema
Dedan
Dedan
Khaibar
Leuke Kome
Yathrib
OPHIR
(Mahd edh-Dhahab)
Myos Hormos
Red Sea
PUNT
Adulis
Dilmun

OKTAN
Uzal
Marib
Shabwa
Timna
SHEBA
HAZARMAVETH
Canneh
Muza
Eden

Remains of a section of what was once thought to be Solomon's Stables at Megiddo. (See on 'Megiddo'.)

trade. Many of these places cannot be located with certainty on a map, but a few can be identified with peoples known from other sources. Figures such as Sheba (the Sabeans of Job 1: 15) and Nebaioth (the eldest son of Ishmael in Genesis 25: 13 and a pastoral tribe in Isaiah 60: 7) stand out. Indeed, Sheba and Nebaioth are linked with Midian, Ephah, and Kedar in Isaiah 60: 4–7, a passage speaking of the wealth of nations being brought to Jerusalem. Other names on the map are supplied from Assyrian or Egyptian records; and some are of ancient sites recovered by archaeological excavations, with evidence of trading activity.

SOLOMON

It is in the portrayal of Solomon that commercial activity plays an important part. His trade in horses and chariots has already been mentioned. His dealings with Hiram, king of Tyre, involved the latter's provision of cedars and cypresses for Solomon's building activities in Jerusalem, in return for which Solomon gave him wheat (1 Kgs. 5: 8–11) and also territory, twenty cities in the Galilee region (1 Kgs. 9: 10–13). Particularly important was his establishment of a fleet of ships at Ezion-geber at the northern end of the Gulf of Aqaba, with access to the Red Sea. This was achieved in partnership with Hiram of Tyre (1 Kgs. 9: 26–8). The significance of this must be seen in conjunction with the much misrepresented story of the visit of the Queen of Sheba from south Arabia. For all her apparent interest in Solomon's wisdom, it is perhaps his commercial wisdom which was particularly attractive and the primary purpose of the relationship was probably trade. She came bearing gold and spices, the two great exports of Arabia to the Mediterranean world, along with precious stones (1 Kgs. 10: 2, 10), and took back unspecified products ('every desire that she expressed'; 1 Kgs. 10: 13). With a fleet based in Ezion-geber, and friendly relations with the Queen of Sheba who controlled the ports of origin in the southern Red Sea, goods could be shipped directly by Solomon's and Hiram's fleets to territory under Solomon's control. This would avoid the necessity (and cost) of transportation overland through Arabia. Every three years the fleets would set out, returning with 'gold, silver, ivory, apes and peacocks' (1 Kgs. 10: 22).

LATER KINGS

There is little to suggest that this trading activity continued to be of major importance, though one reference suggests that it continued for a time. There is an enigmatic mention of the existence of a fleet of ships 'of the Tarshish type' in the time of Jehoshaphat, king of Judah, which was wrecked at Ezion-geber. Jehoshaphat appears to have refused the help of Ahaziah, king of Israel. Ahaziah was Ahab's son, so may have had links with Tyre and therefore have been able to supply Phoenician sailors (1 Kgs. 22: 48–9). What is clear is that it was the Phoenicians who became the great traders around the Mediterranean and beyond. Ezekiel's lament over Tyre (Ezek. 27) gives a summary of the extent of their activities, and some of the place names on the map are taken from this chapter. It suggests that such places were well known to the people of Judah, and it is not impossible that Israelites may have engaged in trade with some of the same peoples.

The Kingdoms of Israel and Judah

According to those who told the stories of the Hebrew kings, the United Monarchy did not outlast the reign of Solomon and there were already hints that the 'unity' was only on the surface, for example, the disaffection of the northern tribes which led to the rebellion of Sheba. Solomon's son Rehoboam was accepted as king in Judah, and went to Shechem to meet a gathering of the northern Israelites. Jeroboam, who had returned from Egypt, led the demands that Rehoboam should lessen the burdens placed on them by Solomon, but Rehoboam refused and was forced to flee to Jerusalem (1 Kgs. 12: 1–18). The biblical narrator, writing from a southern Judahite perspective states, 'So Israel has been in rebellion against the house of David to this day' (1 Kgs. 12: 19). Shechem became the first capital of the northern kingdom of Israel; but whereas in Judah Jerusalem was both the political and religious centre of the kingdom, in Israel Dan and Bethel were established as national shrines by Jeroboam (1 Kgs. 12: 29). At some point Tirzah became the capital of Israel. The mention of Jeroboam's wife coming to Tirzah (1 Kgs. 14: 17) may imply that this happened during his reign. Certainly Baasha is said to have lived in Tirzah (1 Kgs. 15: 21). Subsequently there was another shift of capital to Samaria in the reign of Omri (see below).

The biblical account recalls that, in the fifth year of Rehoboam's reign, Pharaoh Shishak I (Shoshenq) attacked Jerusalem (1 Kgs. 14: 25–6). In the record of his campaign which Shishak had inscribed on the walls of the temple of Amon at Thebes (Karnak), he listed more than 150 towns which he had conquered in the area of Judah and Israel, including Megiddo. A fragment of a limestone stele was found at Megiddo, bearing Shishak's royal cartouches. In addition to external invasion, there are references to friction between Israel and Judah. According to 2 Chronicles 13: 19, Rehoboam's son Abijah (Abijam) took Bethel, Jeshanah, and Ephron and their surrounding villages from Jeroboam. Jeroboam's son, Nadab, was killed by Baasha while Nadab and the Israelite forces were besieging Gibbethon (1 Kgs. 15: 27). Asa had become king of Judah, and the biblical narrator reports, 'There was war between Asa and King Baasha of Israel all their days' (1 Kgs. 15: 16). In preparation for his war with Judah, Baasha fortified Ramah, 5 miles (8 km) north of Jerusalem (1 Kgs. 15: 17). But Asa hired the support of King Ben-hadad of Damascus who invaded Israel and conquered several cities in the far north (Ijon, Dan, and Abel-beth-maacah), the territory around Chinnereth and the region of Naphtali (1 Kgs. 15: 18–20). Asa strengthened Judah's border, apparently using the very stones which Baasha had been using at Ramah to fortify Mizpah and Geba (1 Kgs. 15: 22). In the account of his reign in Chronicles, Asa is credited with the defeat of a huge force led by Zerah the Ethiopian (or Cushite) in the Valley of Zephathah at Mareshah (2 Chr. 14: 9–15). Baasha's son, Elah, was killed at Tirzah by Zimri. When news of this reached the commander of the Israelite troops, Omri, at Gibbethon, he went to Tirzah, and besieged the city. Zimri took his own life and, after the removal of a rival claimant (Tibni) Omri took the throne (1 Kgs. 16: 8–23).

THE HOUSE OF OMRI

Although his reign is dealt with in just six verses in Kings (1 Kgs. 16: 23–8) and no details at all are given in Chronicles, he established an important dynasty. Assyrian records referred to Israel as 'the land of Omri' and continued to do so long after his dynasty ended. He reigned from Tirzah for six years, but then we are told that he bought the hill of Samaria and fortified it, making it his capital (1 Kgs. 16: 24). As a soldier, Omri chose a good strategic site, on a hill which dominated the surrounding countryside, with good access in three directions, west to the coastal plain, north to Megiddo, and east to Shechem and the Jordan valley.

The highest point in the Carmel Hills, the traditional site of Elijah's encounter with the prophets of Baal and Asherah (1 Kgs. 18: 20–40).

The Kingdoms of Israel and Judah

ISRAEL, JUDAH Hebrew kingdoms
ASHER, etc. Tribal areas
SYRIA, etc. Non-Israelite peoples
– – – – – Approximate boundary between Israel, Judah and Philistia

0   10   20 Miles
0   10   20 Kilometres

SYRIA (ARAM)
↑ ZOBAH
Sidon
R. Abana
Damascus
R. Pharpar
Mt. Lebanon
Entrance to Hamath
Mt. Hermon

Zarephath
Ijon
Tyre
Abel-beth-maacah (Abel-maim)
Dan
Kedesh
Yiron
Hazor
SIDONIANS
ASHER
GALILEE
NAPHTALI
Janoah
Merom
BASHAN
MANASSEH
HAURAN
Acco
Chinnereth
Sea of Chinnereth
Karnaim
Ashtaroth
Aphek
Mt. Carmel
R. Kishon
Rumah
Hannathon
ZEBULUN
Gath-hepher
Mt. Tabor
HAVVOTH-JAIR
Edrei
Jokmeam
ISSACHAR
Beth-arbel
Ramoth-gilead
Dor
Megiddo
Shunem
Jezreel
V. of Jezreel
Taanach
THE
GREAT
SEA
Plain of Sharon
Beth-haggan
Tishbe
Borim
Dothan
Ibleam
MANASSEH
Abel-meholah
Brook Cherith
Socoh
Yazith
ISR
GILEAD
EL
Samaria
Tirzah
Mt. Ebal
Siphtan
Lo-debar?
Penuel
MANASSEH
Shechem
Mt. Gerizim
Pirathon
Mahanaim
AMMON
Baal-shalishah
Tappuah
EPHRAIM
Shiloh
Joppa
Zeredah
Jeshanah
Baal-hazor
Ephron
Gimzo
Bethel
Ai
Rabbah
Gath (Gittaim)
Beth-horon
Zemaraim
Mizpah
Gilgal
Jabneel (Jabneh)
Gibbethon
BENJAMIN
Jericho
Mount Baalah
Shikkeron
Aijalon
Ramah
Geba
Baalath?
Timnah
Zorah
Gibeah?
Anathoth
Baal-peor
Heshbon
Bezer? (Bozrah?)
Ekron
Beth-shemesh
Jerusalem
Nebo
Kiriathaim
Ashdod
Gath?
Azekah
Middin
City of Salt?
Medeba
Bethlehem
Nibshan?
V. of Achor
Secacah?
Beth-meon (Baal-meon)
Ashkelon
Adullam
Etam
Tekoa
Br. Kidron
Beth-diblathaim
Libnah
Mareshah
Beth-zur
Zair
PHILISTIA
Lachish
Ascent of Ziz
Sea of the Arabah (Salt Sea)
R. Nahaliel
Jahaz?
Gaza
Hebron
Adoraim
V. of Beracah
Ataroth
Gerar
Ziph
En-gedi
R. Arnon
Dibon
Yurza
Carmel
Aroer
aphia
Wilderness
JUDAH
Sharuhen
SIMEON
Beer-sheba
Great Arad
Gurbaal
Arad of Beth-yeroham?
Valley of Salt
MOAB
Kir-hareseth
Waters of Nimrim
The Negeb
Zoar
Brook Zered
Br. Besor
EDOM
Hazazon-tamar (30° 48')

© Oxford University Press

The Mesha Stele, also known
as the Moabite Stone, inscribed
with a Moabite version of the
events described in 2 Kgs. 3.
A cast taken before it was
broken has enabled missing
text to be reconstructed.

Omri's son, Ahab, married Jezebel, the daughter of the king of Tyre, and became a worshipper of Baal, building a temple and altar for Baal in Samaria (1 Kgs. 16: 31–3). The account of his reign provides the context for the stories of Elijah, such as that of the great contest with the prophets of Baal and Asherah on Mount Carmel (1 Kgs. 18: 20–40). King Ben-hadad of Damascus attacked Israel at Samaria and at Aphek, but was defeated on both occasions (1 Kgs. 20). The Syrians held Ramoth-gilead, and Ahab was not able to take it back, even with the assistance of Jehoshaphat, the king of Judah. It was in battle at Ramoth-gilead that Ahab died. His body was brought to Samaria where he was buried (1 Kgs. 22: 1–40).

Although it is not mentioned in the brief account of his reign, Omri must have gained control over Moab and imposed tribute upon the Moabites; but after Ahab's death Mesha, king of Moab, successfully revolted (2 Kgs. 3: 4–5). This episode is of particular interest because it is one of the few instances where accounts from the two sides in the conflict have been preserved. Mesha's own inscription (sometimes known as the 'Moabite Stone') was found at Dibon. This document speaks of Mesha's conquest of Ataroth and Jahaz and the building or fortifying of other cities, and claims that in his day Israel perished completely and for ever. The biblical account does eventually admit that the battle went against Israel, but only after Mesha had sacrificed his firstborn son: 'And great wrath came upon Israel, so they withdrew from him and returned to their own land' (2 Kgs. 3: 27).

King Jehoram (Joram), Ahab's son, had been assisted by Jehoshaphat, king of Judah, in his conflict with Moab. It was Jehoshaphat who had unsuccessfully attempted to revive Solomon's trading connections with the Red Sea via Ezion-geber (see 'Ancient Trade Routes'). Jehoshaphat was succeeded by his son, also called Jehoram (or Joram), who was unsuccessful in an attempt to subdue a revolt of the Edomites, and it is noted that Libnah also revolted at the same time (2 Kgs. 8: 20–2). Within this general context, the stories of Elisha are set. They suggest a time of tension with the Arameans (Syrians) to the north and mention Aramean attacks on Dothan and Samaria (2 Kgs. 6–7). They also associate Elisha with an act of regicide in Damascus, whereby Ben-hadad was replaced by Hazael (2 Kgs. 8: 7–15). Jehoram of Israel waged war against Hazael of Damascus at Ramoth-gilead, where he was wounded. Afterwards he went to Jezreel to recuperate, where he was visited by Ahaziah who had succeeded Jehoram as king of Judah (2 Kgs. 8: 28–9).

THE HOUSE OF JEHU

One of the most significant acts with which Elisha is credited is the anointing of Jehu, Jehoram's commander-in-chief, to become king in Israel. Jehu made his famous chariot ride from Ramoth-gilead to Jezreel, and killed Jehoram of Israel. Ahaziah of Judah fled, but was wounded at Ibleam and died at Megiddo (2 Kgs. 9: 1–28). Samaria and the rest of Israel fell to Jehu, and he is reputed to have wiped out Baal worship from Israel. But Israelite territory in Transjordan from Bashan and Gilead as far south as Aroer near the River

Arnon was taken by Hazael of Damascus (2 Kgs. 10). Hazael's attempts to enlarge his territory included the taking of Gath and the threatening of Jerusalem, but he withdrew when bought off by Jehoash (Joash), son of Amaziah, now king of Judah (2 Kgs. 12: 17–18). After the death of Hazael, the grandson of Jehu, who was also called Jehoash, recovered the Transjordanian territories which Hazael had taken (2 Kgs. 13: 25). Jehoash also fought against Amaziah of Judah, who had won a victory over the Edomites in the Valley of Salt and taken Sela by storm (2 Kgs. 14: 7), defeated him at Beth-shemesh, and plundered Jerusalem (2 Kgs. 14: 11–14).

Jehoash's son Jeroboam II, in a reign of some forty years, established a time of peace and prosperity in Israel. He is said to have restored Israel's ancient boundaries from Lebo-hamath to the Sea of the Arabah, in accordance with the words of Jonah of Gath-hepher (2 Kgs. 14: 25). It is in his reign that the activity of the prophet Amos and the beginning of the career of Hosea are set. In Judah too there was a lengthy reign, that of Jeroboam's near contemporary Uzziah (Azariah). Little is said about his reign in Kings, but Chronicles credits him with various acts, including restoring Eloth (that is, Elath, Eziongeber) on the Red Sea to Judah, fighting against the Philistines, destroying Gath, Jabneh, and Ashdod and building cities in their territory, fighting against Arabs and Meunites, placing the Ammonites under tribute, and enhancing the fortifications of Jerusalem (2 Chr. 26: 2, 6–9). It was to the year of his death that the prophet Isaiah's call was dated (Isa. 6: 1).

THE LAST DAYS OF ISRAEL

Jeroboam's son Zechariah only reigned for six months before he was killed by Shallum, bringing to an end the dynasty of Jehu (2 Kgs. 15: 10). After a month's reign, Shallum was struck down in Samaria by Menahem of Tirzah (2 Kgs. 15: 14). Menahem sacked Tappuah (Tiphsah) and its territory 'from Tirzah on' (2 Kgs. 15: 16). It is in his reign that we are told that the Assyrian king Tiglath-pileser III (Pul) came against Israel. Menahem gave money to Tiglath-pileser to help confirm his kingship (2 Kgs. 15: 19). The Assyrian threat was becoming a reality. After a reign of only two years, Menahem's son Pekahiah was killed by his captain, Pekah, in Samaria (2 Kgs. 15: 23–6). Pekah of Israel and Rezin of Damascus conspired against Ahaz, who had become king of Judah, and attacked Jerusalem. At the same time the Edomites are said to have recaptured Elath (2 Kgs. 16: 5). Under this pressure from various quarters, Ahaz appealed to Tiglath-pileser for aid, sending him silver, gold, and other treasures (2 Kgs. 16: 7–8). Tiglath-pileser took Damascus, and also Ijon, Abel-beth-maacah, Janoah, Kedesh, Hazor, Gilead, and Galilee, and made all of these conquered territories into Assyrian provinces (2 Kgs. 15: 29; 16: 9). Subsequently Pekah's successor Hoshea rebelled against Assyria, so Shalmaneser V came and captured Samaria in 722, though his successor Sargon also claimed the credit for the capture of Samaria.

The Assyrian Empire

Much of our knowledge of the Assyrians comes from records they left behind, in particular through royal annals. In using these records, it is necessary to bear in mind such tendencies as the wish to minimize setbacks and defeats and maximize victories won and territories conquered. Nevertheless, it is possible to use such material to help to provide a picture of the fluctuating fortunes of the Assyrian Empire and to highlight how it impinged upon the story of the ancient Israelites.

EARLIER CONQUESTS

Tiglath-pileser I, who ruled towards the end of the 2nd millennium BCE, called himself 'king of the world, king of Assyria, king of the four rims of the earth', and claimed conquests from the Lower Zab (a tributary of the Tigris) to the Upper Sea (that is, the Mediterranean). He campaigned in the Nairi region and took tribute from Gebal, Sidon, and Arvad. His army is said to have reached Lake Van, and he is reputed to have crossed the Euphrates twenty-eight times. He controlled all of north Babylonia and he conquered the city of Babylon itself. However, this period of glory seems to have been short-lived and to have been followed by a period of weakness.

A second period of strength came in the 9th century, with the reign of the brutal Ashurnasirpal II from Bit-adini. He crossed the Euphrates, captured Carchemish, overran Hattina (north Syria), and claims to have washed his weapons in the Great (Mediterranean) Sea and exacted tribute from Tyre, Sidon, and Arvad amongst other places. He also went up into the Amanus Mountains. He was succeeded by Shalmaneser III (858–824) who greatly expanded Assyria's borders and boasted of having reached the sources of the Tigris and Euphrates. In the south he invaded Babylonia and entered Babylon, Cuthah, and Borsippa, and to the north he reached Lake Van. In 853 he invaded Syria. Aleppo submitted, but at Qarqar on the River Orontes he was confronted by a coalition of twelve kings, including Ahab of Israel and Hadad-ezer of Damascus. In 841 he crossed the Euphrates for the sixteenth time, defeated Hazael of Damascus, and received tribute from Tyre, Sidon,

Statue of King Ashurnasirpal II from the shrine of Ishtar in Nimrud.

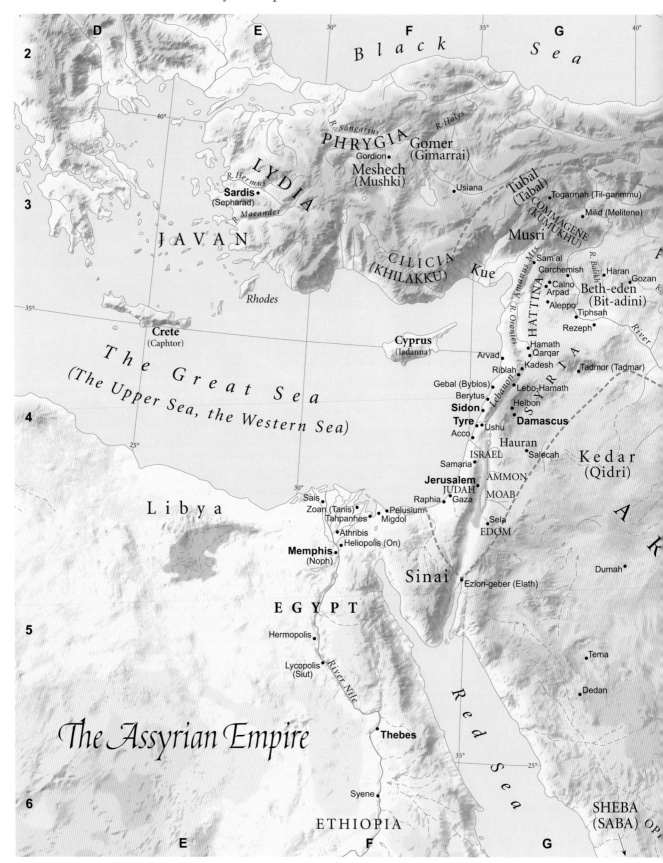

The Assyrian Empire

J
50°
K
L

C a s p i a n   S e a

40°

3

A R A T
RARTU)

•Turushpa
(Tuspar)

Lake Urmia

Minni
(Mannai)

Y
Dur-sharrukin
eh
Arbela
Upper Zab
R I A
Lower Zab
•Arrapkha
R. Adhaim
R. Diyala
River Tigris

MADAI
(MEDES)

•Ecbatana

4

ates
•Sippar •Cuthah
Babylon
•Borsippa •Nippur

Pekod
(Puqudu)

E L A M

•Susa (Shushan)

BABYLONIA
Erech (Uruk)• •Larsa
Ur•

ancient coastline

5

I A

The Lower (Eastern) Sea

50°

55°
25°

– – – – Approximate extent of Assyrian domination
in the latter part of the 8th. century.
(Later, under Esarhaddon (680-669), Assyria conquered Egypt.)

0   100   200 Miles

0   100   200 Kilometres

6

© Oxford University Press

J   K

and Jehu of Israel. The Black Obelisk of Shalmaneser depicts Jehu prostrating himself before the Assyrian king. Later, Adad-nirari III (811–783) received tribute from J(eh)oash of Israel.

ASSYRIAN ASCENDANCY

After a period in which Assyria had been weakened by revolts and the encroachments of Urartu to the north, Tiglath-pileser III (745–727), called Pul in the Hebrew Bible, reasserted Assyrian power. He captured Arvad, invaded Philistia, and received tribute from numerous places and people, including Kumukhu (Commagene), Milid (Melitene), Kue, Samal, Damascus, Tyre, Gebal, the queen of Arabia, and also Menahem of Israel. He reached, but was unable to conquer, Turushpa in Urartu. Having been paid by King Ahaz of Judah to help to counter the attacks being made on his kingdom by Israel and Damascus (2 Kgs. 16: 5–9; see also Isa. 7–8), he conquered Damascus and annexed much of Israel, placing Hoshea on the throne of the northern kingdom.

Soon after Tiglath-pileser was succeeded by Shalmaneser V (727–722), Israel revolted against Assyria. Shalmaneser advanced and imprisoned Hoshea, and besieged and captured Samaria. His successor Sargon II also claimed credit for the defeat of Samaria; in his annals he is reported to have deported 27,290 Israelites to various places in his empire, including the area of the Habor (the river of Gozan) and Media. He rebuilt Samaria, populating it with aliens from Babylon, Cuthah, Avva, Hamath, and Sepharvaim. He faced further difficulties in the west; Hannoo, the king of Gaza, and Re'e (previously misread as Sib'e and equated with the King So of 2 Kgs. 17: 4) the Tartan (commander-in-chief or governor general) of Egypt were defeated at Raphia. In 711, Azuri, the king of Ashdod, withheld tribute, and the revolt spread. So Sargon invaded, captured Ashdod along with Gath and Asdudimmu, and made the area an Assyrian province. Sargon also conquered Babylonia which was under Merodach-baladan, and built a new capital at Dur-sharrukin (Khorsabad), north of Nineveh.

Sargon's son Sennacherib (705–681) had to face revolts in Phoenicia and Philistia, encouraged by Merodach-baladan and by Egypt (see 2 Kgs. 20: 12–19). Sennacherib advanced down the east Mediterranean coastlands; the Phoenician cities capitulated, and Moab, Edom, and Ammon, among others,

The Prism of Sennacherib, containing the annals of the king, including the account of his attack on Jerusalem in 701 BCE, in the time of Hezekiah.

sent tribute. An Egyptian–Ethiopian army was defeated at Eltekeh and Ekron was captured. Judah was invaded, numerous cities captured (see 'The Kingdom of Judah') and Jerusalem besieged. But Sennacherib withdrew without taking the city and King Hezekiah of Judah later sent tribute to Nineveh. Babylonia fell to Sennacherib in 689, and Babylon itself was ruthlessly laid waste.

ASSYRIA'S CLIMAX AND DECLINE

Ultimately Sennacherib was the victim of a conspiracy by two of his sons, Adrammelech and Sharezer, who killed him at Nineveh. Another son, Esarhaddon (681–669), succeeded, and pursued his elder brothers to Hanigalbat west of the Upper Tigris, but they escaped to 'the land of Ararat', that is, Urartu (2 Kgs. 19: 36–7). His early attempts against Egypt met with failure, but subsequently he did enter Egypt, conquered Memphis, and brought Egypt within his empire, though the defeated pharaoh Tirhakah escaped to Napata. Esarhaddon even claimed to have conquered Ethiopia (Cush), and called himself 'king of Assyria, governor of Babylon, king of Karduniash [Babylonia], king of Egypt, Paturisi [biblical Pathros, Upper Egypt] and Ethiopia'. On Esarhaddon's way back from Egypt, Ashkelon submitted to him. According to 2 Chronicles 33: 10–13, Manasseh of Judah was exiled to Babylon, though there is no mention of this in Kings. If this reflects a real happening, it may have been a reprisal for his being involved in revolts in that part of the Asyrian Empire or for withholding tribute. On his north-west frontier, Esarhaddon defeated both Teushpa, king of the Gimarrai (Cimmerians), and the people of Khilakku, and he temporarily stopped the southward advance of the Scythians.

Esarhaddon's successor, Ashurbanipal (669–627), made a first campaign into Egypt, capturing Memphis and occupying Thebes. Then, in a second campaign, he defeated Tirhakah's successor, Tandame, and sacked Thebes. Ashurbanipal is mentioned in Ezra 4: 10 as 'the great and noble Osnappar'. It was under Ashurbanipal that Assyria reached the peak of her cultural development, as witnessed by the royal residences and great library excavated at Nineveh. But the Assyrian grip on Egypt and Babylonia was diminishing, and after the death of Ashurbanipal the decline was rapid. Babylonia, under Nabopolassar, gained independence in *c.*626 after an unsuccessful Assyrian attack on Babylon. To the east, the power of the Medes was increasing, and Asshur fell to them in 614. Nineveh was destroyed by the Medes and Babylonians in 612. (The fall of Nineveh provides the background to the Book of Nahum.) Ashuruballit assumed control over what remained of Assyria in Haran, but Haran too was captured by the Medes and Babylonians in 610 and the might of Assyria was ended.

The Kingdom of Judah

SYRIA (ARAM)

Damascus

R. Abana

R. Pharpar

Sidon

Zarephath

Ahlab

Tyre

Uzu

Dan

MAACAH

Kedesh

Hazor

P H O E N I C I A

Achzib

Acco

Mt. Hermon

R. Jordan

HAURAN

Karnaim

Ashtaroth

I S R A E L

G A L I L E E

Jotbah

Rumah

Sea of Chinnereth

ISRAEL — Former kingdom of Israel conquered by Assyria

– – – – – Approximate boundaries

0   10   20 Miles

0   10   20 Kilometres

T H E

G R E A T

S E A

Mt. Carmel

R. Kishon

Plain of Megiddo

Dor

Megiddo

Taanach

Plain of Sharon

Beth-shan

Ham

G I L E A D

Ramoth-gilead

Ibleam

Dothan

Jabesh-gilead

Abel-meholah

The Arabah

S A M A R I A

Samaria

Tirzah

Shechem

Succoth

Penuel

River Jordan

R. Jabbok

Adam

AMMON

Shiloh

Jazer

Joppa

Bene-berak

Ono

Asor

Lod

Beth-dagon

Rabbah

Mesad Hashavyahu

Gimzo

Bethel

Rimmon

Aiath

Eltekeh?

Mizpah

Michmash

Gilgal

Shittim

Jabneel (Jabneh)

Ramah

Migron

Jericho

Elealeh

Mount Baalah

Gezer

Gibeah?

Geba

Sibmah

Heshbon

Gibbethon

Anathoth

Baalath?

Shikkeron

Kiriath-jearim

Laishah

Gallim

Nebo

Bezer? (Bozrah?)

Ekron

Timnah

Jerusalem

Nob

Ashdod

Beth-shemesh

Medeba

Kiriathaim

Azekah

Beth-haccherem

Beth-diblathaim

Gath?

Socoh

Bethlehem

Beth-meon (Baal-meon)

Ashkelon

Adullam

Netophah

Moresheth-gath

Achzib?

Tekoa

Jahaz?

Libnah?

Keilah

Ataroth

Lachish

Mareshah

Kerioth

P H I L I S T I A

Bozkath

Hebron

Gaza

The Shephelah

Dibon

Beth-ezel

Ziph

Aroer

Beth-gamul

Gerar

Debir

R. Arnon

J U D A H

Yurza

Madmannah

M O A B

Raphia

Sharuhen

Great Arad

Madmen?

Ar

Beer-sheba

Salt Sea (Sea of the Arabah)

Kir-hareseth (Kir, Kir-heres)

Waters of Nimrim

The N e g e b

Zoar

Brook Zered

E D O M

Brook Besor

© Oxford University Pr

The Kingdom of Judah

After the northern kingdom fell in 722, the Assyrian pressure on Judah was great. King Hezekiah of Judah is recorded as having rebelled against Assyrian domination, and he also attacked the Philistines as far south as Gaza (2 Kgs. 18: 7–8). He is remembered for having instituted religious reforms (2 Kgs. 18: 3–6) and, according to 2 Chronicles 30, he summoned people from the whole land, from Dan to Beer-sheba (that is, including the territory of the former northern kingdom), to come to keep the Passover in Jerusalem. In 711, Sargon of Assyria attacked Ashdod and made it an Assyrian province. This may be the context of Micah's prophecy against Philistia and other cities of the area, including Gath, Beth-ezel, Moresheth-gath, Achzib, Mareshah, and Adullam (Mic. 1: 10–15). Hezekiah is also renowned for the steps he took to ensure a secure water-supply for Jerusalem (2 Kgs. 20: 20; 2 Chr. 32: 30) and he may have been responsible for the extension of the city's fortifications (see 'Jerusalem in the 1st Millennium BCE').

Sargon was succeeded by Sennacherib, who continued to exert pressure on Judah. In 701 he invaded and claims to have captured almost all the fortified cities of Judah. It is possible, though not universally accepted, that this invasion is reflected in the graphic verses of Isaiah 10: 27–32 which record a king of Assyria gradually getting closer and closer to Jerusalem. Starting from Rimmon he comes to Aiath, passes through Migron, stores his baggage at Michmash, and lodges at Geba for the night; he then continues past Ramah, Gallim, Laishah, Anathoth, Medmenah, and Gebim whose inhabitants flee for safety. Ultimately, from Nob he shakes his fist against Mount Zion in Jerusalem. The impact of such passages is greatly enhanced by an awareness of the underlying geography. Sennacherib's own annals supplement the account in 2 Kings 18–19. They recorded how Sidon, Acco, Achzib, and other Phoenician cities submitted to him, and how he besieged and captured Joppa, Beth-dagon, Bene-berak, Ekron, Eltekeh, and Timnah. Sennacherib's siege and capture of Lachish is recorded on a series of reliefs which decorated his palace in Nineveh. The similarities between the reliefs and

what has been revealed by archaeology at the site of Lachish suggest that they may have been based on drawings produced by an eyewitness of the events. Sennacherib seems to have used Lachish as the base for his operations against Jerusalem, but he did not actually succeed in taking Jerusalem. However, Hezekiah paid a heavy tribute (2 Kgs. 18: 14–16). In the latter part of his reign, Hezekiah is recorded as having become ill but was cured thanks to the intervention of the prophet Isaiah (2 Kgs. 20: 1–11). He is also said to have received envoys from Merodach-baladan of Babylon (2 Kgs. 20: 12–15).

Hezekiah was succeeded by Manasseh. His long reign is recalled in Kings as a time of religious apostasy which brought Judah under divine judgement (2 Kgs. 21: 1–18). But in Chronicles he is recorded as having sought forgiveness and rectified some of his earlier misdeeds (2 Chr. 33: 10–17). Manasseh was succeeded briefly by his son Amon, who was removed from the scene by his own servants, sparking a reaction from the 'people of the land', probably the significant land-owners, who took reprisals and placed Amon's son Josiah on the throne (2 Kgs. 21: 19–25).

REVIVAL AND REFORM

Josiah's reign is most noted for the religious reform which he instituted. According to the account in Kings, the reform was sparked off by the discovery of a book of the law in the Temple in Jerusalem in his eighteenth year (2 Kgs. 22: 3–23: 23). A somewhat different impression is given in Chronicles; there it is suggested that the reform had begun earlier, and that the law book was discovered whilst repairs were being carried out in the Temple (2 Chr. 34: 1–18). The reform involved cleansing the Temple of all pagan accoutrements, the closure of other sites of pagan worship in Jerusalem, and the removal of priests from the towns of Judah and the defilement of their high places 'from Geba to Beer-sheba' (2 Kgs. 23: 8). It is also claimed that his reforms extended to territories which had formerly belonged to the northern kingdom of Israel and which were perhaps in his control as a nominal vassal of Assyria. He destroyed the altar at Bethel (2 Kgs. 23: 15) and removed shrines from the towns of Samaria (2 Kgs. 23: 19–20; see also 2 Chr. 34: 6–7). But Josiah was killed in battle at Megiddo in 609, in an ill-fated attempt to stop the advance northward of pharaoh Neco, who was apparently seeking to join forces with the retreating Assyrians at the Euphrates (2 Kgs. 23: 29). The pass at Megiddo would have been a natural place to attempt to intercept an army travelling north through the flat coastal plains along the 'Way of the Sea' but needing to follow the narrow valley through the hills.

DECLINE AND FALL

Josiah's son, Jehoahaz, was placed on the throne, but after only three months he was removed by pharaoh Neco and taken to Egypt, where he died; his brother Jehoiakim was made king and paid a heavy tribute to Egypt (2 Kgs. 23: 31–5).

The Gihon Spring which flows into Hezekiah's Tunnel.

The biblical city of Lachish was once thought to be located at Tell el-Ḥesi, but it is now accepted to be Tell ed-Duweir. Evidence of occupation goes back to the Chalcolithic period, by Middle Bronze Age II it had become a significant fortress, and in the Late Bronze Age it was an important city. From the LBA come three successive temples, superimposed one upon the other.

The conquest?

A destruction at the end of LBA (stratum VI) has been associated with the activity of incoming Israelites, and a fairly precise date has been given to this destruction on the basis of an inscription on a bowl. Written in the hieratic Egyptian script, it refers to the fourth year of the reigning pharaoh, presumed to be Merneptah (1213–1203). This piece of 'evidence' has been felt to be crucial in the dating of the Israelite conquest of Canaan, but it must be remembered (*a*) that the pharaoh is not named, and (*b*) that there is no specific evidence as to who brought about the destruction.

Sennacherib's invasion

The Iron Age stratum III also suffered a major destruction, almost certainly to be associated with

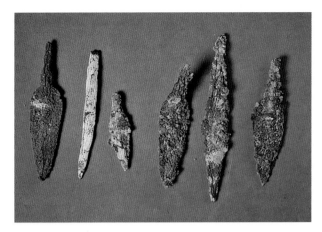

Arrow heads from Lachish, from the time of Sennacherib's siege (701 BCE).

Sennacherib's campaign in Judah of 701 (though it has also been linked with the time of Nebuchadrezzar, and an earlier campaign than that which led to the destruction of stratum II). From this destruction comes evidence of the waging of warfare, such as arrow heads and helmet crests. The association of this destruction with Sennacherib's campaign owes much to the fact that Sennacherib had reliefs depicting the siege made to decorate his palace at Nineveh, and what is depicted on the reliefs fits closely with what has been found on the site of Lachish, notably the siege ramp constructed by the attacking Assyrians. That the picture from Sennacherib's palace is indeed of Lachish is made clear from an inscription naming the city, placed close to the depiction of the enthroned Sennacherib receiving the homage of the people of the city.

The fall of Judah

That the destruction of stratum II is to be associated with the fall of Judah to the Babylonians under Nebuchadrezzar is generally accepted. Among the significant discoveries reflecting this crucial episode are a number of inscribed potsherds, found in one of the gate-rooms of the city. These are the so-called Lachish Letters, mostly written to Yoash, the commander of the garrison at Lachish, by a subordinate named Hoshayahu. The letters give some insights into events at the time, speaking of the activity of an unnamed prophet and suggesting that there were those who were seeking to weaken the resolve of those trying to withstand the Babylonians. One letter makes the point that the sender and those with him are watching for signals from Lachish because they can no longer see those from Azekah. This suggests a point in time just after that envisaged in Jer. 34: 7, where Lachish and Azekah are mentioned as the only two remaining fortified cities of Judah.

Left: Aerial view of Tell ed-Duweir, the site of Lachish.

Right: A helmet crest from Lachish, from the time of Sennacherib's siege.

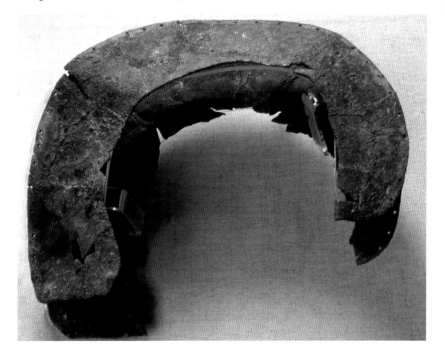

Mount Hermon, the highest point in the vicinity of Palestine, whose snow-capped summit may be alluded to by Jeremiah.

It is in the reign of Josiah and his successors that the activity of the prophet Jeremiah of Anathoth is set (Jer. 1: 1–3). He warned his people of the threat from a foe from the north. This foe was to be the means whereby divine judgement would be brought about upon Judah (for example, Jer. 1: 13–16). The identity of this foe is not made clear; it was the Babylonians who were to capture Judah and Jerusalem but it is objected that their threat had not begun to be real in the early years of Jeremiah. (The fact that Babylon was east rather than north of Judah would not have been a problem since the Babylonian armies would have had to travel around the Fertile Crescent and therefore have approached from a northerly direction.) Another suggestion is that the Scythians or some other group from the north was campaigning in the area. But it is possible that the descriptions in Jeremiah are deliberately imprecise and reflect the fact that when trouble came upon Israel and Judah it often came from the north. Passages such as Jeremiah 4: 13–17 show the enemy getting ever closer, as news of their approach is heard in Dan, then in the hill country of Ephraim, and then in Jerusalem itself (see also Jer. 8: 16). Other geographical statements are used to illustrate the prophet's teaching. Jeremiah contrasts the permanency of the snows of Lebanon and Sirion (probably Hermon) with the inconstancy and disobedience of the people of Judah (Jer. 18: 14–15). Although to God the house of the king of Judah was like Gilead or

120

the summit of Lebanon (places known for their fertile vegetation), it would become like a desert or an uninhabited city (Jer. 22: 6). Jeremiah is said to have declared that because of Judah's unfaithfulness, Jerusalem would suffer the same fate as Shiloh (Jer. 7: 12–14). When Jeremiah was brought to trial for such statements, it was recalled that Micah had made similar pronouncements and not been put to death (Jer. 26: 16–19) so Jeremiah was spared. But not so the prophet Uriah from Kiriath-jearim, who was pursued as far as Egypt, brought back to Judah, and put to death by King Jehoiakim (Jer. 26: 20–3).

The threat of Babylon became a very real one for Judah (for fuller details, see 'The Babylonian Empire'). Jehoiakim was succeeded by his son Jehoiachin, the former perhaps having been removed by his own people in the hope of receiving less severe treatment at the hands of Babylon. But on 16 March 597 (the date is so precise because of details in his own chronicles) Nebuchadrezzar (Nebuchadnezzar) captured Jerusalem, took Jehoiachin and other leading citizens into exile, and placed Zedekiah on the throne. Jeremiah is recorded as having advised not only Zedekiah but the kings of Edom, Moab, Ammon, Tyre, and Sidon to submit to Babylon (Jer. 27: 1–15). But sedition continued, perhaps in part fomented by news of unrest in Babylon. This was the context of Jeremiah's famous letter to the exiles (Jer. 29). In 589, the Babylonians again marched against Judah. Jeremiah is reported to have warned Zedekiah that defeat for Jerusalem was inevitable at a time when all the remaining fortified cities of Judah apart from Lachish and Azekah had fallen (Jer. 34: 1–7). A moment shortly after this is envisaged in one of the inscribed potsherds (ostraca) found in the excavations at Lachish, known as the Lachish Letters. The letter indicates that the senders are watching for fire-signals from Lachish because they can no longer see Azekah, the implication being that the latter city had just fallen.

One of the 'Lachish Letters'. (See on 'Lachish'.)

In 586 the city of Jerusalem was captured and burnt, Zedekiah was taken and blinded, and a second group of deportees was taken into exile. Gedaliah (significantly not a member of the royal family—the Davidic dynasty was at an end) was made governor over those who remained in Judah (2 Kgs. 25: 1–22). Jeremiah, who had been taken to Ramah with other captives, was freed and chose to remain in Judah with Gedaliah (Jer. 40: 1–6). But Gedaliah was murdered at Mizpah, his headquarters, by Ishmael (who *was* of the royal family) apparently at the instigation of the Ammonite king Baalis (2 Kgs. 25: 22–6; Jer. 40: 14; 41: 1–3). A certain Johanan sought to take reprisals near the great pool at Gibeon, but Ishmael managed to escape to Ammon (Jer. 41: 11–15). Johanan and his associates decided to flee to Egypt, against Jeremiah's advice, taking Jeremiah with them (Jer. 41: 17–43: 7). Jeremiah 52: 30 mentions a third deportation of exiles to Babylon, and it is possible that this was a reprisal for the murder of Gedaliah.

The Babylonian Empire

THE BEGINNING OF THE NEO-BABYLONIAN (CHALDEAN) EMPIRE

The Babylonians, more correctly called the Neo-Babylonians or Chaldeans to distinguish them from an earlier era of Babylonian strength, were intimately involved in the fate of Judah and were the subject of many prophetic oracles in the Hebrew Bible, in particular in Jeremiah, Ezekiel, and Isaiah 40–55. Clay tablets preserving the chronicles of Neo-Babylonian kings have provided important information about the period which witnessed the last days of the Assyrian Empire, the rise of Babylonia, the fall of Jerusalem, and the exile of the Jews in Babylon.

After the Assyrians were defeated at Babylon in 626 BCE, Nabopolassar was officially placed on the throne. (The gods of Susa, which the Assyrians had gathered and deposited in Erech, were returned to their own city, confirming the independence of Elam.) In pursuit of his war with the Assyrians, Nabopolassar marched north-west along the Euphrates; Sukhu and Khindanu yielded to him, and plunder was taken from towns in the Balikhu area. To the east of the Tigris he campaigned in the vicinity of Arrapkha and the Assyrians were pursued to the Lower Zab river. An unsuccessful attack was made on Asshur. It was in 614 that the Medes succeeded in taking Asshur, Nabopolassar arriving after the city had fallen. Then, in 612, the Medes and Babylonians together took Nineveh. Sinsharishkun, a son of Ashurbanipal, who had succeeded his brother Ashuretililani on the throne, perished in the fall of Nineveh.

The Babylonian armies continued to undertake campaigns in the upper Euphrates region, reaching as far as Nisibis. In 610, with the help of the Medes and Scythians, they took Haran. The Egyptians had sought to make common cause with the retreating remnants of Assyria, and they made a combined attempt to recapture Haran in 609, but were unsuccessful. (This was the context of the death of King Josiah of Judah as he sought to prevent pharaoh Neco's advance; see 'The Kingdom of Judah'.) Nabopolassar's campaigns led him to the very borders of Urartu. The Egyptians, having failed in their attempt to bolster the remaining Assyrian forces, sought to consolidate control of the territory south of Carchemish, capturing Quramati and Kimukhu. But in 605, the Babylonian crown-prince Nebuchadrezzar defeated the Egyptians at Carchemish, setting fire to the city (the context of Jeremiah's oracle against the Egyptians in Jer. 46: 1–12). Nebuchadrezzar then pressed south along the Mediterranean coastlands (Hatti) as far as the Egyptian border.

THE REIGN OF NEBUCHADREZZAR

When Nabopolassar died, Nebuchadrezzar (604–562) took the throne. His armies continued to maintain control in Hatti and, in December 604, he marched against Ashkelon and destroyed the city. Subsequently, in 601–600, he marched to Egypt and fought a fierce but inconclusive battle there; this battle may be reflected in the oracle in Jeremiah 46: 13–24. Jehoiakim of Judah, probably with Egypt's encouragement, revolted. In December 598, Nebuchadrezzar marched to the 'Hatti-land' and laid siege to Jerusalem. Jehoiakim had died (see 'The Kingdom of Judah') and his son Jehoiachin had become king. On 16 March 597, Jerusalem fell, and Nebuchadrezzar installed Zedekiah on the throne in place of Jehoiachin. The latter, along with other leading citizens (2 Kgs. 24: 15–16), was taken into exile. Tablets found at Babylon, dating from the period 595–570, include references to captives from many places, including Jehoiachin king of Judah and his five sons, and the sons of Aga, king of Ashkelon. Mention is also made of artisans, sailors, and musicians from other cities of Hatti, as well as places (perhaps outside the Babylonian Empire itself) as far afield as Lydia and Ionia in the west to Media and Persia in the east. The presence of captives from Pirindu and Khume resident in Babylon imply that Neduchadrezzar had campaigned in the area which was to become known as Cilicia.

When Judah again revolted in 589, the Babylonian armies returned. The siege of Jerusalem began in 588, and an Egyptian army which came to Judah's assistance was defeated. When Jerusalem fell in 586, Zedekiah was taken before Nebuchadrezzar at Riblah in the land of Hamath, where he was blinded (2 Kgs. 25: 6–7; see on 'The Kingdom of Judah'). It was not only Jerusalem that was placed under siege at this time. Tyre too was besieged, but managed to resist for thirteen years.

THE JEWS IN BABYLON

Available sources make it possible to glean a limited amount of information about the Jews in exile in Babylon. As already noted, references have been found in Babylonian sources to Jehoiachin and his family, and these suggest that provision was made for the exiled king (cf. 2 Kgs. 25: 27–30). Jeremiah's 'Letter to the Exiles' and its repercussions (Jer. 29) suggest that communication was possible between Judah and Babylonia, and that the exiles were in a position to build houses, plant gardens, and get married. The Book of Ezekiel mentions 'the exiles at Tel-abib, who lived by the river Chebar' (Ezek. 3: 15; cf. Ezek. 1:1–3), and refers to Ezekiel's own house where he was able to

Figs ripening on a fig tree. (See on 'Main Crops'.)

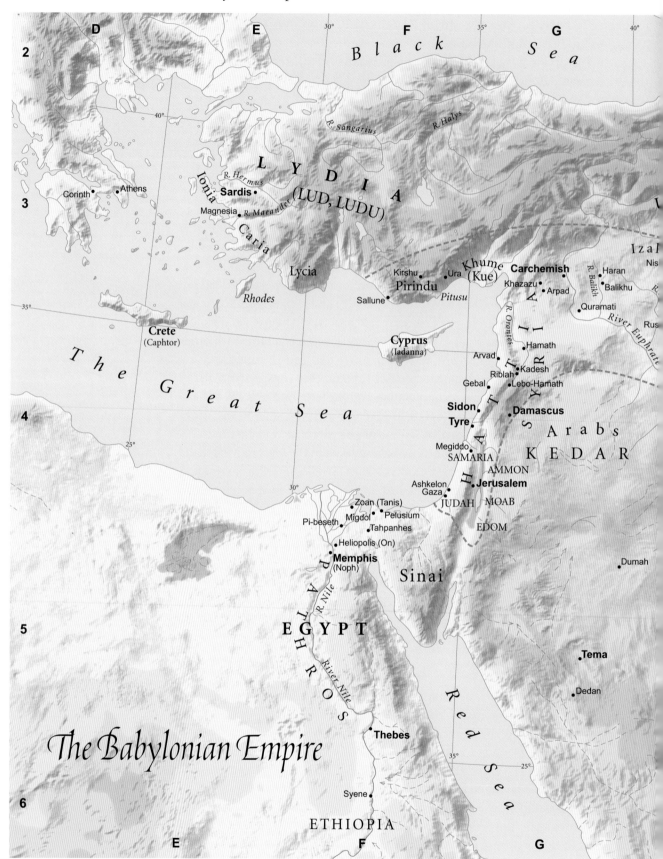

The Babylonian Empire

Caspian Sea

T U
(RAT)

RIA

Mannai
(Minni)

M E D I A

Upper Zab

Lower Zab

•Arrapkha

River Tigris

R. Adhaim

R. Diyala

•Ecbatana

Sallat•   •Der

•   AKKAD
Sippar•

•Cuthah

Babylon• •Kish

BABYLONIA   •Nippur

(CHALDEA)

Erech (Uruk)•

Ur•

E L A M

Susa•

ancient coastline

•Anshan (Tall-i Malyan)

P E R S I A

Persian Gulf

Approximate greatest extent of
Babylonian domination.
(The Halys river marked the border of the Median and
Lydian Empires after the Battle of the Eclipse in 585 B.C.)

0   100   200 Miles

0   100   200 Kilometres

© Oxford University Press

meet the elders of Judah (Ezek. 8: 1). So it seems that not all the exiles were harshly treated, and that some had a fair amount of freedom. On the other hand, Psalm 137 suggests that some who lived 'by the rivers of Babylon' were subjected to torment by their captors.

NEBUCHADREZZAR'S SUCCESSORS

Nebuchadrezzar's son Amel-marduk (562–559), known in the Bible as Evil-Merodach (2 Kgs. 25: 27), was succeeded in turn by Nergal-shar-uṣur (Ner-iglissar; 559–556). It is possible that he is the Nergal-sharezer mentioned as having been present at the siege of Jerusalem in Jeremiah 39: 3, 13. He restored temples at Babylon and nearby Borsippa, and campaigned in the north-western part of the empire against Appuasha of Pirindu who had entered Khume in order to take plunder and captives. He was pursued to Ura and Kirshu, the island of Pitusu was overrun, and Sallune was burnt. His successor, Labashi-marduk, reigned for only a few days. Then Nabonidus (Nabunaid) became king of Babylonia (556–539). He was of priestly descent, and his mother had been taken captive by Nebuchadrezzar at Haran in 610. He too engaged in campaigns in the Mediterranean coastland regions and in Khume, but his particular concern was to ensure control over the caravan routes for southern Arabia. To that end he took the important oasis city of Tema and established it as his royal residence. His son Belshazzar was placed in charge of affairs in Babylon during his father's absence, though strictly speaking he was not actually king as suggested in Daniel 5.

THE FALL OF BABYLON

Meanwhile to the east, Cyrus, originally king of Anshan, had expanded his power and become king of the Medes and Persians. He had conquered Astyages, the Median king, and captured Ecbatana in 550. He did not immediately turn his attention to Babylonia, but first attacked Lydia and, after an indecisive battle at the Halys River, Sardis fell in 546. Subsequently northern Mesopotamia and territories which had belonged to the Babylonian Empire were taken. The Babylonian army was defeated at Opis on the River Tigris and Sippar was taken. In 539, Cyrus' general Gobryas entered Babylon with his troops, apparently welcomed as liberators, and Nabonidus was taken prisoner.

The Persian Empire

THE EMPIRE'S EXPANSION

It was Cyrus, of the Achaemenid family, originally king of Anshan in Persia, who was responsible for bringing into being the Persian (Achaemenian) Empire. This vast empire ultimately stretched from the region of Sogdiana in the north-east to the Aegean Sea in the west and incorporated all of the former Babylonian Empire. One biblical writer went so far as to refer to Cyrus as God's anointed, who was about to bring about God's purposes for his people in exile in Babylon (Isa. 45: 1–7). According to the Book of Ezra, one of his first acts was to permit the return to Judah of the Jewish exiles (Ezra 1: 1–4). It is also indicated that it was from Ecbatana that Cyrus issued a decree, permitting the rebuilding of the Jerusalem Temple and ordering that the costs be defrayed from the royal treasury (Ezra 6: 1–5).

There was further expansion under Cyrus' son, Cambyses (530–522), who invaded Egypt, won a victory at Pelusium, took Heliopolis and Memphis by siege, and marched along the Nile. Other territories in North Africa submitted. Aramaic papyri discovered at Elephantine (Yeb) provide evidence of the existence there at this time of a Jewish military colony.

Darius I (522–486) commemorated victories over his enemies in a huge inscription carved into the cliff face at Behistun. This inscription, in Persian,

The Behistun Inscription: carved on a rock place, the trilingual inscription was vital to the decipherment of Akkadian. The picture shows Darius I with defeated rebels. (See on 'Writing Systems'.)

The Persian Empire

Elamite, and Akkadian, provided the key to the deciphering of Akkadian (see 'Writing Systems'). Darius built Persepolis as his capital, and brought under his control parts of western India which became the province of Hindush. Such a huge empire required an efficient system of communication, and to this end relays of horsemen travelled the Royal Road which ran through a vast tract of the empire. He also developed the existing administrative system based on satrapies, districts under the control of a 'satrap' (the word means 'protector of the country'), a Persian noble who was the king's per-

The Persian Empire

- - - - - Approximate boundary of the Persian Empire

sonal representative. In *c.*513, Darius entered Europe, passing through
Thrace and crossing the Danube. Thrace and Macedonia submitted to him.
When Miletus led an Ionian revolt, it was dealt with severely in 494. In 490 a
Persian expedition which landed in Greece, at Marathon, was defeated by the
Athenians. Subsequently Xerxes (486–465) carried out a full-scale invasion of
Greece, defeating the Spartans at Thermopylae and occupying Athens. But
he met a severe defeat in the naval battle of Salamis, and Greece retained its
freedom.

© Oxford University Press

REVOLTS AND DOWNFALL

Artaxerxes I (465–424) overcame revolts in the north-east (Bactria) and south-west (Egypt) of his empire. It was in his reign that Nehemiah came to Jerusalem (Neh. 2: 1). After the brief (45-day) reign of Xerxes II, Darius II (424–404) succeeded. He subdued rebellions in Media and Lydia, but Egypt was lost. A letter of his, sent *c.*419 to the Jewish colony of Elephantine, directing the proper celebration of the feast of unleavened bread, is among the documents found there. Cyrus, the younger brother of Artaxerxes II (405–359), contested the throne with the support of large numbers of Greek mercenaries, but he was defeated at Cunaxa in 401. Xenophon (in the *Anabasis*) tells of the march of 10,000 Greeks through hostile territory, just 400 of them reaching the sea at Trapezus. It was perhaps in the reign of Artaxerxes II, in 398, that Ezra came to Jerusalem (see Ezra 7, and 'Judah, Yehud, and Judea' below). The biblical account does not make it clear which Artaxerxes was king at the time).

Artaxerxes III (359–338) reconquered Egypt, lost and then regained Phoenicia, and entered into an alliance with Athens against Philip of Macedon. After the short reign of Arses (338–336), Darius III (336–331) came to the throne. But the days of the Persian Empire were numbered as another ambitious military commander rose to power: Alexander 'the Great' of Macedon.

Judah, Yehud, and Judea

RETURN AND REBUILDING

In 538 BCE, after Cyrus had issued decrees permitting them to do so, the exiles began to return to Judah and to rebuild the Temple in Jerusalem (Ezra 1: 1–4; 6: 3–5). Early leaders of groups of returnees were Sheshbazzar (Ezra 1: 8) and Zerubbabel (Ezra 2: 2), both probably members of the house of David. There may have been an early start on the work of restoring the Temple, but work did not begin in earnest until 520, encouraged by the prophets Haggai and Zechariah. It was rededicated in 515 (Ezra 6: 15–18). Jerusalem itself seems to have remained in a state of disrepair, and it was not until 445 that Nehemiah was given permission to return to supervise the rebuilding of the city walls (Neh. 1–2). He is recorded as having gathered a workforce from Jerusalem and nearby towns, including Jericho, Tekoa, Gibeon, Mizpah, Zanoah, Beth-haccherem, Beth-zur, and Keilah (Neh. 3). His efforts met with opposition from Sanballat, the governor of Samaria, Tobiah, an Ammonite official, and Geshem the Arab (Neh. 2: 19; see also Neh. 4: 7). Tobiah may have been governor of Ammon, ruling over central Transjordan. His family home was at modern 'Araq el-Emir, where two inscriptions in Aramaic letters reading 'Tobiah' have been found carved into the façades of halls cut into the cliffs. Geshem may be mentioned on an inscription found at Dedan in Arabia, and his son Qainu is referred to as king of Kedar on a silver bowl inscription found at Succoth in Egypt. Geshem apparently ruled with Persian backing over a sizeable territory which included the Land of Goshen, Sinai, the southern part of what had been Judah, Edom and north Arabia. Among Nehemiah's reforms were the prohibition of intermarriage with the women of Ashdod, Ammon, and Moab, and the requirement that children should speak 'the language of Judah' (Neh. 13: 23-27). It was during the Persian period that Aramaic, the official language of the Persian Empire, and its script gradually replaced Hebrew and its 'palaeo-Hebrew' (or Phoenician) script. Parts of the Books of Ezra and Daniel (and a single verse in Jeremiah) are in Aramaic. The restored Judah was known as Yehud. It was a subprovince of the satrapy of Abar Nahara.

Nehemiah 11: 25–36 purports to provide details of towns and their surrounding villages or countryside outside Jerusalem which were settled by Jews. People of Judah were living in Dibon, Jekabzeel, Kiriath-arba, Jeshua, Moladah, Beth-pelet, Hazar-shual, Beer-sheba, Ziklag, Meconah, En-rimmon, Zorah, Jarmuth, Zanoah, Adullam, Lachish, and Azekah; people from Benjamin lived in Geba, Michmash, Hazor, Ramah, Gittaim, Hadid, Zeboim, Neballat, Lod, and Ono. Whatever the origins of such lists, they reflect a concern by the biblical writers to give geographical information as to where Jews were living. In Ezra 2: 2–70 and Nehemiah 7: 6–73 there are parallel lists of returning exiles. Again their origins are obscure, but it is possible that they reflect a census of the Jewish community carried out some time after the restoration. The lists include people from Gibeon, Bethlehem, Netophah, Anathoth, Beth-azmaveth (Azmaveth), Kiriath-jearim, Chephirah, Beeroth, Ramah, Geba, Michmash, Bethel, Ai, Nebo, Harim, Jericho, Lod, Hadid, and Ono.

The relationship between the careers of Ezra and Nehemiah is problematic. The biblical writers seem to suggest that Ezra arrived first in 458, followed by Nehemiah in 445/444, and that for a period they were active at the same time. But there are problems with such an understanding, and a possible solution is that Ezra arrived in 398 and needed to repeat or reinforce some of Nehemiah's earlier reforms.

In the latter part of the period of Persian domination, it is possible that Judah was granted a fair amount of local autonomy. This is suggested by the discovery in Palestine of coins bearing the name 'Yehud' (Judah), dating from the late 5th and early 4th centuries. The same inscription is found on official seals stamped on jar-handles.

THE HELLENISTIC AND SELEUCID PERIODS

After its descriptions of the activities of Nehemiah and Ezra, the Hebrew Bible falls silent with regard to records of events set in subsequent years. (See 'Alexander's Empire and its Aftermath' for comments on what was happening in the lands surrounding Judah/Yehud.) Eventually the story is taken up in the Books of Maccabees which form part of the collection variously known as the Apocrypha or Deuterocanonical books.

Alexander the Great and his successors fostered the spread of Greek culture (Hellenism). After Alexander's death in 323, his empire was split and Judah/Yehud initially came under the control of the Ptolemies of Egypt. Subsequently it came into the hands of the Seleucids, in the time of Antiochus III (the Great) (223–187). It was the attempt of one of his successors, Antiochus IV (Epiphanes), to proscribe the practice of Judaism and force the Jews to adopt a thoroughgoing Hellenism that sparked off the Maccabean revolt. Antiochus Epiphanes plundered Jerusalem and desecrated the Temple. Instructions were given for pagan altars to be set up throughout the land. On 25 Chislev (December) in 168 or 167, pigs were offered as sacrifices on the altar of Zeus which had been erected in the Temple (1 Macc. 1). This period

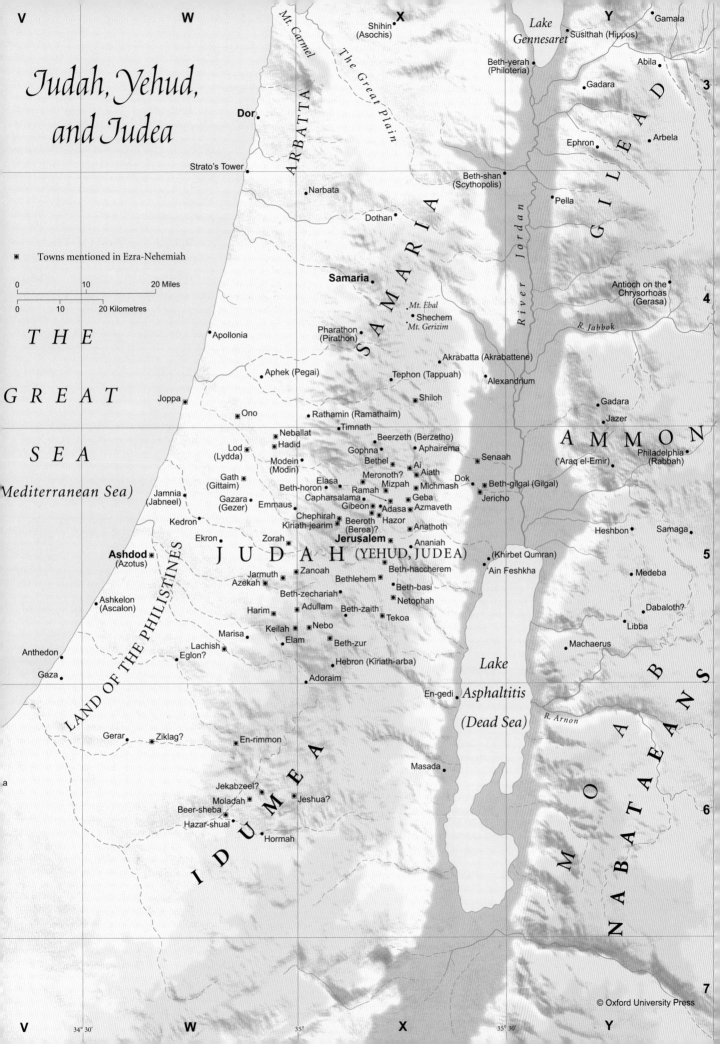

Judah, Yehud, and Judea

V   W   X   Y

3

Mt. Carmel

The Great Plain

Shihin (Asochis)

Lake Gennesaret

Gamala

Suslthah (Hippos)

Abila

Beth-yerah (Philoteria)

Gadara

Arbela

Ephron

ARBATTA

Dor

Strato's Tower

Narbata

Beth-shan (Scythopolis)

Dothan

Pella

GILEAD

■ Towns mentioned in Ezra-Nehemiah

0   10   20 Miles

0   10   20 Kilometres

Samaria

SAMARIA

Mt. Ebal

Shechem

Mt. Gerizim

Antioch on the Chrysorhoas (Gerasa)

4

River Jordan

R. Jabbok

THE

Apollonia

Pharathon (Pirathon)

Akrabatta (Akrabattene)

GREAT

Aphek (Pegai)

Tephon (Tappuah)

Alexandrium

Gadara

Jazer

AMMON

Joppa

Shiloh

SEA

Ono

Rathamin (Ramathaim)

Timnath

Neballat

Beerzeth (Berzetho)

Senaah

(Mediterranean Sea)

Hadid

Gophna

Aphairema

Philadelphia (Rabbah)

Lod (Lydda)

Modein (Modin)

Bethel

Ai

('Araq el-Emir)

Jamnia (Jabneel)

Gath (Gittaim)

Elasa

Meronoth?

Aiath

Dok

Beth-gilgal (Gilgal)

Kedron

Gazara (Gezer)

Beth-horon

Ramah

Mizpah

Michmash

Jericho

Emmaus

Capharsalama

Geba

Azmaveth

Ekron

Chephirah

Gibeon

Adasa

Zorah

Kiriath-jearim

Beeroth (Berea)?

Hazor

Anathoth

Heshbon

Samaga

5

Ashdod (Azotus)

JUDAH (YEHUD, JUDEA)

Jerusalem

Ananiah

(Khirbet Qumran)

Jarmuth

Zanoah

Beth-haccherem

Medeba

Azekah

Bethlehem

'Ain Feshkha

Ashkelon (Ascalon)

Beth-zechariah

Beth-basi

Harim

Adullam

Netophah

Dabaloth?

Marisa

Keilah

Nebo

Beth-zaith

Tekoa

Libba

Elam

Beth-zur

Machaerus

Lachish

Anthedon

Eglon?

Hebron (Kiriath-arba)

Gaza

Adoraim

LAND OF THE PHILISTINES

En-gedi

Lake Asphaltitis (Dead Sea)

R. Arnon

MOAB

Gerar

Ziklag?

En-rimmon

Masada

NABATAEANS

a

Jekabzeel?

IDUMEA

Jeshua?

Moladah

Beer-sheba

6

Hazar-shual

Hormah

© Oxford University Press

7

V   W   X   Y

34° 30'   35°   35° 30'

of oppression and persecution of the Jews is the probable context of the Book of Daniel.

An elderly priest named Mattathias, of the family of Hasmon, refused to sacrifice a pig at Modein, and fled with his five sons to the hills, where they were eventually joined by others who wished to remain loyal to their faith (1 Macc. 2: 1–48). After the death of Mattathias, his son Judas, known as Maccabeus ('the Hammerer') led those who were in rebellion. They achieved victories over armies led by Apollonius (1 Macc. 3: 10–12) and by Seron, 'the commander of the Syrian army' (1 Macc. 3: 13–25). This was followed by the defeat of a large force raised by Lysias, who had been left in charge of affairs west of the Euphrates while Antiochus was raising revenue in the east, and which had camped near Emmaus. A plan by a section of the army, led by Gorgias, to enter Judas' camp was foiled, and the enemy were routed and pursued to Gazara, the plains of Idumea, Azotus, and Jamnia (1 Macc. 3: 38–4: 25). The following year, an army reputed to be even larger was defeated at Beth-zur and Lysias was forced to withdraw to Antioch (1 Macc. 4: 26–35). This provided the opportunity for the Temple to be cleansed, and it was rededicated on 25 Chislev 165 or 164 (1 Macc. 4: 36–59). Judas also fortified Jerusalem and Beth-zur (1 Macc. 4: 60–1). Subsequently Judas defeated the Idumeans at Akrabattene, entered Ammon, and captured Jazer (1 Macc. 5: 3–8). He was then able, with his brother Jonathan, to go to the help of persecuted Jews at Dathema in Gilead, while another brother, Simon, went to the assistance of Jews in Galilee, pursuing the enemy as far as Ptolemais, then taking Jews from Galilee and Arbatta into Judah (1 Macc. 5: 9–23). Judas and Jonathan crossed into Transjordan and campaigned against various cities in the Gilead region including, according to 1 Maccabees 5: 26, Bozrah, Bosor, Alema, Chaspho, Maked, and Carnaim. He also campaigned in Idumea—taking Hebron—and in the land of the Philistines (1 Macc. 5: 65–8).

After the death of Antiochus IV, Judas attacked the Seleucid garrison in Jerusalem, but he suffered defeat at Beth-zechariah, and Beth-zur surrendered to the enemy (1 Macc. 6: 18–63). After the brief reign of Antiochus V, Demetrius I became king, chose Bacchides to deal with Judas and his brothers, and appointed Alcimus as high priest (1 Macc. 1: 1–11). Bacchides was unsuccessful and withdrew, and subsequently Nicanor was sent to quell Judas' opposition. Nicanor, however, was killed in battle at Adasa (1 Macc. 7: 26–50). Later Demetrius sent Bacchides a second time, and in the ensuing battle at Elasa, near Beth-horon, in 161 or 160, Judas fell (1 Macc. 9: 5–22).

THE HASMONEAN HIGH PRIESTHOOD AND KINGSHIP

After the death of Judas, Jonathan assumed the leadership, and he and his followers lived for a time in the Wilderness of Tekoa. There he was attacked by Bacchides, who also fortified a number of cities—Jericho, Emmaus, Beth-horon, Bethel, Timnath, Pharathon, Tephon, Beth-zur, and Gazara—and placed garrisons within them (1 Macc. 9: 32–53). Eventually peace was established between Jonathan and Bacchides, and Jonathan ruled from Michmash

(1 Macc. 9: 70–3). Subsequently Jonathan was allowed by Demetrius I to forti- fy Jerusalem, and he was appointed high priest (1 Macc. 10: 1–21). But later, in the reign of Demetrius II, Jonathan was imprisoned at Ptolemais (1 Macc. 12: 44–8) and eventually killed at Baskama in 143 or 142 (1 Macc. 13: 23–4).

Jonathan was succeeded by his brother Simon, who fortified Joppa, Beth- zur, and Gazara (1 Macc. 14: 33–4). He also succeeded in driving the enemy from the citadel (the Acra) in Jerusalem and replacing them with Jews (1 Macc. 14: 36–7). He was confirmed in the high priesthood (1 Macc. 14: 38–45). Simon and two of his sons were murdered at Dok, but a third son, John Hyr- canus, who was at Gazara, escaped and ruled as high priest, bringing the Jew- ish state to the height of its power under the Hasmoneans, and reigning from 135 or 134 to 104 (1 Macc. 16: 11–24). John Hyrcanus' son Aristobulus (104–103) was the first Hasmonean ruler to assume the kingship. After him ruled

Qumran: the ruins of the settlement and cliffs in which were some of the caves con- taining the Dead Sea Scrolls.

Alexander Jannaeus (103–76), Alexandra (76–67), and Aristobulus II (67–63). In the year 63, Pompey entered Jerusalem and the Romans took control, establishing the province of Judea.

THE QUMRAN COMMUNITY

During the latter half of the 2nd century BCE, a group of people, in all probability belonging to one of the major religious movements of the time, the Essenes, established themselves at Qumran and the nearby spring at 'Ain Feshka, on the north-west shore of the Dead Sea. It was this group which was responsible for the writing and/or preserving of the Dead Sea Scrolls.

Alexander's Empire and its Aftermath: The Hellenistic Period

It was the rise to power of Alexander the Great of Macedon which brought about the downfall of the Persian Empire. In 334 he crossed the Hellespont, defeated the Persians at the River Granicus, forced the surrender of Miletus, and won the battle of Issus against Darius III in 333. The way was open to take Phoenicia and Egypt. He again defeated Darius on the plain of Gaugamela, between Nineveh and Arbela. Alexander continued to Susa and Persepolis, which submitted, and pursued Darius to Ecbatana, Rhagae (Raga/ Rages), and on into Hyrcania where Darius was put to death by his own troops. Alexander was able to extend his sphere of control as far east as the River Indus and beyond. He established or rebuilt many cities, a number of which were named Alexandria after him, including those in north Egypt, in Syria near Issus, and several in the eastern provinces. Alexander died in Babylon in 323.

ALEXANDER'S SUCCESSORS

After his death there was rivalry among his generals for control, resulting in a time of confusion and warfare. Eventually, Ptolemy secured Egypt, Cyrene, Cyprus, and the Mediterranean coastlands, and Ptolemaic dominion initially seems to have extended to Lycia, Ionia, and the Aegean. The bulk of Asia Minor was held by Antigonus, Lysmachus controlled Thrace, Cassander held Macedonia and Greece, and Seleucus secured Babylonia. After Antigonus was defeated at Ipsus (301), Seleucus gained control of Syria and was given the area which included Judah (Coele-Syria), but in fact Ptolemy had secured control of Coele-Syria and Phoenicia. Later Seleucus gained Asia Minor, and established his capital at Antioch.

PTOLEMAIC AND SELEUCID CONFLICTS

After the death of Seleucus I (312/311–281) a long series of wars began between the Ptolemies and the Seleucids. Eventually, Antiochus III, known as 'the Great' (223–187) became the Seleucid ruler and gradually succeeded in

Alexander's Empire:
The Hellenistic Period

- - - - Approximate boundary
of Alexander's Empire

establishing Seleucid control over. the region of Palestine. He sought to foster good relations with the Jews, supplying aid for the maintenance of the Temple and its sacrificial cult, and defending the status of Jerusalem and the Jewish religion. But Antiochus was defeated by Rome in the battle of Magnesia (190), as a result of which he lost Asia Minor and was placed under a heavy financial burden by the Romans. To raise money he followed the example of

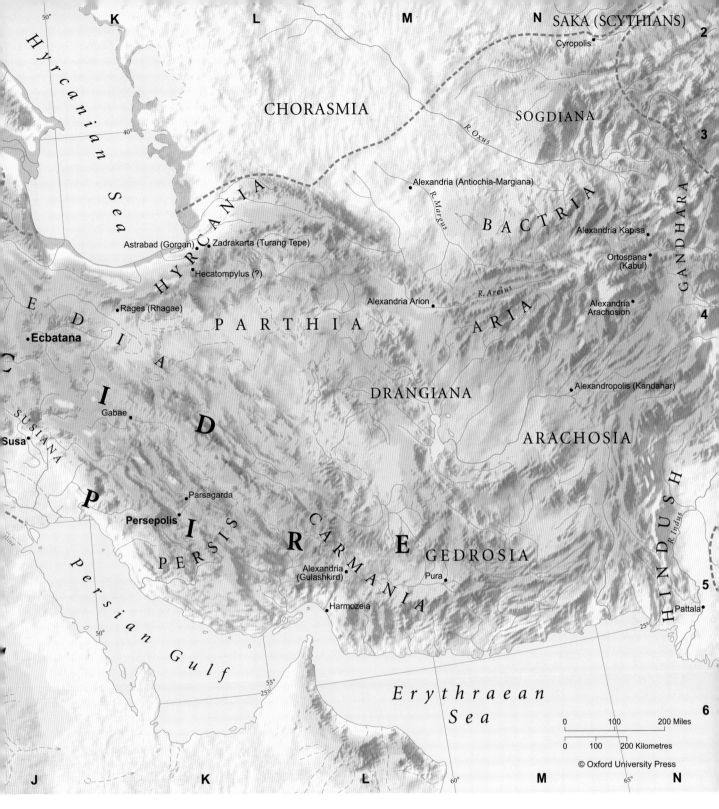

other Seleucid rulers in plundering wealthy sanctuaries, and it was apparently whilst attempting to take treasures from one such sanctuary that he died. His son Seleucus IV (187–175) was succeeded by Antiochus IV, known as 'Epiphanes' (175–164), who became the arch-persecutor of the Jews and their faith. He had formerly lived in Rome, but he usurped the throne with the assistance of the king of Pergamum. (This episode may be alluded to in

Daniel 11: 21, and the chapter as a whole may reflect the rivalries between the Ptolemaic and Seleucid rulers.)

Matters came to a head in 169, when Antiochus Epiphanes, forced by the Romans to cease interest in Egypt, sought to promote unity throughout his large kingdom by imposing Hellenistic culture, including Greek religion. In Palestine this meant that the practice of Judaism was proscribed and the Jews were compelled to accept Hellenization. The crowning insult was the setting up of a statue of Zeus in the Jerusalem Temple, and the sacrificing of a pig, in December 167 (1 Macc. 1: 54).

It was under Simon, one of the brothers and successors of Judas Maccabeus, and his successor, John Hyrcanus, that the Jews achieved relative freedom from Seleucid domination.

Jerusalem in the 1st Millennium BCE

The city of Jerusalem was established at a point where three valleys meet, the Hinnom valley (or Gehenna) to the west and south, the Kidron valley to the east, and between them the Central (later Tyropoeon, or Cheesemakers') valley. The earliest city seems to have occupied the southern part of the ridge between the Kidron and the Central valleys, below which was a perennial spring, the Gihon. A second water-supply, the spring of En-rogel, was just to the south of the junction of the three valleys, but this would have been less close at hand and therefore less useful to the city's inhabitants.

The site of the earliest city was well protected by the valleys to the east, south, and west, and seems to have been strongly fortified. Indeed, the biblical account of its capture by David suggests that the previous inhabitants, the Jebusites, considered it to be inviolable and defensible by 'even the blind and the lame' (2 Sam. 5: 6). The precise means whereby this 'stronghold of Zion' was captured and became the 'city of David' (2 Sam. 5: 7) is not clear, but may have involved gaining access via the water-system. Steps had been taken to provide access to the water-supply from within the city's walls by the construction of a sloping passage, a shaft, and a tunnel cut through the rock to bring the water to the base of the shaft. A Hebrew word (ṣinnôr) is used in 2 Sam. 5: 8 which is only used once elsewhere in the Hebrew Bible (Ps. 42: 7) and may refer to some sort of water channel. Here it is often translated 'water-shaft' (for example, NRSV, REB), but a vertical shaft seems an unlikely means of access for armed soldiers. Perhaps the implication is that someone gained entry by stealth and admitted David's soldiers, but this is not stated and the parallel account in 1 Chronicles 11: 4–7 makes no mention of the ṣinnôr. The account goes on to describe how 'David built the city all around from the Millo inward' (2 Sam. 5: 9), suggesting that he added to the fortifications. The precise significance of the term Millo is unclear. It seems to mean 'Filling', and has been thought to refer to retaining walls supporting terraces which held the rock-fill in place, or perhaps even to be associated with the so-called 'stepped stone structure' which acted as a retaining wall for the fortifications. The acropolis area at the northern end of the city of David was probably the feature known as the Ophel (Isa. 32: 14 (NRSV 'hill'); 2 Chr. 27: 3). There was a saddle between the Ophel on the southern hill and the hill to the north, and it is also possible that the Millo was located in this saddle.

Solomon too is credited with building the Millo and the walls of Jerusalem in addition to his own palace and the Temple (1 Kgs. 9: 15), extending the city to the north to encompass much of the area occupied today by the Temple Mount or Haram esh Sharif. The site of the Dome of the Rock is traditionally thought to be the location of Solomon's Temple. Thereafter, the city underwent further expansion, particularly to the west, and various kings of Judah are credited with adding to or strengthening the fortifications (Uzziah (2 Chr. 26: 9), Jotham (2 Chr. 27: 3), Hezekiah (2 Chr. 32: 5), and Manasseh (2 Chr. 33: 14)). We are also told that Jehoash, a king of Israel, destroyed a section of the wall of Jerusalem (2 Kgs. 14: 13).

It is to Hezekiah that a particularly significant contribution to Jerusalem's defences is credited. There is evidence that a conduit had been made to bring water from the Gihon Spring to a pool below the southern end of the city, but much of its length was unprotected, and it would therefore be of little use in time of siege, for example. Hezekiah ordered that a tunnel be cut through the rock and a pool prepared inside the extended fortifications to the south, the Pool of Siloam, thereby achieving an internal water-supply for the city (2 Kgs. 20: 20; 2 Chr. 32: 2–4, 30). This tunnel was rediscovered in 1880, with an inscription on its wall which provided a clue as to its method of construction

Jerusalem: the 'City of David' excavations, showing the 'stepped stone structure', probably constructed in the 10th century BCE as a retaining wall for the fortifications.

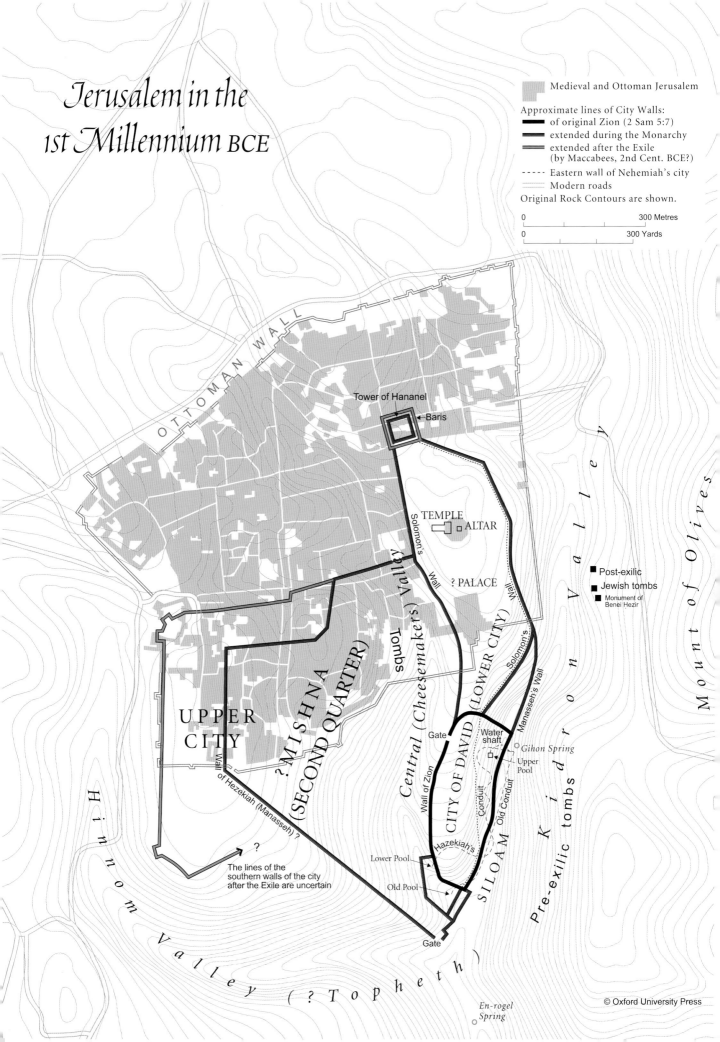

Jerusalem in the
1st Millennium BCE

Medieval and Ottoman Jerusalem
Approximate lines of City Walls:
of original Zion (2 Sam 5:7)
extended during the Monarchy
extended after the Exile
(by Maccabees, 2nd Cent. BCE?)
- - - - - Eastern wall of Nehemiah's city
Modern roads
Original Rock Contours are shown.

0   300 Metres
0   300 Yards

OTTOMAN WALL

Tower of Hananel
Baris

TEMPLE
ALTAR

? PALACE

Solomon's Wall

Solomon's Wall

Valley (Cheesemakers') Valley

Tombs

?MISHNA (SECOND QUARTER)

Central (Cheesemakers') Valley

(LOWER CITY)

Manasseh's Wall

UPPER
CITY

Wall of Hezekiah (Manasseh)?

Post-exilic
Jewish tombs
Monument of
Benei Hezir

Gate

Water
shaft

Gihon Spring
Upper
Pool

Wall of Zion

CITY OF DAVID

Conduit

Old Conduit

Hezekiah's

SILOAM

Kidron Valley

Pre-exilic tombs

Mount of Olives

Lower Pool

Old Pool

The lines of the
southern walls of the city
after the Exile are uncertain

Hinnom Valley (?Topheth)

Gate

En-rogel
Spring

© Oxford University Press

The Siloam Inscription, originally carved into the wall of Hezekiah's Tunnel, describing how it was hewn out by workers starting each end and working towards each other.

(though the inscription itself does not mention Hezekiah or give any pointer as to the date). It appears that two groups of workers began at either end and worked towards each other and that they were in danger of missing each other until sounds from one tunnel were heard in the other and they hewed out the intervening rock to complete the project. This was a remarkable achievement given not only the length of the tunnel (583 yds or 533 m) but its meandering route. It is possible that there was already an underground stream or fissure in the rock through which water seeped and which could be followed.

After Jerusalem's destruction at the hands of the Babylonians in the 6th century BCE, it is Nehemiah that the biblical narrative credits with the rebuilding of the city walls (Neh. 2: 17–6: 19). The likelihood is that those who returned occupied only the eastern hill, approximately the area taken by David and expanded by Solomon, and it was this area that Nehemiah's walls encircled. Remains suggest that the wall on the eastern side of Ophel followed the crest of the hill. During the bulk of the Persian and Hellenistic periods (6th–2nd centuries BCE), Jerusalem probably continued to occupy just the area of the Temple Mount and the City of David.

In the 2nd century BCE, according to the First Book of Maccabees, the Seleucid king Antiochus Epiphanes came to Jerusalem with a large army. 'He plundered the city, burned it with fire, and tore down its houses and its surrounding walls' (1 Macc. 1: 31) He also refortified the City of David and established a citadel there (verse 33). Under the Maccabees, the Temple Hill was refortified; their counterpart to the Greek citadel was a castle (known as Baris), at the north of the area, possibly the same as the Tower of Hananel, mentioned in Jeremiah 31: 38. During the Maccabean period, it seems that there was expansion of the city to the west, to encompass the south-western hill, though the location of the southern walls in particular is uncertain.

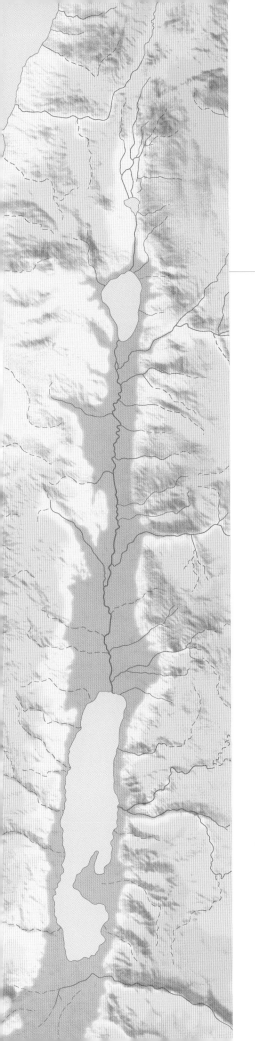

The New Testament

The Kingdom of Herod and his Successors

PROVINCE OF SYRIA

MARE INTERNUM
(Mediterranean Sea)

Sidon
Sarepta
Tyre
R. Leontes

ABILENE

Damascus
(a city of the De...

Paneas
Danos (Caesarea Philippi)

ITURAEA

Ulatha

Bathyra?

TRACHONIT...

BATANAEA

Ptolemais

Mt. Carmel

GALILEE

Chorazin
Capernaum
Gennesaret
Bethsaida-Julias

Magdala
(Taricheae)
Sea of Galilee

Sepphoris
Gabae (Hippeum)
Nazareth
Hippos

Raphana
(a city of the Decapolis)

GAULANITIS

Gamala

Dion?

AURANITIS

Wadi Yarmuk
Gadara
Abila

Dora

The Great Plain

HEROD

Caesarea
(Strato's Tower)

Plain of Sharon

Scythopolis
Pella

DECAPOLIS

Sebaste (Samaria)
Neapolis
Mt. Ebal
Mt. Gerizim

SAMARIA

Apollonia
Sozusa

Antipatris

Alexandrium

River Jordan

Gerasa
Amathus

R. Jabbok

KINGDOM OF

Joppa

Phasaelis

Gadara

Thamna

Lydda

Gophna

Archelais

Philadelphia (Rabbah)

PEREA

Jamnia

Gazara
Emmaus (Nicopolis)

Jericho
Cyprus

Jerusalem
Bethany
Hyrcania
Bethlehem

Azotus

JUDEA

Betharamphtha

(Kh. Qumran:
settlement of
Dead Sea sect)

Medeba

Ascalon
(Free City)

Betogabri

Herodium

Wilderness of Judah

Marisa

Agrippias
(Anthedon)

Gaza

Hebron

Lake Asphaltitis

Callirrhoe
Machaerus

Adora

Engaddi (En-gedi)

R. Arnon

IDUMEA

(Dead Sea)

Raphia

Masada

KINGDOM

Bersabe
(Beersheba)

Malatha

NABATAEAN KINGDOM

Mampsis

- - - - Boundary of Herod's kingdo...
         at its greatest extent
- - - - Divisions, CE 6-37
■ Fortresses

0   10   20 Miles

0   10   20 Kilometres

© Oxford University Pre...

The Kingdom of Herod and his Successors

HEROD THE GREAT

In 63 BCE, the Roman general Pompey entered Jerusalem as conqueror and brought to an end the rule of the Hasmonean dynasty. An Idumean named Antipater was made ruler of Galilee in return for his services to the Romans, and his sons Herod and Phasael shared in the exercise of power. After a period of conflict and the deaths of Antipater (by poisoning) and Phasael (by suicide), Herod achieved power, gaining control first of Galilee, Samaria and Idumea in 39 BCE, and ultimately of the whole of the area in 37 BCE when he captured Jerusalem. In c.30 BCE he was confirmed as king of the Jews by Octavian. His rule extended over the whole of Jewish territory including Judea, Samaria, and Galilee, as well as the district of Perea to the east of the Jordan and regions to the north-east of Galilee including Auranitis, Trachonitis, and Batanaea. His kingdom was bounded in the north by the province of Syria (which was under the rule of a Roman governor) and in the south-east by the Nabataean kingdom with its capital at Petra. To the east lay the Decapolis, a league of self-governing cities, most of which (for example, Scythopolis, Pella, and Philadelphia) were outside Herod's kingdom. Ascalon was a free city, and not included in his kingdom, as was the case for a certain period with Gaza and Joppa.

Although not of Jewish descent, Herod was a Jew by religion. Nevertheless, he went as far as a Jew could in aligning himself with the power of Rome and the ways of the pagan world. His reign was noted for the construction of many large public building works, including the development of the former Strato's Tower into the harbour at Caesarea Maritima, and a number of fortresses including Masada, where he also had a palace constructed, and Herodium, where tradition says that he was buried. Building work was also undertaken at other places including Samaria, which he renamed Sebaste after Caesar Augustus (Greek *Sebastos*), and most notably in Jerusalem with the construction of a huge temple platform and the Temple itself.

It was before the death of Herod in 4 BCE that Jesus was born. According to Matthew 2: 1 and Luke 2: 4 his birth took place in Bethlehem.

Aqueduct at Caesarea, from the time of Herod, constructed to bring water from the hills.

HEROD'S SUCCESSORS

After the death of Herod, his kingdom was divided between three of his sons: Archelaus received Judea and Samaria; Herod Antipas received Galilee and Perea, and Philip received Ituraea. Herod Antipas and Philip established their capitals, which they named in honour of Rome, at Tiberias (after Tiberius) and at Caesarea Philippi. Archelaus reigned in Jerusalem until the year 6 CE when he was deposed. Judea, along with Samaria, was placed under the rule of a Roman governor who was directly responsible to the emperor. The holder of this office from 26 to 36 was Pontius Pilate. The governor was supported by Roman troops and was based in Caesarea Maritima; but there was also a Roman headquarters (*praetorium*) in Jerusalem (Mark 15: 16).

The Ministry of Jesus and the Beginnings of the Church

THE GOSPELS

Although he is often known as Jesus of Nazareth (for example, Matt. 21: 11; Mark 1: 24; Luke 18: 37; John 18: 5; Acts 2: 22), two of the Gospels place his birth in Bethlehem (Matt. 2: 1 and Luke 2: 4). Luke accounts for this with reference to a registration of the population, carried out in the time of Augustus, when people were required to return to their ancestral homes to be registered. Hence Joseph, a descendant of David, travelled to Bethlehem, and it would have been important for those who claimed that Jesus was the Messiah, a descendant of David, to establish this connection. But it seems that it *was* in Nazareth that he was brought up and lived until he was about 30 years old (Luke 4: 16). Nazareth was probably a very humble village. It is not mentioned in the Hebrew Bible nor by Josephus, but it is named in an inscription from the early Roman period found at Caesarea, and Eusebius mentions a village in Galilee called Nazareth in his *Onomasticon*.

The Church of the Nativity: Bethlehem. The star in the crypt marks the spot where, according to tradition, Jesus was born.

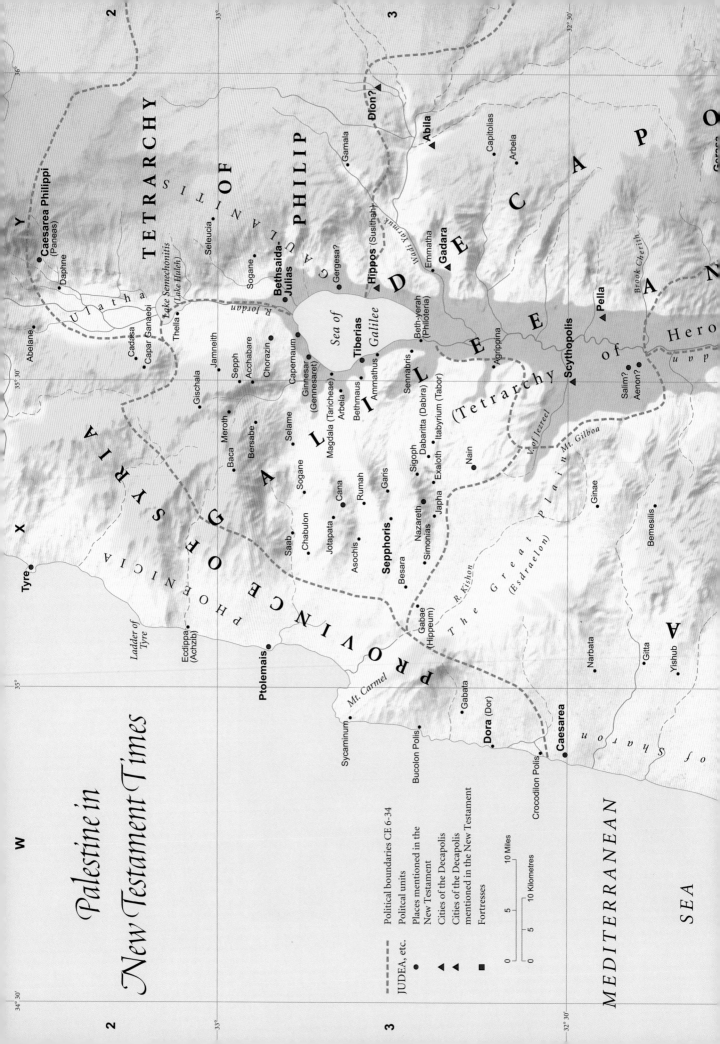

Palestine in New Testament Times

Legend:

Political boundaries CE 6-34
JUDEA, etc.   Political units
●   Places mentioned in the New Testament
▲   Cities of the Decapolis
◀   Cities of the Decapolis mentioned in the New Testament
■   Fortresses

Scale:
0   5   10 Miles
0   5   10 Kilometres

Map labels:

W

TETRARCHY

PHILIP

TETRARCHY OF PHILIP

GAULANITIS

Caesarea Philippi (Paneas)
Daphne
Abelane
Abelane
Capar Ganaeoi
Cadasa
Thella
Seleucia
Sogane
Lake Semechonitis
Lake Semechonitis (Lake Hûleh)
Ulatha
R. Jordan
Bethsaida-Julias
Gamala
Gergesa?
Gischala
Jamneith
Seloph
Acchabare
Chorazin
Capernaum
Meroth
Baca
Bersabe
Selame
Sogane
Ginnesar (Gennesaret)
Magdala (Taricheae)
Arbela
Bethmaus
Ammathus
Sea of Galilee
Tiberias
Beth-yerah (Philoteria)
Sennabris
Sigoph
Dabaritta (Dabira)
Itabyrium (Tabor)
Saab
Chabulon
Jotapata
Cana
Rumah
Garis
Exaloth
Japha
Nain
Asochis
Besara
Nazareth
Simonias
Sepphoris

PHOENICIA

PROVINCE OF SYRIA

GALILEE

Tyre
Ecdippa (Achzib)
Ladder of Tyre
Ptolemais
Gabae (Hippeum)
Gabata
Gabata
Mt. Carmel
R. Kishon
The Great Plain (Esdraelon)
Mt. Gilboa
Ginae
Narbata
Gitta
Yishub
Bemesilis

DECAPOLIS

Dion?
Abila
Gadara
Hippos (Susithah)
Emmatha
Capitollas
Arbela
Wadi Yarmuk
Pella
Brook Cherith
Agrippina
Scythopolis
Salim?
Aenon?
GILEAD (Tetrarchy of Herod)
of Hero[d]
Heron

Sycaminum
Bucolon Polis
Dora (Dor)
Crocodilon Polis
Caesarea

MEDITERRANEAN SEA

of Sharon

X
Y
2
3
2
3

35°
35° 30'
36°
34° 30'
33°
33°
32° 30'
32° 30'

© Oxford University Press

I S S

Philadelphia
(Rabbah)

Medeba (Madaba)

Esbus

Zia

P

Gadara

E

Betharamphtha
(Livias Julias)

R

E

A

(ntipas)

Calirrhoe

R. Nahaliel

Machaerus

N A B A T A E A N   K I N G D O M

Areopolis (Rabbathmoab)

Areopolis (Rabbathmoab)

R. Arnon

R
(arah)
River

Coreae

Acrabbein

Alexandrium

Phasaelis

Archelais

Jericho

Cyprus

Taurus

Lake

Asphaltitis (Dead Sea)

Mahnayim

Anathu Borcaeus

Selo (Shiloh)

Ephraim (Aphairema)

Capharsalama?

Michmash

(Kh. Qumran:
settlement of
Dead Sea sect)

Hyrcania

Kidron

Wilderness of Judea

Engaddi (En-gedi)

Tephon

Berzetho

Gophna

Bethel

Ailon?

Anathoth

Adasa

Gabaon

Gabath Saul

Colonia Amasa
(Emmaus?)

Mt. Scopus

Bethphage

Bethany

Beth-basi

W. Murabba'at

Masada

X

Arus

Thamna (Timnath)

Lower Beth-horon

Upper Beth-horon

Berea?

Jerusalem

J U D E A

Bethlehem

Beth-zur)

Etam

Herodium

Thecoa (Thekoa)

Terebinthus (Mamre)

Aristobulias

Tephon

Ilon

Sappho

Cariathiareim

Emmaus
(Nicopolis)

Bethsura (Beth-zur)

Aulos

Hebron

Adora

?Caparorsa

(under Roman administration)

Capparetaea

Antipatris (Pegai)

Tower of Aphek

Rathamin
(Arimathea?)

Adida

Modein

Beth-zechariah

Caphartobas

Gemmaruris

Mampsis

Malatha

I D U M E A

Brook of Kanah

D

U

Betogabri

Lydda

Gazara

Kedron

Bethletepha

Capharabis

W

Joppa

Jamnia

Accaron
(Ekron)

Bersabe
(Beersheba)

Iamnitarum Portus
(Jamnia Harbour)

Azotus

Wadi Qubeiba)

Azotus Paralius
(Azotus-on-Sea)

Ascalon
(Free city)

Maiumas Ascalon
(Baths of Ascalon)

Agrippias (Anthedon)

Gaza

To Province of Syria

Brook Besor

Bethsura (Beth-zur)

R. Belus (Kedron)

R. Nahaliel

Thecoa (Thekoa)

The Church of the Annunciation in Nazareth, said to mark the spot where the angel Gabriel appeared to Mary (Luke 1: 26-38).

The first three (synoptic) Gospels suggest that Jesus' ministry (prior to its final days in Jerusalem) was centred on Galilee, with Capernaum having a prominent place in the accounts (for example, Matt. 8: 5; Mark 1: 21; 2: 1; Luke 4: 23). Matthew 4: 13 suggests that he left Nazareth to make his home in Capernaum. There are also references to journeys further afield, for example, to 'the region of Tyre' (or possibly 'regions of Tyre and Sidon', Mark 7: 24). Mention is also made of a visit to the territory of the Decapolis, but there is some uncertainty as to whether it was to the area of Gadara or Gerasa or even Gergesa (see Matt. 8: 28; Mark 5: 1; Luke 8: 26). Mark reports that people came to hear Jesus from Judea, Jerusalem, Idumea, and beyond the Jordan, and also from the regions of Tyre and Sidon (Mark 3: 8). The fourth Gospel sets visits to Jerusalem and Judea early in its account (for example, John 2: 13, 23; 5: 1), also placing there Jesus' baptism in the Jordan, the call of some of the first disciples (John 1: 19–42), and the conversation with Nicodemus (John 3: 1–22). John also refers to Jesus passing through Samaria and visiting the well at Sychar (John 4: 4–5).

All the Gospels agree in placing the final days of Jesus' life in and around Jerusalem. The implication of Luke 17: 11 may be that he skirted Samaria and travelled through Perea, recrossing the Jordan to pass via Jericho (Luke 19: 1) to Jerusalem. There he was betrayed, crucified, and buried. It was also in or near Jerusalem that some of the first post-resurrection appearances are set, including those to Mary Magdalene (John 20: 14), the two disciples on the road to Emmaus (Luke 24: 13–35), the assembled disciples (Luke 24: 36–49; John 20: 19–22), and Thomas (John 20: 24–9). Resurrection appearances are also located in Galilee (Matt. 28: 16–20; John 21: 1–21). The gathering of the disciples which is the setting for the ascension is located on the Mount of Olives (Acts 1: 12).

THE SURROUNDINGS OF JESUS' MINISTRY

With the exception of Jerusalem, the places associated with Jesus in the Gospel accounts were not particularly important in the wider context of the times. On the other hand, cities which *were* important, such as Sepphoris, the most important town in Galilee and not far from Nazareth, are not mentioned in the Gospels. Tiberias on the shores of the Sea of Galilee is only mentioned in the context of giving an alternative name for the lake (John 6: 1). There is no reference to Caesarea Maritima, the headquarters of the Roman provincial governor, nor to the city of Samaria / Sebaste. (Samaria is mentioned only as a district.) A possible explanation for this is that Jesus

Fishing boat at the point where the River Jordan exits the Sea of Galilee.

Capernaum: remains of the 4th–5th-century CE synagogue. The town features prominently in the accounts of Jesus' ministry.

avoided such places because of their non-Jewish character. But it is appropriate to note that Jesus' activity took place in this wider context which included such places with their Hellenistic and pagan ways, typical of the east Mediterranean world of the time. The Gentile world was all around.

THE BEGINNINGS OF THE CHRISTIAN CHURCH

The activity of the apostles and the earliest Church was centred not in Galilee but in Jerusalem, where the disciples had initially remained after the death of Jesus. From there it began to spread outwards, as reflected in the words placed in the mouth of Jesus prior to the ascension that disciples are to be witnesses 'in Jerusalem, in all Judea and Samaria, and to the ends of the earth' (Acts 1: 8). Mention is made of apostles visiting Samaria (Acts 8: 4–5, 14), and the coastal area from Gaza and Azotus as far north as Caesarea Maritima (Acts 8: 26–40). There were Christian believers in Lydda and Joppa (Acts 9: 32, 36), and as far afield as Damascus where the new faith had apparently come to be known as 'the Way' (Acts 9: 2). Thus began an expansion which was to see Christianity spread far beyond Jerusalem and Judea. But until at least 70 CE, the church in Jerusalem and Judea seems to have retained a special position (see, for example, Acts 11: 1; 15: 1–6; 21: 17–18; 1 Cor. 16: 3; 1 Thess. 2: 14).

An event of profound significance, which must have had its impact on the early Church, was the fiercely fought revolt of the Jews against Rome, which broke out in 66. This led to Jerusalem being placed under siege and eventually being taken and destroyed in 70. This revolt was the context of the desperate last stand of the Jewish resistance at the former Herodian fortress of Masada, where they managed to hold out until 73. A graphic account of this episode is given by the Jewish historian Josephus in his work *The Jewish War*.

The Roman Empire: The Background of the New Testament

THE ROMAN EMPIRE

The broad context for the setting of the New Testament is the Roman Empire which had been inaugurated by Augustus Caesar. Formerly known as Octavian(us), he had put an end to a period of civil war and brought a welcome era of peace to the Roman and Hellenistic worlds as a result of his victory over Mark Antony in a naval battle at Actium in 31 BCE. He was declared 'Augustus' in 27 BCE and lived until 14 CE. His successors Tiberius, Gaius (nicknamed Caligula), Claudius, and Nero ruled over an empire which incorporated the parts of Europe roughly bounded by the Atlantic (but including Britain), the Rhine, and the Danube, Asia Minor, the Mediterranean coastlands as far east as the upper Euphrates and the Arabian Desert, and Africa north of the Sahara. There were certain frontier wars and, at the end of that period, the revolt of the Jews (66–70) and, after the death of Nero, a time of civil strife in 69 (sometimes known as the 'year of the four emperors': Galba, Otho, Vitellius, and Vespasian). But to a large extent the empire was at peace, permitting unrestricted travel.

Provinces were governed by proconsuls or legates, responsible to the Roman Senate in peaceful areas (for example, Gallio in Achaia; Acts 18: 12) or personally to the emperor in military and frontier provinces (for example, Quirinius in Syria; Luke 2: 1–2). Client kingdoms, under native kings appointed and controlled by Rome, were established in certain difficult areas which were not considered ready for provincial status. One such was the kingdom of Herod the Great (see 'The Kingdom of Herod and his Successors'). The eastern frontier was garrisoned against the nations beyond, in particular the Parthians who had destroyed a Roman army at Carrhae (the former Haran) in 53 BCE. However, throughout the New Testament period the Syrian frontier was quiet. The description of the day of Pentecost in Acts 2: 9–11 reflects an awareness of a time of relative peace and ease of travel. Jews from Parthia, Media, Elam, and Mesopotamia as well as those from Asia Minor, North Africa, and other parts of the Roman Empire are all said to have been present in Jerusalem at the same time.

THE EARLY EXPANSION OF THE CHURCH

The early spread of the Church from Jerusalem was initially through Judea and beyond, as far as Damascus (see 'The Ministry of Jesus and the Beginnings of the Church'). The expansion continued and those who were scattered as a result of persecutions in the aftermath of the death of Stephen are said to have preached to Jews in Phoenicia, Cyprus, and Antioch (Acts 11: 19). Antioch was the chief city of the province of Syria, and was an important base for further expansion. To the east lay Edessa and Mesopotamia (including Babylon where there was a sizeable Jewish colony). The New Testament, written in Greek, records the spread of Christianity through the Greek-speaking provinces of the empire as far as Rome itself. But there was also expansion in Syria and to the east among those who spoke Syriac, an Aramaic dialect. Syriac-speaking Christianity centred on Edessa.

PAUL

Paul, previously called Saul, was the son of Jewish parents (his father being a Roman citizen). He was born in the Greek-speaking city of Tarsus in Cilicia, and trained in Jerusalem under the Rabbi Gamaliel (Acts 22: 3). His conversion on the road to Damascus, where there were already Christians, and his beginning to preach, is described in Acts 9: 1–22. Galatians 1: 17–18 suggests that after his conversion he spent time in 'Arabia', returned to Damascus, and that he visited Peter in Jerusalem three years later. He was subsequently brought from Tarsus to Antioch by Barnabas (Acts 11: 25–6). Thereafter he began his series of journeys by land and sea, preaching the good news 'from Jerusalem as far around as Illyricum' (Rom. 15: 19). (See 'Paul's Journeys'.) Throughout, Paul maintained contact with the Church and its leaders at Jerusalem, and visited Jerusalem, probably in 57, after which (he indicated in Romans 15: 28) it was his intention to visit Rome and then travel to Spain.

But the account in Acts records that in Jerusalem, as a result of Jewish hostility, Paul was arrested (Acts 21: 30). He was transferred to Caesarea (Acts 23: 33) where he eventually appealed to Caesar (Acts 25: 11). He was transported by sea, under Roman escort, via Myra in Lycia and along the south coast of Crete (Acts 27: 5–8) and on towards Italy. As a result of a severe storm he was shipwrecked on the island of Malta (Acts 28: 1), but three months later he was conveyed by sea via Syracuse in Sicily to Puteoli on the coast of Italy, and thence to Rome (Acts 28: 11–14). There he remained under house arrest (Acts 28: 16). He was probably executed under Nero.

THE CHURCH IN ROME

It seems likely that when Paul arrived in Rome there was already a reasonably strong church there, to which he had written his epistle. This suggests that Christianity had expanded in ways not mentioned in Acts, probably thanks to the activity of other apostles and the movement of believers around the Empire. Claudius (41–54) is said to have expelled all the Jews from Rome.

E   S c y t h i a n s   F   G   H   J

BOSPORAN
KINGDOM

— · —	Boundary of Roman Empire (c.CE 65)
— — —	Provincial boundaries (c.CE 65)
ASIA, etc	Roman Provinces
— — —	Selected Roman roads (route between Rome and the East)

0   100   200 Miles

0   100   200 Kilometres

Istros
Tomi
Chersonesus

E u x i n e   S e a
(Pontus Euxinus)

Odessus
Mesembria

COLCHIS

Way
Byzantium
Bosphorus
Heraclea
Nicomedia
Nicaea
exandria)
Prusa
Dorylaeum

Amastris
BITHYNIA and PONTUS
Gangra
Ancyra
Tavium
Gordium
Pessinus

Sinope
Amisus
Side
Amasea
Comana
Trapezus

Lesser
Armenia

KINGDOM

OF

ARMENIA

Artaxata
R. Araxes

myttium
A
ergamum
Thyatira
Sardis
Philadelphia
phesus
Laodicea
letus
Colossae

ASIA
PHRYGIA
GALATIA
Antioch
Iconium
Lystra
PISIDIA
PAMPHYLIA
Derbe

CAPPADOCIA
Caesarea (Mazaca)
Archelais

Melitene

Tigranocerta
L. Van
MEDIA
ATROPATENE
L. Urmia

LYCIA
Attalia
Perga
Patara
Myra
Rhodes

Cilicia
Trachea
Tarsus
Seleucia
CILICIA

Commagene
Zeugma
Europus
(Carchemish)
OSROENE
Edessa
Carrhae (Haran)
Samosata
Nicephorium

Nisibis
GORDYENE
Ninus
Arbela
ADIABENE

MESOPOTAMIA

PARTHIAN

MEDIA

R. Tigris

IRE
E

CYPRUS
Salamis
Paphos

Antioch
R. Orontes
Apamea
Epiphania
Emesa

Tripolis

and SYRIA

R. Euphrates

Palmyra

Dura-Europus

EMPIRE

ELAM

Berytus
Sidon
Tyre
Ptolemais
Caesarea
Joppa
Gaza

Area
Abilene
Damascus
Caesarea Philippi
Tiberias
Samaria
Jerusalem
Judea

Nabataean Kingdom

*Arabian
Desert*

Seleucia
Babylon
Ctesiphon

ancient coastline

Canopus
lexandria
Naucratis
Sais
Pelusium

Heliopolis
Memphis
Babylon

EGYPT
R. Nile
Oxyrhynchus

Petra
Aila (Aelana)
Mt.
Sinai

Dumah

*The Roman Empire:
The Background
of the New Testament*

F   *Red Sea*   G   Tema   H   J

Aquila and Priscilla, natives of Pontus, were among those expelled from Rome at this time and they came to Corinth where Paul met them (Acts 18: 2). The Roman historian Suetonius suggests that this expulsion was the result of disturbances caused by a certain Chrestus; this may indicate that Christianity was already causing dissension in the Jewish community.

Tradition associates Peter with the founding of the church in Rome, and perhaps Peter and Paul should be regarded as co-founders. The closing verses of Acts suggest that Paul spent two years in Rome, continuing his preaching ministry (Acts 28: 30–1). By 64 the Christians in Rome were numerous enough for Nero (54–68) to accuse them of having started a disastrous fire in the city. Although it is widely believed that they were innocent, many were put to death at the instigation of the emperor. Tradition says that Peter and Paul were included among their number. The church in Rome became the chief centre of Christianity in the West, and continued to be so for many years. Mark's Gospel has been thought to have been written there, perhaps incorporating traditions which may have come from Peter. There is an enigmatic reference to Christians from Italy in Hebrews 13: 24.

Jerusalem in New Testament Times

HEROD THE GREAT

The reign of Herod was noted for the public building works which he instigated (see 'The Kingdom of Herod and his Successors'). This was true not
least of Jerusalem. Josephus's account of his works suggests that the city was
transformed from a rather unpretentious religious centre to one of the most
impressive of Roman provincial cities. New structures included a hippo-
drome, an amphitheatre, a theatre, baths, and other public buildings. Most
notable of all was the reconstruction of the Temple and its precinct. The new
Temple mount dominated the Kidron and Central (Tyropoeon) valleys. It
was constructed with retaining walls which reached to a considerable height,
made of massive stone blocks, reflecting remarkable workmanship. Remains
of these walls make it possible for the extent of this precinct to be placed
accurately on the map, and some of its gates to be located. But the inner
courts and the Temple building itself have disappeared, so reconstructions
are conjectural, based on brief descriptions given by Josephus and later Jewish writers.

Herod also enlarged and converted the old Maccabean castle (or 'Baris'),
making it a fortified residence for himself and renaming it as the Antonia
Tower. (It is possible that this was the 'barracks' to which Paul was taken after
his removal from the Temple (Acts 21: 30–5). Herod also built a larger royal
palace on the western hill, and the city wall which it adjoined was strengthened by the addition of three great towers named Hippicus, Phasael, and
Mariamne. Phasael is still partly standing, and helps to identify the site of the
palace, in the north-west corner of the Maccabean city; traces of the other
two towers have been excavated. Beyond the city's western wall, across the
Hinnom valley, lies the four-chambered tomb, with a rolling stone to seal the
entrance, which was built by Herod for his own family. The tomb is referred
to by Josephus and was discovered in 1892.

Excavations in the areas immediately to the south and south-west of the
Temple platform have revealed important features of the Herodian city,
including the course of the street which ran adjacent to the retaining walls

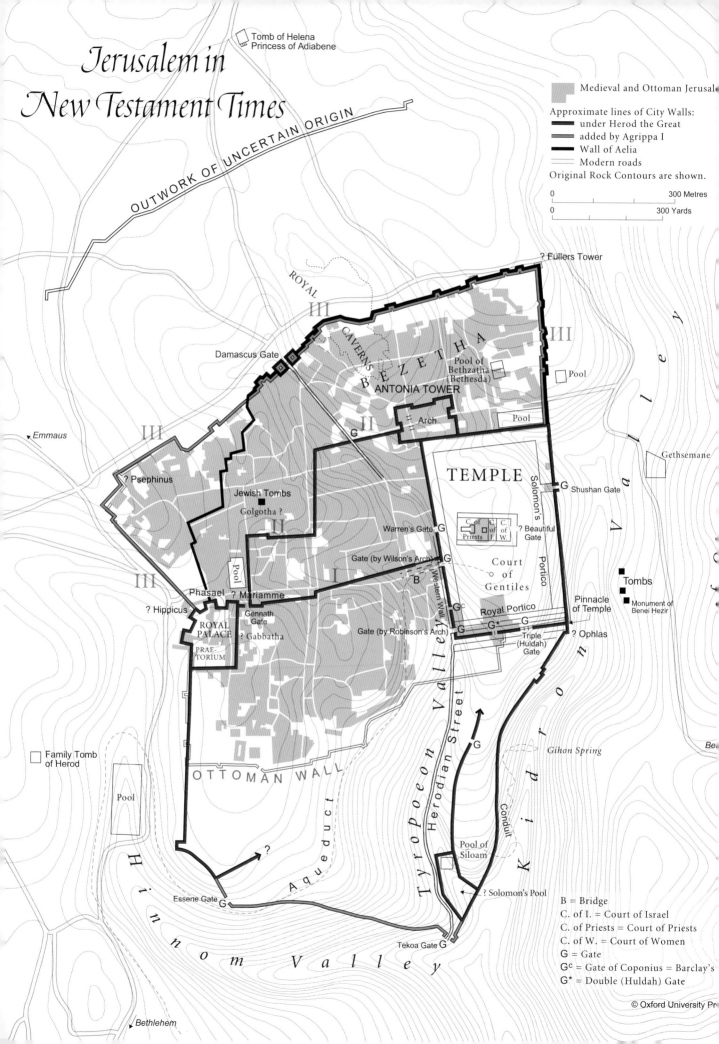

Jerusalem in
New Testament Times

Tomb of Helena
Princess of Adiabene

OUTWORK OF UNCERTAIN ORIGIN

ROYAL

III

CAVERNS

BEZETHA

Damascus Gate

ANTONIA TOWER

Pool of
Bethzatha
(Bethesda)

Pool

III

? Fullers Tower

Pool

III

Emmaus

Arch

Pool

G II

TEMPLE

Solomon's

G Shushan Gate

Gethsemane

? Psephinus

Jewish Tombs

Golgotha ?

Warren's Gate G

C. of
Priests

C.
of
I.

C.
of
W.

? Beautiful
Gate

II

Gate (by Wilson's Arch) G

G

Court
of
Gentiles

Portico

Tombs

III

Pool

I

B

Western Wall

Gᶜ

Royal Portico

Monument of
Benei Hezir

Phasael

? Mariamme

Gʷ

Pinnacle
of Temple

? Hippicus

Gennath
Gate

ROYAL
PALACE

? Gabbatha

PRAE-
TORIUM

Gate (by Robinson's Arch) G G* G

Triple
(Huldah)
Gate

? Ophlas

Kidron

Family Tomb
of Herod

Pool

OTTOMAN WALL

Aqueduct

Gihon Spring

Pool of
Siloam

Conduit

Herodian Street

Tyropoeon Valley

G

Essene Gate G

? Solomon's Pool

Tekoa Gate G

Hinnom Valley

Bethlehem

along the lower west side and along the southern side of the precinct. On the south it adjoined a 'plaza', an open area where pilgrims could congregate before entering the gates of the Temple via a monumental staircase, part of which has been preserved. On the western side, in the vicinity of the Western (formerly 'Wailing') Wall, there is evidence of arches which supported means of access to the Temple precincts. 'Wilson's Arch' was part of the support of a bridge which crossed the Tyropoeon valley. It was previously thought that 'Robinson's Arch' also supported a bridge, but excavations have now made it clear that it was part of the support of a staircase which led up to the Temple. Excavations on the western hill overlooking the Temple have revealed evidence of buildings from the Hasmonean and Herodian periods, but the southern wall which ran across the Tyropoeon valley seems to date from the time of Agrippa I.

The 'Western Wall', part of the structure of the huge platform built to support Herod's Temple in Jerusalem. The courses of massive stones which were part of the original structure can be seen; a similar number of courses are below the present ground level. To the left, the tops of three arches which originally supported a viaduct can be seen.

BIBLICAL SITES

Of the places in Jerusalem mentioned in the New Testament it is only possible to locate a few with certainty. It is likely that Pilate's headquarters, also known as the praetorium (Matt. 27: 27) or 'palace' (Mark 15: 16) was in fact the same as Herod's palace on the western hill. If that is the case, then the 'Stone Pavement', also called Gabbatha (John 19:13) must have been a paved open space in that vicinity, perhaps just inside the Gennath Gate. It therefore can-

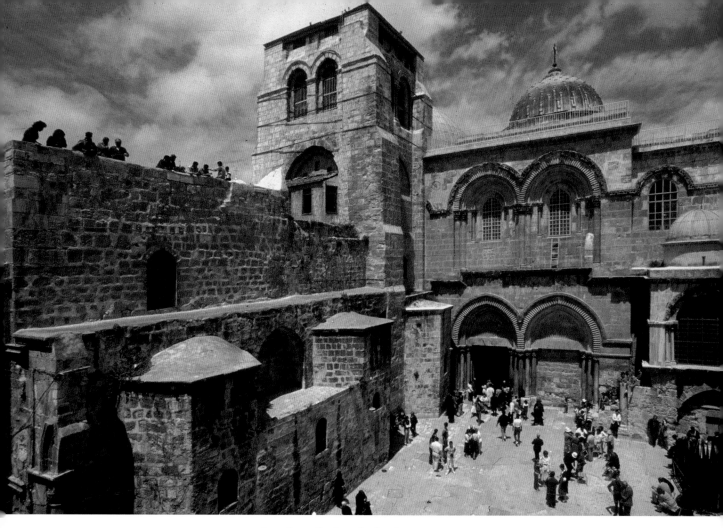

The Church of the Holy Sepulchre, Jerusalem: the church contains the traditional sites of the crucifixion and burial of Jesus.

not be identified with the famous stone pavement which is preserved on the site of the Antonia Tower, close to the Roman triple arch which is known traditionally as the 'Ecce Homo Arch' but which probably dates from the 2nd century CE (though a 1st-century date has been defended). A further corollary is that the 'Via Dolorosa', the traditional route taken by Jesus from his trial to his crucifixion, does not represent an actual route that would have led from the place of judgement to the place of execution. The site of 'The Place of the Skull', or Golgotha (Matt. 27: 33; Mark 15: 22; John 19: 17; see also Luke 23: 33) is uncertain, but a tradition which goes back at least to the 4th century, and which may be correct, places it in a area of Jewish tombs one of which is claimed as the tomb in which Jesus' body was placed. Traditional sites of both the crucifixion and the tomb are now venerated inside the Church of the Holy Sepulchre.

Within the Temple area, the 'Beautiful' gate (Acts 3: 10) may have been the main eastern entrance to the Court of the Women. Solomon's Porch or Portico (John 10: 23; Acts 3: 11; 5: 12) may have formed one side of this court or may have been a colonnaded walkway on the eastern side of the outer court. Tradition has associated the 'Pinnacle of the Temple' (Matt. 4: 5; Luke 4: 9) with the south-eastern corner of the Temple platform. Two pools mentioned in the New Testament, Bethzatha or Bethesda (John 5: 2) and Siloam (John 9: 7) can be located by extant remains. It is noteworthy that, in the same vicinity as the former, a temple dedicated to the Roman god of healing, Aesclepius, was built after the destruction of the Second Temple and was a feature of the Roman city, Aelia Capitolina. This suggests the possibility of an ongoing connection of that location with healing.

CITY WALLS

The map of 'Jerusalem in New Testament Times' shows in red the walls as they are thought to have existed in the time of Herod the Great. (It is noteworthy that at the time the traditional site of Golgotha lay outside the city walls.) Marked in blue are those of Herod Agrippa I, who added a third, northern, wall in the time of Claudius (41–54 CE). All these lines are partly conjectural and the northernmost (marked III) is much disputed. Here it has been made to coincide with the existing Ottoman wall for two reasons: (1) the Damascus Gate is known to stand on the foundation of an older gate built in the same style as the Temple enclosure that may have belonged to Agrippa's wall; (2) Josephus states that the northernmost wall passed through the royal caverns. The only caverns which exist on the northern side of the city are the quarry-caves known as 'King Solomon's Caves', and the Ottoman wall passes through the middle of them. Agrippa's wall was completely destroyed by the Romans in 70 CE, after the Jewish Revolt, and, except at the Damascus Gate and in some reused stones, nothing can be seen of it today. Somewhere at its north-west corner stood the tower of Psephinus, an octagonal structure of considerable height.

Much of the oldest masonry visible in the wall line which exists today belongs to a reconstruction dating to the 3rd or 4th century CE, when Jerusalem was still a Roman city and named Aelia Capitolina. This rebuilding began at the tower of Phasael and reached the Damascus gate by a shorter line than that of Agrippa's wall. This is marked in black on the map.

The unattached double line further to the north shows the line of a massive 'outwork' which was thought to be Agrippa's wall. But there are no known royal caverns on or near its path, and the rough materials used conflict with Josephus's description. In addition, numismatic and ceramic evidence suggests a date between 60 and 100 CE, which is too late for Agrippa. A possible explanation for its origin is that it was a defensive fortification hastily erected by Jewish insurgents at the time of the Jewish revolt in 66 CE. The wall marked II is that which Josephus described as beginning at the Gennath Gate and ending at the Antonia Tower. Its line is partly authenticated by some rock scarps and masonry remains, now deeply buried.

Paul's Journeys

The spread of Christianity into Asia Minor, and through the lands around the Aegean Sea, was due in no small part to the journeys undertaken by Paul, and his letters of guidance and encouragement to various churches. He travelled through these Greek-speaking regions which were predominantly Gentile; but there were Jewish communities and synagogues in many cities, which were often Paul's first port of call.

THE FIRST JOURNEY

Paul set out in the company of Barnabas from Antioch in Syria. From Seleucia they sailed to Salamis on the island of Cyprus, then travelled overland to Paphos. Thence they crossed to Perga in Pamphylia, and journeyed inland to Antioch in Pisidia, Iconium, Lystra, and Derbe, and back via the same cities to Attalia, where they embarked to return to Syrian Antioch (Acts 13–14). Opinion is divided as to whether the Epistle to the Galatians is addressed to the churches of southern Galatia, established on this journey, or those of northern Galatia founded on his second journey.

THE SECOND JOURNEY

Paul again set out from Antioch, this time with Silas rather than Barnabas (Acts 15: 36–41). They travelled overland to Derbe and Lystra, where they met Timothy who joined them, and on through Galatian Phrygia and north-westwards through Mysia to the coast at Troas (Acts 16: 1–8). At this point, the Acts' account reports that, prompted by a vision, Paul crossed over via Samothrace into Macedonia, landing at Neapolis and travelling on first to Philippi and then, via Amphipolos and Apollonia, to Thessalonica and Beroea (Acts 16: 9–17: 14). Paul then travelled on to Athens, initially leaving Silas and Timothy behind, and it was while waiting for them that Paul made his speech on the Areopagus (Acts 17: 15–33). He journeyed on to Corinth, where he was joined by his companions, and stayed some considerable time, establishing the church there, before setting sail first to Ephesus, then on to Caesarea, visiting Jerusalem before returning thence to Antioch (Acts 18: 1–22).

Ephesus: the Library of Celsus, built c.135 CE in honour of the governor of the Roman province of Syria.

Adriatic Sea

ITALY

Rome

MACEDONIA

Philippi
Amphipolis   Neapolis
Berea   Apollonia
Thessalonica   San

Aeg

ACHAEA

Delphi
Corinth   Athens
Cenchrea

Ionian
Sea

SICILY

Malta

Phoe

Mediterranean

Paul's 1st Journey
Paul's 2nd Journey
Paul's 3rd Journey

CYRENAICA

Paul's Journeys

Istanbul

B l a c k   S e a

BITHYNIA

PONTUS

Ankara

GALATIA

CAPPADOCIA

MESOPOTAMIA

Kaymakli

MYSIA

PHRYGIA

LYCONIA

CILICIA

Pergamum

Thyatira

Philadelphia

Hierapolis

PISIDIA

Pisidian Antioch

Iconium

Tarsus

River Euphrates

Sardis

Coloesse

Smyrna

Laodicea

Lystra

Derbe

Seleucia

Antioch

Ephesus

PAMPHYLIA

Samos

Perga

Attalia

Samos

Miletus

LYCIA

Cyprus

Salamis

SYRIA

Patmos

Cos

Myra

Cos

Rhodes

Patara

Paphos

Sidon

Damascus

Rhodes

Tyre

Salmone

Ptolemais

Sea of Galilee

R. Jordan

Caesarea

Jerusalem

Dead Sea

S e a

EGYPT

Alexandria

© Oxford University Press

Cairo

1

2

3

A

D

E

THE THIRD JOURNEY

Paul again went from Antioch overland through Galatian Phrygia and journeyed on to Ephesus, establishing the church there, and remaining for some time (Acts 18: 23–19: 41). While there he seems to have maintained contact with the church in Corinth via messengers, and it is possible that he visited Corinth himself. Paul left Ephesus after a disturbance caused when Demetrius, the silversmith, took exception to his denunciation of the making of images for the temple of Artemis. He then travelled through Macedonia and on into Achaia, where he remained for three months, before returning via Philippi whence he sailed to Troas and joined delegates from a number of churches who were also heading for Jerusalem. They sailed via Assos, Mitylene, 'opposite Chios', and Samos, and reached Miletus. There Paul summoned the elders of the Ephesian church so that he could take his leave of them. He and his companions then sailed via Cos, and Rhodes, to Patara where they found a ship bound for Tyre. From Tyre Paul sailed via Ptolemais to Caesarea and, despite warnings that he should not do so, continued his journey to Jerusalem (Acts 20: 1–21: 17). There he was arrested and eventually transported to Rome (see 'The Roman Empire: The Background of the New Testament').

The Cradle of Christianity

The early development of Christianity owed much to the church in Jerusalem and its outreach into Judea and surrounding areas (see 'The Ministry of Jesus and the Beginnings of the Church') and the travels and letter-writing of Paul (see 'Paul's Journeys'). Witness to this is found predominantly in Acts and the Pauline Epistles. Acts also mentions Apollos, a native of Alexandria who had been 'instructed in the Way of the Lord' and who 'taught accurately the things concerning Jesus' (Acts 18: 24–19: 1; see also 1 Cor. 1: 12). This suggests the presence of a church in Alexandria, but its origins are unknown.

It has been suggested that Paul may have been released from his first imprisonment in Rome and that he subsequently made further journeys,

Patmos: the Monastery of St John, marking the traditional site of the writing of the Book of Revelation.

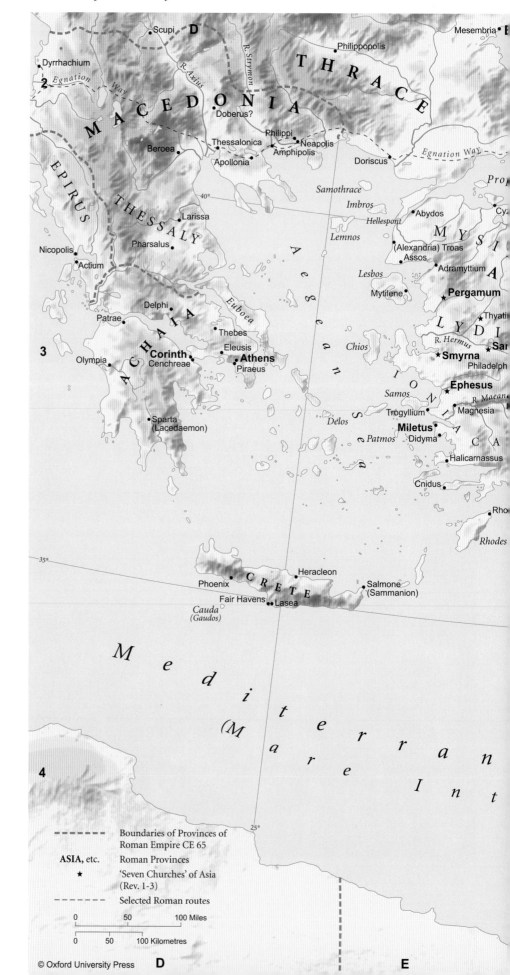

Boundaries of Provinces of
Roman Empire CE 65

ASIA, etc.   Roman Provinces

★   'Seven Churches' of Asia
(Rev. 1-3)

Selected Roman routes

0   50   100 Miles

0   50   100 Kilometres

© Oxford University Press

The Cradle of Christianity

visiting again Troas, Miletus, and Corinth (2 Tim. 4: 13, 20), leaving Titus in Crete (Tit. 1: 5) and intending to spend the winter in Nicopolis (Tit. 3: 12). That suggestion was based on the assumption that Paul wrote the Pastoral Epistles, but this view is no longer widely held. Nevertheless, these letters suggest an awareness of Christian communities in those cities. The salutation in 1 Peter 1: 1 suggests that the letter was addressed to Christians in Pontus, Galatia, Cappadocia, Asia, and Bithynia. In about 112 Pliny, the governor of Bithynia, found many Christians there, some of whom had been converted over twenty years earlier. John, the writer of Revelation, may have been banished to the island of Patmos during the persecutions under the emperor Domitian (81–96). In the early chapters of Revelation, John addresses the 'seven churches that are in Asia' (Rev. 1: 4): Ephesus, Smyrna, Pergamum, Thyatira, Sardis, Philadelphia, and Laodicea. Tradition associates the ongoing activity of the apostle John with Ephesus.

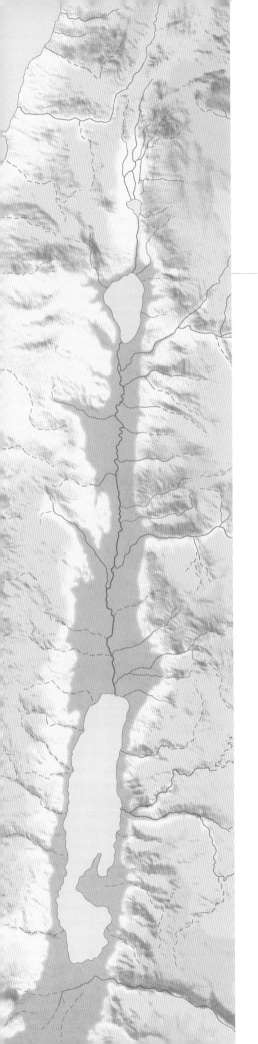

Archaeology in Bible Lands

Archaeology in the Ancient Near East

It is thanks in part to the numerous archaeological excavations and surveys that the wider world of the Bible has become known. (The two maps of archaeological sites here do not reflect any one period, but give an indication of some of the principal locations of archaeological excavations). The section of this atlas on 'Israel and the Nations' has demonstrated that those people with whom the Bible's story is principally concerned frequently came into contact with their nearer neighbours and with those from further afield. The biblical story suggests that there was considerable movement around the ancient world, as peoples moved into new territories, armies conquered new lands, and trade was carried out. The fortunes of those who lived in the area of Palestine were often affected by the changing relative strengths and weaknesses of the great empires around them. Dynasties rose and fell, great cities were built and destroyed, religious ideas developed and legal systems were enacted. People were shaped by the past and by those with whom they came into contact. And just as the biblical writers were at pains to set the stories of the people of Israel and Judah and of the early Christians in the context of the wider world, so the reader of the Bible needs an awareness of the world beyond the bounds of Palestine.

THE BEGINNINGS OF CIVILIZATION

The word 'civilization' literally implies people living together in towns, and some of the earliest evidence for this development comes from the Palestine region itself. At Einan, in the Huleh valley, there have been found remains of human habitation consisting of round pits, whose sides were reinforced with stone walls and in the centre of each of which were stone-lined hearths. There were also many burial pits. These dwellings are dated to the Natufian period which ended in about 8500 BCE. The earliest remains from Jericho also belong to the Natufian culture. The Natufian period gave way to the Neolithic, more specifically the Pre-Pottery Neolithic era, and at Jericho a settlement of round houses developed and was surrounded by a wall—the earliest

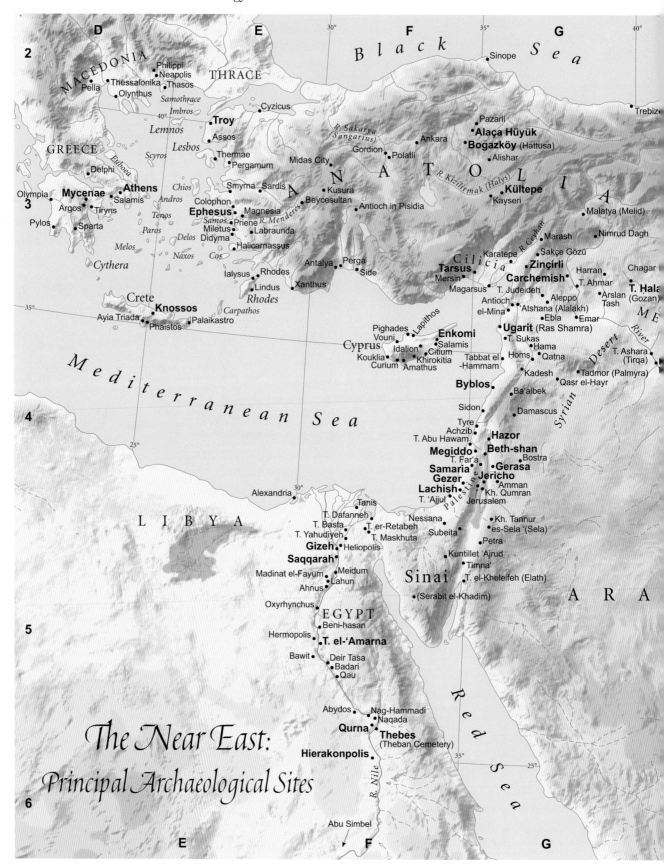

The Near East:
Principal Archaeological Sites

K

L

J

50°

C a s p i a n   S e a

40°

3

Van

Lake
Urmia

Geoy Tepe

Shah Tepe
TurangTepe

Tepe Hissar

Tepe Gawra
Khorsabad
Nineveh
Nimrud (Calah)

M E D I A

Jarmu

Hamadan (Ecbatana)

shur Nuzi

Behistun

Samarra

Tepe Giyan

Siyalk

4

T. Asmar
ar Quf Khafajeh
T. Harmal Ctesiphon
Sippar

Musyan

P E R S I A

'Uqeir Jemdet Nasr
Babylon Kish
Borsippa

Susa

Nippur
Bismaya
Fara (Shuruppak)
Erech (Uruk) Telloh (Lagash)
T. el-'Ubeid Larsa
'Ur
Eridu

Bishapur

Persepolis

Sarvistan

5

ancient coastline

P e r s i a n   G u l f

50°

55°
25°

T. = Tell (mound, city site)

Kh. = Khirbet (ruin)

0   100   → 200 Miles

0   100   200 Kilometres

6

© Oxford University Press

J

K

known walled settlement. On the west, a round tower was constructed. These early fortifications date from the 8th millennium BCE. Probably the key reason for the development of this early settlement was the fact that Jericho was located by an oasis. This enabled irrigation and therefore crop production, providing a constant food supply for the people and their animals, at a time when other people were still forced to move periodically in search of their livelihood. Thus the people of Jericho were among the pioneers of a revolution whereby humans ceased to rely on hunting and what was grown in the wild, and began to control the resources of nature.

Some 4,000 years later in the valleys of the Nile, and the Tigris and Euphrates, another revolution occurred which was also based on irrigation. In each of these fertile areas there were constant supplies of water, providing the assurance of a good livelihood to any group of people capable of collab-

Jericho: round tower from the Neolithic period (8th millennium BCE).

orating to exploit them (see 'Israel and the Nations'). In these regions, for the first time, people submitted themselves and their labour to centralized political powers, recognizing the need for permanent authority and regarding this as having the sanction of the gods. So there emerged the first dynastic rulers, the first organizers of society on a large scale. This social revolution was associated with another, the development of writing. Prosaically, the impetus for this development may, in part at least, have been the necessity to compile lists. People who submitted themselves to central organization needed to be sure that they received a fair share of what had been produced or that they had contributed a fair share of the dues. Writing was a device for recording such things as produce, possessions, and payments, thereby confirming transactions and avoiding disputes. Writing was thus an essential instrument in the process of civilization.

THE BRONZE AGE

After the discovery of writing at the end of the 4th millennium BCE, city life developed and technical knowledge increased, but there were also intervals of depopulation and decline. The pattern recurs with considerable consistency throughout the ancient Near East, in Persia, Mesopotamia, Anatolia, the Levant, and Egypt. It is therefore possible to speak in general terms of a 'Bronze Age' which lasted from *c.*3300 to *c.*1200 BCE, applying roughly to all those regions. It was broken, by two periods of recession, into three phases, known as Early Bronze Age (EBA, *c.*3300–2000), Middle Bronze Age (MBA, *c.*2000–1550), and Late Bronze Age (LBA, *c.*1550–1200). The Early Bronze Age was the time of the building of the great pyramids in Egypt, and of the flourishing of the Sumerian civilization in southern Mesopotamia (modern Iraq) whose high level of craftsmanship is known from, among other discoveries, objects found in the royal tombs at Ur. The Middle Bronze Age was the time of the lawgiver, Hammurabi the Great of Babylon, of the early Hittite rulers (probably of Indo-European origin) in Anatolia, and the flowering of the Minoan culture in Crete. The Late Bronze Age was, in Egypt, the time of the great warrior pharaohs of the 18th Dynasty and also of the religious reformer Akhenaten. In Anatolia, a great Hittite empire rose and declined, and in Upper Mesopotamia the kingdom of Mitaanni was established by another group of Indo-European origins, the Hurrians. On the Mediterranean coast, the kingdom of Ugarit reached its zenith, able to exploit its potential as a port and commercial centre. Seafaring peoples occupied and travelled among the coastlands and islands of the Aegean and east Mediterranean, including the earliest known Greek-speaking colonists, the Achaeans. And in general this was a time when commerce, literacy, and craftsmanship flourished.

THE IRON AGE

The end of the Bronze Age was a time of cataclysm throughout western Asia, with earlier civilizations being brought to an end, and peoples seeking new lands in which to settle. The tradition of the Greek siege of the Anato-

Palestine:
Principal Archaeological Sites

T. Tell (Arabic), Tel (Hebrew): mound; city site

Kh. Khirbet (Arabic): ruin

W. Wadi: watercourse

Biblical names, when known, are given first and
Arabic names are then bracketed.
Hebrew names, when given, follow the Arabic name.

0   5   10 Miles

0   5   10 Kilometres

W   **X**   **Y**   **Z**

Tyre (es-Sur)

Zarephath
Sarepta
(Sarafand)

Sidon (Saida)
33°33'N

Caesarea Philippi (Paneas), (Banias)
Dan (T. el-Qadi; T. Dan)

T. Anafa

Kedesh (T. Qades)

Einan

Shelomi
el-Basseh

Qal'at el-Qurein

Kafr Bir'im
Yiron (Yarun)

el-Jish (Gischala)
Kh. en-Nabratein

Jisr Banat Ya'aqub
Hazor (T. el-Qedah; T. Hazor)

T. et-Taba'iq

Achzib
(ez-Zib; T. Akhziv)

Nahariyeh

Kabri

Tarshiha
Suhmata

el-Buqei'a
Kh. et-Tuleil

Merom (Meirun)
Kh. Shema

Chorazin (Kh. Kerazeh)

Capernaum (T. Hum)
Heptapegon ('Ain Tabgha)
Chinnereth (T. el-'Ureimeh)
prehistoric caves
Kh. el-Minya

*Sea of
Galilee*

Kh. el-'Asheq (En-Gev)

Susithah (Hippos) (Qal'at el-Husn)

Beth-yerah (Kh. el-Kerak)

el-Hammeh
Gadara (Umm Qeis)

T. es-Sumeiriyeh

Ha-Yonim

Cabul (Kabul)

Acco (T. el-Fukhkhar)

Mishal? (Tell Keisan)

Jotapata (Jotbah)
(Kh. Jefat)

Cana
(Kh. Qana)

Umm el-'Amad

Sepphoris (Saffuriyeh)

Magdala (Taricheae)
(Mejdal; Migdal)
Arbela
(Kh. Irbid)

Tiberias

Jabneel (Tel Yin'am;
Tell en-Na'am)

'Ubeidiya

Kishion (Kh. Qasyun;
Tell Qishyon)

Beth-shan Scythopolis (T. el-Husn)

Pella (Kh. Fahil)

Ramoth-gilead
(T. Ramith)

Rihab

Qal'at er-Rabad

Syaminum (T. es-Samak;
T. Shiqmona)

Rosh Maya
(Kh. Rushmiya)

Nahal Oren

Mugharet Abu
Usba' 'Athlit
(Pilgrims' Castle)

W. el-Mughara
(prehistoric caves)

Dor (et-Tantura)

Caesarea

Hadera

Beth She'arim
(Sheikh Abreiq)

Hazorea
(Tell Qiri)

Mugharet el-Kebara

T. el-Mubarak

Neve Sha'anan (Iraq ez-Zigan)

T. Harbaj

T. el-'Amr
'Isfiyeh

T. Abu Hawam

Nazareth

Japhia (Yafa)

Jokneam (T. Qeimun; T. Yoqneam)

R. Kishon

'Affuleh

Beth Alpha (Beit Alfa)

Megiddo (T. el-Mutesellim)

Jezreel (T. Yizre'el)

Beth Hashitta

Rehob (T. es-Sarem; T. Rehov)

Dothan (T. Duthan)

T. el-Mubarak

Meser

Migdal (T. edh-Dhurur; T. Zeror)

Hepher? (Tel Hefer, Tell Ifshar)

Taanach (T. Ta'annak)

*Mt. Tabor
(Jebel et-Tor)*

Tirzah T. Far'a

2   33°   34° 30'   35°   35° 30'   36°   **3**   32° 30'   **2**

Inset map

Dhat Ras

Kh. Tannur

Bozrah

Petra
Tawilan
Beidha

*Dead
Sea*

S   h   e   r   a

A   r   a   b   a   h

Umm el-Biyyarah

Er-Ram

Timna

H. Bodeda
T. el-Kheleifeh

*Gulf of
'Aqaba*   35°

Beer-sheba
T. Isdar

Kurnub

Yeroham

Subeita

Nessana
Abdah

Ramat Matred

'Ain Qedeis

N   e   g   e   b

'Ain Qudeirat

0   10   20   30 Miles

0   10   20   30   40 Kms

31°   30°

u   u

© Oxford University Press

Z

Rabbah Philadelphia ('Amman)

32°

T. Umm Hamad?

Zarethan (T. Umm Hamad?)

R...

'Araq el-Emir

Heshbon (Hesban)

Kh. el-Mekhayet

Medeba (Madaba)

Baal-meon (Ma'in)

Kh. Iskander

Mt. Pisgah (Ras Siyagha)

Beth-haram (T. Iktanu)

Tuleilat el-Ghassul

Machaerus (Kh. Mukawer)

Dibon (Dhiban)

Aroer ('Ara'ir)

Balu'a

Y

'Ader

Kir-Hareseth (el-Kerak)

Bab ed-Dra'

R. Arnon

Callirrhoe

31° 30'

36°

35° 30'

Alexandrium (Qarn Sartabeh)

Shiloh (Seilun)

Mugharet Abu Shinjeh

T. Abu Habil

Gilgal? (Kh. el-Mafjar)

Jericho, O.T.

Jericho

Jericho, N.T.

Deir el-Quruntul

'Ain ed-Duyuk

Deir el-Qilt

Deir Mar Jiryis

Kh. Qumran

En-Eglaim ('Ain Feshkha)

caves

Middin (Kh. Abu Tabaq)

Nibshan? (Kh. el-Maqari)

Dead

Sea

Bethel (Beitin)

Ai (et-Tell)

Khan el-Ahmar

Jerusalem (el-Quds)

Beth Haccherem (Ramat Rahel)

Kh. el-Mird

Kh. es-Siyar'

W. el-Murabba'at

caves

En-gedi

Masada (es-Sebbeh)

Nahal Hever

Cave of the Letters

X

W. Tseelim

Gibeon (el-Jib)

Gibeah? (T. el-Ful)

Shuqba

Modein

el-Qubeibeh

'Ain Karim

Manahath

Bethir (Battir)

Bethlehem

Herodium (J. Fureidis)

Umm Qatafa (prehistoric caves)

Kh. Asideh

Beth-zur (Kh. Tubeiqa)

Mamre (Ramat el-Khalil)

Hebron (Kiriath-arba) (el-Khalil)

'Ain el-Ma'mudiyeh

Mizpah (T. en-Nasbeh)

Qaryat el-'Inab

T. Beit Mirsim

Debir (Kh. Rabud)

Eshtemoa (es-Samu')

Jattir (Kh. 'Attir, H. Yatir)

En-rimmon? (Tel Halif, Kh. Khuweilifeh)

Beer-sheba (T. es-Saba', T. Beer Sheva)

Hormah? (Tel Masos, Kh. el-Meshash)

Arad (T. el-Milh, Tel Malhata)

Arad (T. 'Arad)

Mampsis (Kurnub)

31° 01'N

35°

T. Makmish

T. el-Qasileh

Aphek (T. Ras el-'Ain)

Benei Berak

Joppa (Jaffa)

Gath-rimmon? (T. el-Jerisheh)

Eben-ezer? ('Izbet Sartah)

T. Qudadi

Dhahrat Humraiyeh

el-Jisr

Eltekeh? (T. esh-Shallaf)

Gath (Gittaim) (T. Ras Abu Humeid)

Gezer (T. Abu Shusheh)

Emmaus ('Imwas)

Timnah (T. el-Batashi)

Beth-shemesh (T. er-Rumeileh)

Beit Jimal

Bethletepha (Beit Nattif)

Kh. el-Hubeileh

Moresheth-gath? (T. el-Judeideh)

Beth Gubrin (Beit Jibrin)

Mareshah (T. Sandahannah)

Azekah (T. Zakariyeh)

Gath? (T. es-Safi)

Libnah? (T. Bornat)

Lachish (T. ed-Duweir)

Eglon? (T. el-Hesi)

Ekron (Kh. El-Muqanna', T. Miqne)

T. el Kheidar, T. Mor...

Ashdod (Esdud, T. Ashdod)

Azotus-Paralius (Minet el-Qala')

Ashkelon (Ascalon)

Ziklag?

W

T. Abu Matar, Kh. Beter

6

5

6

6

Gaza Maioumas

Gaza (el-Ghazza)

Beth-eglaim (T. el-'Ajjul)

T. er-Ruqeish

Deir el-Balah

Yurza (T. Jemme)

Sharuhen (T. Far'ah)

34° 30'

34° 30'

same scale

V

31° 30'

32°

5

6

lian city of Troy may reflect this turbulent time. Among those on the move were the so-called 'Sea Peoples', who may have originated in the Aegean region and who sought to invade Egypt but were repulsed. They included the Philistines who settled in the coastal strip which ultimately came to reflect their name, the Plain of Philistia. Some have seen the biblical traditions of the arrival of a new group, the Israelites, into the Palestine area and the destruction of cities belonging to earlier inhabitants, as reflecting this period. But that the beginning of the Iron Age coincided with the emergence of a people which can appropriately be called Israelite (or 'Proto-Israelite') has been widely accepted.

Archaeology and the Bible

DEFINITIONS: 'ARCHAEOLOGY' AND 'BIBLICAL ARCHAEOLOGY'

A literal meaning of the word 'archaeology' might be 'the study of antiquities'. But in practice the word has come to refer to the recovery of and the study of the material remains of an ancient culture, including its written records. Since the biblical writings are set in the context of ancient cultures and are the product of ancient cultures, the importance of archaeology in shedding light on those cultures and thereby aiding the study of the Bible cannot be over-emphasized. The term 'biblical archaeology' has been thought by some to be inappropriate, implying that there is a special sort of archaeology which is 'biblical' and which differs from other archaeology. There is the caricature of the 'biblical archaeologist', with spade in one hand and Bible in the other, looking for evidence of what he or she is reading about! Some prefer an alternative term, for example 'Syro-Palestinian Archaeology' (so William Dever). But the term 'biblical archaeology' is often simply used as a convenient short-hand term to refer to those results of archaeology which are relevant to the study of the Bible, and as such it can be defended. The term also has the advantage of embracing archaeology from a much wider area than Palestine. Nevertheless, archaeology in Palestine will often provide a more direct witness to the peoples of Israel and Judah, in that they shed light on some of the places in which they lived, and the objects they made and used. Although the known amount of written material from Palestine has increased considerably in recent years, it is still the case that relatively little such material has been preserved when compared with some of the archives of tablets or monumental inscriptions of certain other peoples. An obvious exception is what is often referred to as the 'library' from Qumran comprising the Dead Sea Scrolls.

WHAT CAN BE EXPECTED OF 'BIBLICAL ARCHAEOLOGY'?

The question is an important one, because sometimes exaggerated claims have been made, of the 'archaeology proves (or disproves) the Bible' type. It is perhaps because archaeology has been thought to be more 'scientific' than other critical, exegetical, and theological approaches that words like 'proof' have been used. But it is essential to bear in mind that there is often as much interpretation involved in the understanding of an archaeological discovery as there is in the understanding of a biblical passage. The ancient identity of a site may be unknown or uncertain. A piece of ancient writing may be fragmentary, difficult to read or translate, and even if the translation is clear the precise significance may not be. The purpose or function of an artefact or structure may not always be easily or correctly understood.

Despite the difficulties and the need for caution, archaeology's contribution to the study of the Bible has been immense, not least in providing information about the wider context of the world in which those who produced the Bible lived and in which the biblical traditions are set. The section on 'Israel and the Nations' has shown that the fortunes of the inhabitants of Palestine often depended on the relative strengths and weaknesses of the great powers of the ancient Near East. The biblical writings were produced in the wider literary context of the ancient Near East. The suggestion that some biblical writings may show parallels to or even dependency upon those of other ancient peoples has sometimes been found to be disturbing, as though questioning or devaluing their special nature. Yet archaeology has made it possible to appreciate that the writers were able to draw upon a great variety of different types of literary expression and that their own claim to belong to an older and wider world is indeed justified. Judaism and Christianity developed in the midst of many and varied religious beliefs and practices, learning from some of them and coming into conflict with some of them.

THE PRACTICE OF ARCHAEOLOGY

A Bible atlas is not the place to go into detail about archaeological methods and techniques, but some brief comments are appropriate. Some archaeological work involves the making of surveys, involving predominantly the careful study of surface remains. More often the approach involves excavation, frequently of a 'tell'. A tell is an artificial mound, built up often over many centuries as a result of successive settlements being built on the same spot. After a town had been destroyed or fallen into ruin, new buildings would be erected above the remains of the former structures. Although stone might be used for foundations, for supporting columns, or in high-status buildings, much construction would have been of mud brick which would weather into a layer of soil. The successive layers of occupation are known as 'strata'. The careful digging of trenches or, more frequently recently, square 'sections' enables the successive strata of an occupied site to be examined and a relative chronology produced. The careful preservation of the baulks (the soil left between trenches or sections) allows the charting of the vertical 'wall' and the checking of the stratigraphy. (The development of this technique is associated particularly with Kathleen Kenyon.) Domestic objects show developments and variations which may be pointers to relative dating. In particular the study of pottery types has proved of immense value

The Tell of Beth-shan.

for dating purposes. The use of pottery chronology was developed by Flinders Petrie and refined by W. F. Albright. Sometimes a discovery within a stratum will enable it to be dated accurately. Examples include a stele of Seti I found at Beth-shan, and a statue base of Rameses VI discovered at Megiddo. A cartouche, bearing the name of a pharaoh, or a coin indicating the ruler in whose reign it was minted, may be valuable pointers to the date of a stratum.

Scientific techniques are now available to aid the archaeologist, and archaeology has become a much more multidisciplinary science. For example, Carbon 14 (radiocarbon) dating may be used for estimating the age of ancient organic material, including human remains. Analysis of pollen grains in soil (palynology) can be of value for dating as well as providing information about plant life, crops, etc. (See below on 'Human, animal, and plant remains'.) There is a method, using thermo-luminescence, for determining the date of the firing of ceramics. The use of magnetometry can help to locate buildings and objects under the surface of the ground. The availability of high-quality photography enables the stages of excavation and the location of objects to be recorded, a technique which represents a major advance on the drawings and sketches of earlier excavations. This is very important because archaeology is, of necessity, a destructive science. Once the digging has been done, it cannot be undone.

For the purpose of considering various types of archaeological discovery, it is convenient to divide them into several broad categories; buildings and artefacts; tombs and burial practices; human, animal, and plant remains; and written documents.

Buildings and artefacts

Archaeology can shed light on the nature of ancient towns and cities, revealing the types of fortification, wall, and gateway constructed to defend a city. Different types of wall, such as the 'casemate' and the 'offset-inset' were used. Walls of the 'casemate' type have sometimes been associated in particular with the early monarchic period in Israel. A variety of types of city gate were developed, including the six-room gates which have been thought to be evidence of Solomon's building activity at Hazor, Gezer, and Megiddo. Major buildings on a site, often in prominent positions, may be, for example, palaces, official residences, administrative headquarters, or sanctuaries. Sometimes their function will not be clear, while at other times there may a clue to the nature of the building. The presence of an altar for sacrifice (perhaps with animal bones in the vicinity, as in the circular 'high place' at Megiddo) or an incense altar (such as that from Taanach, decorated with animals and sphinxes) will suggest a cultic usage. Or jars with official stamps on their handles (such as those stamped *lmlk*, 'to/for the king', at Lachish), probably used for the collection of taxes in kind, may suggest an administrative building.

Archaeology also reveals the types of dwelling in which people lived. One which deserves particular mention is the so-called 'four-roomed' house which became popular in the Iron Age and has often been thought to be typically Israelite. A 'standard' house of this type would have a doorway leading into a room (which has sometimes been thought to be a courtyard) on either side of which and parallel to it, separated by pillars or walls, were two more rooms, with a fourth room running along behind the other three. There was probably more than one storey. There were variations on this basic pattern, and the actual number of rooms might differ. Sometimes, where convenient, the house would abut the city wall, using it as the rear wall of the house.

In addition to dwellings, other structures or installations may shed light on the way of life of the people, for example, storehouses, grain silos, and places for the production of olive oil. Sometimes methods of securing a water supply are revealed, such as the digging and plastering of cisterns. At Qumran water was preserved in a system of cisterns, some of which were stepped, raising the question whether they were simply intended for water storage or whether they might have been used for ritual washing. More elaborate provisions might include the construction of aqueducts, such as that which brought water into Caesarea Maritima. Access to water from within a city's fortifications was important in times of siege, and in some places, such as Hazor and Megiddo, this involved the hewing of tunnels through solid rock to gain access to a spring. A remarkable example is 'Hezekieh's Tunnel' in Jerusalem (see 'Jerusalem in the 1st Millennium BCE').

But the function of a building may not always be certain, as witnessed by the debate which continues to surround the identification of certain structures at Megiddo, originally suggested to be Solomon's Stables. (See on 'Megiddo'.)

Archaeology has also revealed numerous smaller artefacts which help to build up a picture of the way of life of the people. These include pottery vessels of various shapes, sizes, and quality and, as already noted, these may be of considerable importance for dating purposes. Among other types of find are tools and weapons, jewellery, ornaments, statuettes, and coins.

Tombs and burial practices

Archaeology has revealed a great variety of types of burial, from simple interments or cave burials to elaborate tombs, with evidence from right across the historical and indeed prehistorical spectrum. The presence of various objects placed alongside the bodies suggests a belief in the necessity of making some sort of provision for the dead, though the extent to which such funerary goods provide evidence for a belief in an afterlife is uncertain. Burials from the Middle Paleolithic period were in pits, with the body in a contracted position. From the Natufian culture come contracted burials but also burials involving just the skull. In the Neolithic period, burials were sometimes made beneath the floors of houses. From this period come the famous

Excavations in progress: an anthropoid coffin (*c.*14th–13th century BCE) being unearthed at Deir el Balaḥ.

plastered skulls from Jericho (see below on 'Human, animal, and plant remains'). A remarkable feature of burials from the Chalcolithic period was the use of clay ossuaries. These boxes were often in the shape of houses and were used for the storage of bones after the decomposition of the flesh. In the Early Bronze Age, many tombs comprised a shaft leading into a burial chamber, but there is also evidence of the construction of megalithic tombs. Stone-built tombs, sometimes inside towns and close to houses, are known from the Middle Bronze Age. In the Negeb, the construction of tumuli, covering stone cists in which the body would have been placed, was widespread. Shaft tombs were widely used in the Late Bronze Age.

The Iron Age saw the development of multi-chamber tombs, with benches along the walls on which the bodies would be laid, and sometimes with places for the collection together of disconnected bones. Thereafter, a variety of types of tomb continued to be used, ranging from small individual graves to rock-hewn structures and extensive catacombs. Examples of some differing styles of tomb construction are to be found in the Kidron valley. Many Roman period tombs comprised a corridor leading from a forecourt into one or more chambers in whose walls were burial recesses (*loculi*). From Jerusalem come some elaborate examples such as the so-called 'Tombs of the Kings' and the tomb of Queen Helena of Adiabene. The outer doors of some such tombs would be blocked by a rectangular stone slab, but others would have been closed by a large circular stone which would be rolled in a groove. In the 1st century CE, a new type of tomb was developed, involving benches inside arched recesses (*arcosolia*). The use of ossuaries was widespread in the early Roman period.

Human, animal, and plant remains

The discovery of human and animal remains has always been a feature of archaeology. Cemeteries and tombs have yielded human bones, and the discovery of animal bones has sometimes been a pointer to the identification of a site as a place of sacrifice. At Lachish, for example, a tomb in a large cave contained the remains of about 2,000 bodies, some of which showed signs of charring, suggesting the possibility that they were deposited there after some attack on the city, perhaps at the time of Sennacherib's campaign in 701 or when it fell to the Babylonians *c*.597. A feature of some of the skulls found at Lachish is that they may show evidence of trepanning, the surgical removal of a segment of bone to relieve pressure on the brain. A somewhat different example of the discovery of human remains is that of the plastered skulls found at Jericho and a number of other sites, dating from the Pre-Pottery Neolithic B period (that is, from the late 8th millennium to the early 6th millennium BCE) and perhaps reflecting some form of ancestor cult.

In recent years, the application of archaeozoology (the study of animal remains) and palaeoethnobotany (the study of botanical remains – including palynology, the analysis of pollen grains in soil) has begun to make an increasing impact on the study of the ancient Near East in general and the

Levant in particular. They shed light, for example, on the ancient environments, the domestication of plants and animals, diet, various cultural practices, and even such things as trade (showing, for example, whether wood used for building was local or imported). Of particular interest for the study of the Bible has been evidence for the domestication of and the eating of the pig, in view of the biblical prohibitions (for example, Lev. 11: 7). Evidence suggests that, after the Middle Bronze Age, apart from its use by the Philistines, the eating of the pig was not common until the Hellenistic period. The date of the domestication of the camel has been an issue in the context of the discussion of the dating of certain biblical traditions and whether references to camels are anachronistic. Evidence suggests the presence of camels in the Levant in the 3rd millennium, though it is not clear whether these were wild or domestic. After the beginning of the 1st millennium BCE, camel bones begin to appear in a number of places, although they are still relatively rare. From Tell Jemme, south of Gaza, there is evidence of significant use of the camel from the 8th to the 7th centuries, perhaps reflecting its position close to major trade routes, and that camel numbers increased in the Persian period. More generally, the use of the camel seems to have become more widespread in the Levant during the Persian period.

Written documents

Written documents revealed by archaeology are of a great variety of types and what follows is illustrative – in no sense exhaustive – and only attempts to deal with the principal types. Particular mention will be made of some examples of documents relevant to the study of the Bible.

Inscriptions were carved on the walls of buildings and other structures, or even into the rock of a cliff or a tunnel or a tomb. The 'Behistun Inscription' (see on 'Writing Systems') was carved high on a rock face. In Egypt, carvings on the walls and columns of temples and other buildings, and texts painted on the inner walls of pyramids and burial chambers have provided a major source of information about Egyptian history and religion. Inside 'Hezekiah's Tunnel' in Jerusalem was the famous 'Siloam Inscription' describing the tunnel's construction (see 'Jerusalem in the 1st Millennium BCE'). Approximately contemporary was the inscription carved into the lintel of a rock-cut tomb at Silwan (Siloam), overlooking the Kidron valley and Jerusalem. The damaged inscription suggested that the tomb was that of someone whose name ended -*yahu* (usually anglicized as -*iah* in personal names) and who was (literally) 'over the house', that is, a steward. In Isaiah 22: 15–16, this precise description (NRSV 'master of the household') is used of the royal steward Shebna, who is criticized for 'cutting a tomb on the height'. Although the form of the name used in Isaiah does not have the ending preserved on the inscription, it is likely that it is an abbreviated form of the fuller name Shebaniah, and it is therefore possible that the tomb inscription refers to the person mentioned in Isaiah. From the theatre at Caesarea comes an inscription carved on stone which, although damaged and incomplete, almost certainly

One of the most important advances in human civilization was the invention of writing. The ancient Near East saw the development of several systems of writing. Before the end of the 4th millennium BCE two important systems had developed, one at each end of the Fertile Crescent.

Cuneiform

In the southern part of Mesopotamia, the Sumerians had begun to use simple depictions of objects, drawn on clay tablets with a pointed stylus of reed or wood. The fact that these pictures were accompanied by what were

Clay tablet inscribed with a pictographic script and indications of numbers.

probably indications of numbers suggests that they were perhaps lists. In the course of time, the pictures were simplified to a limited number of strokes which, because of the method of writing using a stylus on a clay tablet, were 'wedge-shaped', i.e. cuneiform. Gradually the signs came to stand not only for the name of the object portrayed, but for the sound conveyed by the name. This cuneiform script was adopted by the Akkadians to write their Semitic language which, by the second millennium, had become virtually a lingua franca throughout much of the ancient Near East. The Akkadian language was deciphered as a result of the discovery of a huge trilingual inscription carved into the rock on a cliff face at Behistun, in what is now Iran, recording the successes of Darius the Great (522–486) over his opponents after his succession to the throne (see p. 125). The

three languages of the inscription were Old Persian, Elamite, and Akkadian. An officer in the English army, Major Henry Rawlinson, managed at no little risk to his life to copy the Old Persian and Akkadian inscriptions between 1843 and 1847, and the former proved to be the key for the decipherment of the latter.

Hieroglyphs

In Egypt, another script based on the drawing of pictures was developed. This came to be known as 'hieroglyphic'. Signs which originally represented a simple object were grouped together to express more complicated ideas, and gradually they too came to represent sounds. The decipherment of hieroglyphics came about as a result of Napoleon's 1798 campaign to Egypt. In the course of excavations in preparation for the construction of a fort near Rosetta in the Nile Delta region, there was discovered a black basalt slab with writing on

The Rosetta Stone.

it. This turned out to be a record of a decree issued by the priests of Memphis early in the 2nd century BCE. The inscription was bilingual, even though the writing was in three sections, the topmost in the hieroglyphic script, the middle in the demotic script (a more everyday form of Egyptian handwriting), and crucially the bottom section was in Greek. Although it was surrendered to the British in 1801 and taken to the British Museum, it was a Frenchman, Jean François Champollion who, building on earlier work on the proper names in the inscription, was able to use the 'Rosetta Stone' in achieving the essentials of the decipherment of hieroglyphics.

Alphabets

A major advance in the development of writing systems can also be observed in the ancient Near East. The cuneiform and hieroglyphic scripts required large numbers of signs to write them, hence the development of systems based on the simplest consonantal sounds. Early in the 20th century, inscriptions were found in or around the turquoise mining centre of Serabit el-

Proto-Sinaitic script from Serabit el-Khadim.

Khadim in the Sinai peninsula. These were thought to have been written by Semitic workers employed by the Egyptians and to date from the 15th century BCE. The picture-signs were perhaps borrowed from the Egyptians, but the important advance was that they represented a single consonantal sound, probably that the first consonant of the name of the depicted object. These 'Proto-Sinaitic' inscriptions represent one of the earliest known examples of an alphabet.

Further north, and certainly by the 14th century BCE, the scribes of Ugarit were using the cuneiform method for writing their own Semitic language. It is possible that it was developed from an earlier linear script, adapted to

the cuneiform method. It comprised about 30 relatively simple signs. (For a picture, see on 'Ugarit'.) It can appropriately be described as an alphabet since almost all the signs represent a single consonantal sound.

The linear alphabetic method of writing was adapted for the writing of Phoenician, Hebrew, and Aramaic and other languages or dialects such as Moabite. Probably the earliest example of the Old (or palaeo-) Hebrew script is the 'Gezer Calendar' dating from about the 10th century BCE. (For a brief description and a picture, see on 'Climate, Flora and Fauna: main crops'.) Other examples of its use can be seen in the Siloam Inscription (see on 'Jerusalem in the 1st Millennium BCE') and in the Lachish Letters (see on 'Lachish'). A fine example of this script is the seal of Shema, the servant of Jeroboam, the original of which was found at Megiddo. The 'square' characters familiar from the Hebrew Bible and other documents such as the Dead Sea Scrolls (though there are a few examples of palaeo-Hebrew in those texts) were adopted from the Aramaic script. Aramaic was widely used throughout the Persian Empire and the Aramaic script gradually supplanted the Old Hebrew script for the writing of Hebrew, just as Aramaic began to replace Hebrew as the everyday spoken language.

It was the Greeks who made the further development of introducing vowels to the alphabet. They had encountered Phoenician, probably in the context of trade, and adopted their script. Since they did not need all the consonantal sounds of Phoenician, they retained those which were required but used others to represent vowels. Thus the first letter of the Phoenician alphabet which was a consonant (the equivalent of Hebrew 'àlep) became in Greek *alpha*, the 'a' vowel. The Greek alphabet was adopted and adapted by the Romans for the writing of Latin.

Cast of a seal from Megiddo, showing a lion and bearing the inscription '(Belonging) to Shema, Servant of Jeroboam'.

mentions Pontius Pilate. An inscription from Herod's Temple in Jerusalem, written in Greek, warns Gentiles not to enter the court of Israel on pain of death. (See Acts 21: 27–9, which record that Paul was accused of having introduced a Gentile into the Temple, thereby defiling it.)

A number of important inscriptions take the form of stelae or obelisks, inscribed standing stones set up to record, for example, the deeds of a king. The earliest mention of a people 'Israel' is to be found on the Stele of Merneptah, set up in Egypt towards the end of the 13th century BCE and claiming to record the victories of the pharaoh. From the 9th century comes the stele of Mesha, king of Moab, sometimes known as the 'Moabite Stone'. This inscription, found at Dibon in Moab, mentions the Israelite king Omri, and gives a contemporary account from a Moabite perspective of events recounted in 2 Kings 3. King Jehu is mentioned on the 'Black Obelisk' of Shalmaneser III, which was erected by the Assyrian king at Calah early in the second half of the 9th century. Not only is Jehu mentioned, there is even a picture of him prostrating himself before Shalmaneser and bringing tribute – an event not mentioned in the biblical narrative. From Tel Dan come fragments of a victory stele, dating from the 9th century and written in Aramaic, which mentions the 'king of Israel' and the 'house of David'. The interpretation of the phrase translated as 'house of David' has been a matter of considerable debate, but it is possible that this inscription contains the first piece of extrabiblical evidence for the existence of King David. A stele which does include some account of the deeds of a king, but whose primary purpose was somewhat different, is the Stele of Hammurabi. This was set up by the great king of Babylon who reigned in the first half of the 2nd millennium BCE, and contains his famous Law Code, one of a number of ancient Near Eastern law codes with which the biblical laws can be compared.

A great many ancient documents take the form of clay tablets which provided a convenient surface for the writing of the cuneiform script (see on 'Writing Systems'). Mention can only be made of a limited number of examples here. Before turning to tablets of what might be termed 'conventional shape', that is, square or rectangular with writing on the obverse and reverse, it should be noted that clay was also used for documents of other shapes. For example, the six-sided clay 'Prism of Sennacherib' contains annals which report his early military campaigns, including that of 701 BCE in which he claims to have besieged 46 fortified cities of Judah and surrounded King Hezekiah in Jerusalem (see 2 Kgs. 18: 13–19: 36). Interestingly he does not specifically mention his siege of Lachish (see on 'Lachish'). The 'Cyrus Cylinder', also made of clay, contains an account by the Persian king of his conquest of Babylon in 539. This document does not specifically mention the Jewish exiles, but it does refer to Cyrus' policy of returning captive peoples to their homelands.

The numerous clay tablets found in the course of archaeological excavations in the ancient Near East contain a great variety of types of material, including administrative texts, legal documents, letters, ritual texts, myths, and epics. One advantage of conventionally shaped tablets was that they could be 'filed' in sequence and stored in archives. At Ebla, for example, tablets were discovered still in the rows in which they had been stored despite the collapse of the shelving on which they were presumably placed. Other major archives have been found in such places as the Amorite city of Mari on the Euphrates and the Hurrian city of Nuzi, east of the Tigris. The majority of the Mari texts probably date from the 18th century BCE and shed light on events and the way of life at that time. Of particular interest is the fact that the texts refer to a number of types of person and activity which might appropriately be described as 'prophetic'. The texts from Nuzi date from the 16th and 15th centuries and provide evidence of Hurrian culture. Both the Mari and Nuzi texts have been used in discussions about the extent to which the stories of the Patriarchs in the Bible reflect any historical reality. In particular, apparent similarities were noticed between practices mentioned in legal texts from Nuzi and in the biblical narrative. But the extent of such parallels has been overstated, and the importance of the Mari and Nuzi texts lies in the evidence they provide of life in the first half of the 2nd millennium BCE.

At Ugarit were found numerous clay tablets, in archives in the royal palace, in business premises, and private houses, and from what may perhaps appropriately be described as a temple library (see on 'Ugarit'). From Emar, on the Euphrates south east of Aleppo, come tablets from the 13th century, including a number, found in the ruins of a temple, which describe religious rituals. From the library of King Ashurbanipal in Nineveh, dating from the 7th century BCE, are tablets containing copies of the Babylonian account of creation, *Enuma Elish*, and of the *Epic of Gilgamesh*. These stories, which go back to much earlier originals, have been thought to contain some parallels with the creation and flood stories in Genesis.

Another medium for writing was the ostracon, or potsherd. A piece of broken pot could provide a suitable flat surface on which to write, using perhaps a brush, or a pen made from a sharpened stick, and soot mixed with water and gum arabic for ink. Pieces of pot might be used for recording deliveries of produce, such as was the case with the 8th-century ostraca from Samaria which provide useful information about personal and place names of the period. Or they might be used for writing letters. Particularly noteworthy are the Lachish Letters (see on 'Lachish').

It is perhaps appropriate to mention here that sometimes inscriptions are found as part of the decoration on storage jars (*pithoi*). A particularly important example comes from Kuntillet 'Ajrud, dating from the end of the 9th or beginning of the 8th century. The jar was decorated with depictions of various animals and a stylized tree and also two standing figures and a seated figure playing a lyre. There is also an inscription, close to the standing

Tablet XI of the Epic of Gilgamesh, from Nineveh, dating from the 7th century BCE. The tablet contains one of the Mesopotamian versions of the Flood Story.

figures, which contains the phrase, 'I bless you by Yahweh of Samaria and his *asherah*'. Another storage jar from Kuntillet 'Ajrud bears an inscription which mentions 'Yahweh of Teman and his *asherah*'. (A roughly contemporary inscription from Khirbet el-Qom, carved in stone and originally in a burial cave, contains the request that a certain Uriyahu may be blessed by Yahweh, and saved from his enemies by 'his *asherah*'.) The significance of these inscription has been much debated, in particular whether the term *asherah* refers to a cult object or to the goddess of that name and, if the latter, whether this is evidence for the belief that Yahweh had a consort. Such inscriptions are very important for the study of the religious beliefs of the time.

Another important writing material is associated particularly with Egypt: papyrus, prepared from strips of the pith of an aquatic reed. This produced an excellent surface for writing or illustrations. An advantage of papyrus was that it could be folded. Examples of papyrus documents relevant to the study of the Bible include the following: the Egyptian text 'The Wisdom of Amenemope' which has close parallels with parts of the Book of Proverbs; the papyri from Elephantine on the Nile, dating from the 5th century BCE and written in Aramaic, which shed light on the life and religion of the Jewish colony that established itself there; and the papyrus fragment of the Gospel of John, dating from the early part of the 2nd century CE and probably the earliest known New Testament manuscript.

The use of parchment was an important development in the production of written manuscripts. It was made from the skins of sheep and goats, tanned and cut into sheets. These might in turn be sewn together to produce scrolls. Especially noteworthy among parchment documents are the Dead Sea

A section of the 'Temple Scroll' from Qumran, showing where two pieces of parchment have been joined, how the text is written in columns, and how the upper part of the columns has been damaged.

Scrolls, the library of the Jewish group (probably Essenes) based at Qumran, close to the shore of the Dead Sea, from the 2nd century BCE to the 1st century CE. They include not only important community documents but the earliest known manuscripts of considerable sections of the Hebrew Bible. These scrolls have been of immense value for the study of the biblical text and of the beliefs and practices of a branch of Judaism which flourished at the turn of the millennia. Parchment came to be used for the production of the codex, that is, sheets bound together in book form. The Codex Sinaiticus, dating from the 4th century CE, was so-called because it was found at the Monastery of St Catharine in the Sinai peninsula in 1844. It was written on parchment in Greek uncial (capital) letters. The codex originally contained the text of the Septuagint, the New Testament, and a number of Deutero-canonical works, though now some 300 pages are missing from the Septuagint section. It has made an important contribution to the study of the text of the Bible.

Mention has been made above of inscriptions in tombs, and it also appropriate to mention that on some ossuaries (boxes carved out of stone, in which bones would be stored after the flesh had decayed) were inscriptions usually indicating the name or names of those whose bones were inside. These seem to have been used in and around Jerusalem from the latter part of the 1st century BCE until the early 2nd century CE. The suggestion that some of them bear Christian symbols, particularly crosses, is no longer thought to be a likely explanation of the marks. Excitement over the apparent discovery of an ossuary bearing an inscription mentioning 'James the brother of Jesus' is widely held to have been misplaced because the inscription was a hoax.

Extra-biblical texts and the Bible

The rich variety of types of written material from the ancient Near East enables the world from which the Bible emerged and in which the Bible is set to be seen in clearer focus. Much attention has been paid to the myths and legends of the Mesopotamians and the Canaanites, not least because of the Bible's own suggestion that the people of Israel and Judah emerged from Mesopotamian ancestry, settled among Canaanites, and were exiled in Babylon. But the mythology of other ancient peoples such as the Egyptians and the Hittites, now known as a result of archaeological activity, have also been welcomed as shedding light on the religious beliefs of the ancient Near East. Light has been shed on religious practices thanks to the discovery of ritual texts, sacrifice lists, divinatory texts, prayers, and incantations. There are texts which refer to the practice of prophecy, and others which belong to the Wisdom tradition. Ancient law codes reveal that sophisticated legal systems had developed, and that it was believed that the law had divine sanction. The discovery of ancient Near Eastern treaties and the analysis of their form has given rise to the suggestion that this treaty-form is reflected in some passages which present one of the profoundest of the Bible's religious themes, that of covenant.

It is not only in what might broadly be termed the field of religion that ancient textual material is relevant to the study of the Bible. Annals and lists of rulers can help with the establishing of chronology and shed light on the political world. Administrative documents, even the most mundane, provide clues as to the way of life of those who produced them. Lexical texts contribute to the study of the languages of the biblical world and, from time to time, on the languages of the Bible, Hebrew, Aramaic, and Greek.

CHRONOLOGY

DATES	PERIOD	SYRIA-PALESTINE	EGYPT	MESOPOTAMIA	ASIA-MINOR
c.43,000–18,000 BCE	UPPER PALEOLITHIC				
c.18,000–8500 BCE	EPIPALEOLITHIC				
c.8500–4500 BCE	NEOLITHIC				
c.4500–3300 BCE	CHALCOLITHIC		Early stages of urbanization throughout the Near East		
c.3300–2000 BCE	EARLY BRONZE AGE				
3300–3100 BCE	Early Bronze I		Earliest forms of writing Full urbanization Sumerian culture develops		
3100–2700 BCE	Early Bronze II	In Egyptian sphere	Political unification Early Dynastic period	Floruit of Sumerian culture	
2700–2300 BCE	Early Bronze III	Flourishing city-states	Old Kingdom Dynasties 3–5	Sargon of Akkad Naram-Sin of Akkad Gudea of Lagash	
2300–2000 BCE	Early Bronze IV	Decline/abandonment of city-states	First Intermediate Period	Third Dynasty of Ur	
c.2000–1550 BCE	MIDDLE BRONZE AGE				
2000–1650 BCE	Middle Bronze I–II	Revival of urbanism Invention of alphabet	Middle Kingdom Dynasties 11–12	Amorite kingdoms Shamshi-Adad of Assyria (c.1813–1781) Hammurabi of Babylon (c.1792–1750)	Rise of Hittites
1650–1550 BCE	Middle Bronze III		Second Intermediate/ Hyksos Period		
c.1550–1200 BCE	LATE BRONZE AGE	In Egyptian sphere Rise of Mitanni in north Ugarit flourishes Collapse of city-states	New Kingdom Dynasties 18–19 Thutmose III (1479–1425) Akenhaten (1352–1336) Seti I (1294–1279) Rameses II (1279–1213) Merneptah (1213–1203) Sea Peoples' invasions begin		Hittites challenge Egypt for control of Syria Hittite empire collapses Trojan War

DATES	PERIOD	SYRIA-PALESTINE	EGYPT	MESOPOTAMIA
c.1200–586 BCE	IRON AGE			

c.1200–1025 BCE	Iron I	Israel emerges in Canaan
		Philistines settle on SW coast
		Small city-states develop in
		   Phoenicia, Syria,
		   Transjordan
			Rameses III
			(1184–53)
				Resurgence of Assyria
				Tiglath-pileser I
				(1114–1076)

c.1025–586 BCE	Iron II			

c.1025–928 BCE	Iron IIA	United Monarchy in Israel
		   Saul (1025–1005)
		   David (1005–965)
		   Solomon (968–928)		

c.928–722 BCE	Iron IIB	Divided Monarchy
		Israel Judah
		Jeroboam I Rehoboam
		 (928–907) (928–911)
		Omri
		 (882–871)
		 capital at Samaria
		 Ahab Jehoshapat
		 (873–852) (867–846)
		 Jehu Athaliah
		 (842–814) (842–836)
		     Jehoash
		     (836–798)
		Jehoash
		 (800–788)
		Jeroboam II
		 (788–747)
		Hoshea Ahaz
		 (732–722) (743/735–727/715)
			Shishak I invades Palestine	Rise of Neo-Assyrian empire(925)
				
				Shalmaneser III (858–824)
				  Battle of Qarqar (853)
				
				Adad-nirari III (811–783)
				
				Tiglath-pileser III (745–727)
				  Assyrian conquest of the Levant
				Shalmaneser V (727–722)
				  Samaria captured (722)

c.722–586 BCE	Iron IIC	Judah
		 Hezekiah
		  (727/715–698/687)
		 Manasseh
		  (698/687–642)
		 Josiah (639–609)
		
		 Jehoahaz (609)
		
		Jehoiakim (608–598)
		Jehoiachin (597)
		Zedekiah (597–586)
		 Capture of Jerusalem (586)
			Egypt conquered by
			 Assyria (671)
			Psammetichus I (664–610)
			
			Neco II (610–595)
				Sargon II (722–705)
				Sennacherib (705–681)
				 Attack on Judah and
				  siege of Jerusalem (701)
				Esarhaddon (681–669)
				Ashurbanipal (669–627)
				Rise of Babylon
				Assyrian capital of
				 Nineveh captured (612)
				Nebuchadrezzar II
				 (604–562) of Babylon

DATES	PERIOD	SYRIA-PALESTINE	MESOPOTAMIA	GREECE AND ROME
c.586–539 BCE	NEO-BABYLONIAN		Nabonidus (556–539)	
539–332 BCE	PERSIAN	Some exiles return from Babylon (538) Second Temple built (520–515) Nehemiah governor of Judah (c.445–430)	Cyrus II (the Great) (559–530) Capture of Babylon Cambyses (530–522) Capture of Egypt (525) Darius I (522–486) Xerxes (486–465) Artaxerxes I (465–424) Artaxerxes II (405–359)	Greeks repel Persian invasions Peloponnesian War (431–404)
332–63 BCE	HELLENISTIC	Seleucus I (312/311–281) controls Syria and Mesopotamia Ptolemy I (323–282) controls Egypt, Palestine, Phoenicia Antiochus III (223–187) gains control of southern Syria, Phoenicia, and Judea from Ptolemy IV (202–198) Antiochus IV Epiphanes (175–164) Revolt of the Maccabees (167–164) Hasmonean rule of Judea (165–37) John Hyrcanus (135–104) Alexander Janneus (103–76) Salome Alexandra (76–67)		Alexander the Great (336–323) Defeats Persians at Issus (332) Occupies the Levant and Egypt Rome gains control over Greece (c.188–146; 146: sack of Carthage and Corinth)

DATES	PERIOD	EASTERN MEDITERRANEAN	ROME
63 BCE–330 CE	ROMAN	Pompey conquers the Levant (66–62) Enters Jerusalem (63) Herod the Great king of Judea (37–4) Rebuilds Second Temple (Herod) Antipas (4 BCE–39 CE) Life of Jesus of Nazareth (c.4 BCE–30 CE) Pontius Pilate governor of Judea (26–36) (Herod) Agrippa I (39–44) (Herod) Agrippa II (49–92) First Jewish Revolt in Judea against Rome (66–73) Jerusalem captured (70) Jewish revolts in Egypt, Libya, Cyprus (115–118) Second Jewish Revolt in Judea against Rome (132–135)	Julius Caesar named dictator (49); assassinated (44) Octavian (Augustus) defeats Antony at Actium (31) (emperor 27 BCE–14 CE) Tiberius (14–37 CE) Gaius (Caligula) (37–41) Claudius (41–54) Nero (54–68) Vespasian (69–79) Titus (79–81) Domitian (81–96) Nerva (96–98) Trajan (98–117) Hadrian (117–38)

ILLUSTRATION SOURCES

The author and publishers wish to thank the following for their kind permission to reproduce the following illustrations (*l* = left, *r* = right, *t* = top, *b* = bottom):

The Art Archive, 68 *l* (Dagli Orti), 68 *r* (National Museum Damascus, Syria/Dagli Orti)

www.bridgeman.co.uk, 48 (Bildarchiv Steffens), 69 *r* (Museum of Latakia, Latakia, Syria, Peter Willi)

The Trustees of the British Museum, 9, 43, 45, 70 *b*, 112, 119 t, 121, 192 *r*, 195

©Corbis, 11 (Hulton-Deutsch Collection), 70 *t* (Michael S Yamashita), 127 (Roger Wood), 171 (Michael Boys)

Sonia Halliday Photographs, 10 (Jane Taylor), 13, 23 *t*, 24, 25 (Jane Taylor), 26 *t* (Barry Searle), 41 (Prue Grice), 55, 74, 75, 81, 101 (Jane Taylor), 116, 120, 135, 148, 153, 166, 180 (Jane Taylor), 187

Collection of the Israel Antiquities Authority. Photo © The Israel Museum, Jerusalem, 119 *b*

Juergen Liepe, 39

© Photo RMN/Franck Raux   106

Zev Radovan, www.BibleLandPictures.com, 21, 22, 23 *b*, 26 *b*, 31, 32, 34, 37, 51, 52, 57, 59, 62, 86, 88, 89, 93, 96, 97, 104, 109, 118, 123, 142, 144, 149, 152, 154, 163, 164, 189, 192 *l*, 193, 196

Scala, Florence, Paris, Louvre ©1995, 69 *l*

Science Photo Library/Earth Satellite Corporation, 6, 18–19

Picture research by Sandra Assersohn

Chronology (199–201) reproduced from Michael D. Coogan (ed.), *The Oxford History of the Biblical World* (1998), by permission of Oxford University Press, Inc.

ACKNOWLEDGEMENTS

The Fourth Edition of the *Oxford Bible Atlas* has been revised throughout from the Third Edition, which was prepared by John Day. Day worked on the First Edition (Oxford University Press, 1962), edited by Herbert G. May with the assistance of G. N. S. Hunt in consultation with R. W. Hamilton.

Special thanks must be expressed to a number of people who have been instrumental in bringing this work to completion: Terry Hardaker (of Oxford Cartographers, www.oxfordcarto.com) for his work on the maps, Sandra Assersohn for researching the illustrations, Ann Hall and Alan Lovell for preparing the indexes, Lucy Qureshi (formerly of OUP) for co-ordinating the project during much of the production time, and Dorothy McCarthy, Sue Tipping and Rachel Woodforde (all of OUP) who have contributed in their various ways to the production of the volume. All have shown a real commitment to, and enthusiasm for, the preparation of this fourth edition. Their advice, encouragement and, not infrequently, their patience are gratefully acknowledged.

FURTHER READING

Bartlett, J. R., *The Bible: Faith and Evidence*, London: British Museum, 1990.

Barton, J., and Muddiman, J. (eds.), *The Oxford Bible Commentary*, Oxford: Oxford University Press, 2001.

Borowski, O., *Daily Life in Biblical Times*, Atlanta: Society of Biblical Literature, 2003.

Coogan, M. D. (ed.), *The Oxford History of the Biblical World*, New York and Oxford: Oxford University Press, 1998.

Davies, P. R., *In Search of 'Ancient Israel'* (Journal for the Study of the Old Testament Supplement Series 148), Sheffield: JSOT Press, 1992.

Dever, W. G., *What Did the Biblical Writers Know and When Did They Know It?*, Grand Rapids, Michigan and Cambridge, 2001.

Duling, D. C., *The New Testament: History, Literature and Social Context* (4th edn.), London and Belmont, Calif.: Wadsworth, 2003.

Esler, P. F. (ed.), *The Early Christian World* (2 vols.), London: Routledge, 2000.

Freedman, D. N. (ed.), *The Anchor Bible Dictionary* (6 vols.), London and New York: Doubleday, 1992.

Fritz, V., *An Introduction to Biblical Archaeology* (Journal for the Study of the Old Testament Supplement Series 172), Sheffield: JSOT Press, 1994.

Hallo, W. W., and Younger, K. L. (eds.), *The Context of Scripture* (3 vols.), Leiden and New York: Brill, 1996.

King, P. J., and Stager, L. E., *Life in Biblical Israel*, Westminster John Knox Press, Louisville / London, 2001.

Murphy-O'Connor, J., *The Holy Land* (3rd edn.), Oxford: Oxford University Press, 1992.

Negev, A., and Gibson, S. (eds.), *Archaeological Encyclopedia of the Holy Land* (revised and updated edition), New York and London: Continuum, 2001.

Richard, S. (ed.), *Near Eastern Archaeology: A Reader*, Winona Lake, Ind.: Eisenbrauns, 2003.

Rogerson, J. W., and Davies, P. R., *The Old Testament World* (rev. edn.), London and New York: T. & T. Clark / Continuum, 2005.

Soggin, J. A., *An Introduction to the History of Israel and Judah* (rev. edn.), London: SCM Press, 1993.

Notes on the Index of Place Names

PLACE NAMES

Place names, ancient and modern, are listed alphabetically. Many biblical names are followed by alternative names. Such Arabic and Hebrew names are *italicized*.

Acre (Acco/Ptolemais/*Tell el-Fukhkhar*/[*T. ʿAkko*])

Here, **Acre** is followed by an alternative biblical name, the Greek name given to the city, the Arabic name, and finally, in square brackets, the anglicized Hebrew name used in modern Israeli publications. Anglicized Hebrew names often differ from names used in the RSV.

It should be noted that some modern towns and villages in Israel are not on the same site as the biblical place of the same name. For example, the modern village Benei Beraq is not at the Biblical Bene-berak: **Bene(-)berak** (*Ibn beraq*/[*Ḥorvat Bene-beraq*]).

Some of the alternative names listed are not shown on any map. They have been included for information only.

Ḥorvat and Khirbet *mean* 'ruin'.

Tel *and* Tell *mean* 'a mound over an ancient site'.

T., *Tel*, and *Tell* are **all** listed under T.

PAGE NUMBERS

Page numbers follow a grid reference for each entry:

Tarsus
  E2 169
  F3 100, 128, 138, 159, 173, 178

The above indicates that on page 169 the town will be found in 'square' **E2**, whilst on pages 100, 128, etc it will be found in the 'square' **F3**. An entry such as:

Deir el-Balaḥ (*insert*) 183

indicates that Deir el-Balaḥ has no grid reference and is to be found in a box set within the map on page 183.

Bold page numbers indicate a whole map, as in:

Judah (region and kingdom) **133**

INDEX OF PLACE NAMES

207

GENERAL INDEX

Notes: Page numbers in **bold** indicate major references; those in *italics* indicate *captions* to illustrations and maps. Further page references for place-names can be found in the Gazetteer.